American Labor
and European Politics

American Labor and European Politics

The AFL as a Transnational Force

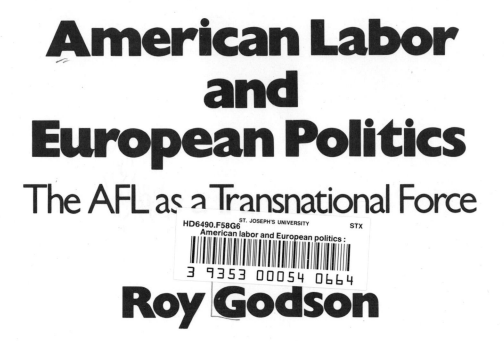

Roy Godson

Crane, Russak & Company, Inc.
New York

American Labor and European Politics

Published in the United States of America by

Crane, Russak & Company, Inc.
347 Madison Avenue
New York, New York 10017

ISBN 0-8448-0919-5 (hardcover)
ISBN 0-8448-0920-9 (paper)
LC 76-491

Printed in the United States of America

For Christine, Joe, and Ruth

Contents

Chapter

Acknowledgments

Maybe some people produce books by themselves. Certainly I did not. Without a great deal of moral, intellectual, and material support from other people, I could not have written this book.

In the late 1960s, I began teaching international relations at Carnegie Mellon University and serving as education director of the World Affairs Council of Pittsburgh. The executive director of the council, former ambassador Max Bishop, first pointed out that although fragments of the story were scattered about, few people recognized the singular role the AFL had played in postwar Europe. Dr. Philip Mosely, Director of Columbia University's European Institute and my mentor, agreed that this was an important and fitting subject for a doctoral dissertation. Mosely guided the research and, together with R. Daniel McMichael, author, foundation executive, and friend, made it possible for me to take leaves of absence to complete the research in Europe. After Mosely's very sad death in 1971, Dr. Donald Puchala helped me to negotiate the shoals of the rather stormy political and intellectual atmosphere at Columbia.

A number of other people also saved me from serious error and made helpful suggestions that I have tried to incorporate into the manuscript. Apart from numerous American and foreign trade union officials, politicians, and scholars, I really have to thank Charles Lichenstein, a great editor, and Dr. Daniel Horowitz, surely one of the best analytical minds in the foreign affairs bureaucracy.

Last but by no means least, I owe a great deal to Frank R. Barnett, president, and Dr. Frank N. Trager, director of studies, of the National Strategy Information Center, Inc., who recognized the importance of the subject and the need for greater public understanding of American labor's role in international affairs. Without their personal encouragement and the support of the National Strategy Information Center, this book probably would not have seen the light of day.

Abbreviations

AFL   American Federation of Labor

AFL-CIO   American Federation of Labor–Congress of Industrial Organizations

AID   Agency for International Development

AUCCTU   All-Union Central Council of Trade Unions (of the Soviet Union)

BMCO   Bureau Central de la Main d'Oeuvre

CFTC   Confédération Française des Travailleurs Chrétiens

CGIL   Confederazione Generale del Lavoro (Italy)

CGT   Confédération Générale du Travail

CIA   Central Intelligence Agency

CISL   Confederazione Italiana dei Sindacati Lavoratori (Italy)

CP   Communist party

DGB   Deutcher Gewerkschaftsbund (Federal Republic of Germany)

ECSC   European Coal and Steel Community

ERP   European Recovery Program

FO   CGT Force Ouvrière

FTUC   Free Trade Union Committee (of the AFL)

IAM   International Association of Machinists

ICFTU   International Confederation of Free Trade Unions

IFTU   International Federation of Trade Unions

ILGWU   International Ladies' Garment Workers Union

ILO   International Labor Organization

ILRC   International Labor Relations Committee (of the AFL)

IMF   International Metalworkers Federation

ITF	International Transport Workers' Federation
ITS	International Trade Secretariats
IWW	Industrial Workers of the World
JLC	Jewish Labor Committee
NATO	North Atlantic Treaty Organization
NVV	Nederlands Verbond van Vakverenigingen (Netherlands)
OECD	Organization for Economic Cooperation and Development
OEEC	Organization for European Economic Cooperation
OSS	Office of Strategic Services
PTT	Fédération des Portes, Téléphones et Télégraphe
SPD	Sozial Demokratishe Partei (Federal Republic of Germany)
TUAC	Trade Union Advisory Committee (of the OEEC and later of the OECD)
TUC	Trades Union Congress (Great Britain)
UD	Union Départmentale
UIL	Unione Italiana del Lavoro (Italy)
UMWA	United Mine Workers of America
WFTU	World Federation of Trade Unions

Chapter 1

Introduction

Contemporary world politics, typically perceived, is "politics among nations." Nation-states and their governments are the only important actors on the international stage; presidents, prime ministers, and cabinet officers the only people worth watching in the dramas of international affairs. According to this point of view, multinational corporations, trade unions, foundations, and religious and even political organizations are not considered significant in deciding who gets what, where, when, and how. These nongovernmental entities are props or, on occasion, instruments in the hands of the real actors on the world stage. The props may add to the total production but should not divert attention from the principals.

During the past few years, however, numerous scholars and political practitioners have questioned this view.[1] They maintain that nongovernmental entities

[1] Among the leading theoretical works that have stressed the necessity of altering the "state-centric paradigm" that has dominated the American study of international relations are Joseph Nye and Robert Keohane, eds., *Transnational Relations and World Politics* (Cambridge: Harvard University Press, 1971) and George Modelski, *Principles of World Politics* (New York: Free Press, 1972). However, very few empirical studies employing the transnational approach have been published so far.

can be and indeed have been significant actors in their own right. To understand
the major events of the past and the world scene today, they argue, it is essential
to examine the policies of these nongovernmental organizations and their interactions with governments. For example, to understand events in a number of
Latin American countries and such European countries as Spain and Italy, it has
been and remains essential to take account of the activities of the Roman Catholic church. Similarly, students of the Middle East, whether concerned about the
British Mandate period after World War I or the present day, have to consider
the activities of Jewish and other nongovernmental organizations. Actions of the
Palestine Liberation Organization, the Zionist groups, and many other organizations sometimes affect the politics of the area as much as do actions of the
governments of Egypt and Israel or, for that matter, the United States and the
Soviet Union. And, more to the point, all may be seen as interacting in one
grand drama that extends well beyond the Middle East proper.

If this is true, those who want to understand or to shape world politics must
be concerned with nongovernmental organizations. These organizations can, and
do, alter the course of events. To ignore them will not only make it difficult for
one to understand the world; it will also mean that one will lose an opportunity
to shape its future.

In this book, an attempt will be made to demonstrate that one type of
nongovernmental organization, the trade union, can play an enormously important role in world politics.[2] For years, trade unions have been involved in the
most sensitive political and security issues of the day, not only in their own
countries but across national borders as well. They have been major actors in
propaganda drives, elections, and efforts to change government policy. They
have also been participants in sabotage, espionage, coups d'état, and revolutions.
Indeed, trade unions have been among the most significant nongovernmental
organizations involved in shaping major events in the twentieth century.

The main focus of the study will be the activities of American trade unions
in restoring and maintaining the European and world balance of power in the
decade following World War II. The argument will be made that the American
Federation of Labor was a significant actor in its own right; that European trade

[2]An organization is nongovernmental to the extent that it is a free association of
individuals, groups, and institutions; it is independently financed; and its leaders are selected
by, and responsible only to, the members of the organization. The membership can comprise solely individuals from one state—a national nongovernmental organization (NNGO) or
individuals and groups from more than one state—an international nongovernmental organization (INGO). An NNGO or an INGO becomes an actor in world politics when it affects
the movement of tangible or intangible goods across national boundaries.

Trade unions are nongovernmental organizations to the extent that they meet these
criteria. Labor organizations created or controlled by totalitarian or authoritarian governments, such as those in Soviet Russia or what was formerly Franco's Spain, in this sense are
not trade unions or nongovernmental actors.

unions were important actors as well; and that the interaction of these non-governmental entities with each other and with European, the United States, and the Russian governments in substantial part determined the course of postwar history.

Specifically, it will be argued that the AFL helped maintain the postwar balance of power by helping to prevent the Soviet Union from dominating the European continent. The AFL was able to do this by helping to build new, noncommunist trade union structures and thus to undercut Russian control of the European labor movement. This result, in turn, strengthened democratic pluralism in Western Europe and impeded Stalin's ability to use Moscow-oriented labor leaders to destroy democracy, upset the balance of power, and thus dominate the Continent.

There will be a description of why and how the AFL became involved in Europe and particularly in a key country, France. Although the American unionists were motivated to some extent by economic and humanitarian considerations, the major reason for their action was political. The AFL leadership was seeking to maintain democratic trade unionism, preserve the power equilibrium of the Western nations and the Soviet Union, and promote economic and social justice in the United States and abroad. This meant preventing the Russians from gaining control of Western Europe and either precipitating war with the United States or, ultimately, destroying democracy and genuine trade unionism in the United States.

To achieve these objectives, the AFL launched a broad range of activities. First, the American unionists ran up the warning flag: the Soviet Union and its allies in Western Europe—local Communist parties—were not to be trusted. Sooner or later, the AFL warned, the Communists would move to dominate Western Europe and snuff out the reviving democracies. The Russians and their allies would use a variety of means to these ends, the AFL said, including trade union organizations. If they were successful, workers in Western Europe would suffer the same fate as workers behind the Iron Curtain—forced labor and the destruction of trade union rights. In English, French, German, and Italian, the AFL made its views known throughout the world. AFL publications, some of them in Russian, were even smuggled, at great risk, by sailors and workers on barges into the ports and canals of Eastern Europe and the Soviet Union itself.

At the same time, the American trade unionists started redirecting some of the resources they had used during the war in aid of the victims of nazism to the partisans of postwar democracy. Food parcels and other types of material assistance were channeled by the AFL to workers who were struggling to rebuild the democratic trade union movement. In such countries as France, food parcels were a welcome addition to the meager postwar diet. In others—Germany, for example—they were an outright necessity for thousands of workers and their families barely eking out a living in the ruins of Central Europe.

The AFL also began to help finance European union leaders who requested assistance. Many of the prewar leaders were impoverished. They had returned from Nazi concentration camps or from the Resistance to find their prewar organizations largely destroyed.

In addition to the task of rebuilding the unions, democratic European labor leaders were faced with another pressing problem. They were opposed by powerful rivals within the house of labor. Before the war, Communists were a distinct minority in the leadership of the labor movement. After the war it was a different story. Communist cadres began moving into prominent leadership positions in France and Italy even before the fighting ended. The Communists were centrally directed and well funded. They were skilled organizers. Shortly after the war, they emerged as the dominant faction in the main trade union bodies in both countries.

Some noncommunist union leaders argued that the democratic elements could peacefully coexist with the Communists in the same union, that continuation of wartime Resistance unity would enable the workers of Europe to overcome economic and social injustice just as they had overcome Fascist and Nazi oppression, and that cooperation with the Soviet Union and parties friendly to it was essential for postwar stability and security. These leaders believed that the noncommunists could avoid being controlled by the Communists and that the unions would not be used to support Russian political and military objectives.

Other noncommunist leaders were less sanguine. They believed that coexistence in the same organization would be disastrous. Unity with the Communists, they argued, was incompatible with genuine trade unionism. It would not produce very much in the way of immediate economic benefits because the Communist union leaders were subservient to Russian-controlled Communist parties—unless, of course, economic benefits for workers happened to be "the party line" at a given time. Moreover, they felt that it would be very dangerous to allow Communists to control or even share substantially in the control of one of the major institutions in democratic society, the trade union. Sooner or later, these noncommunist union leaders argued, the Russians would use local Communist allies to support their political-military policies in Europe, just as they had done before World War II.

To get help in rebuilding the unions and to avoid working with the Communists, these union leaders turned to the AFL. In France and Italy in particular, a faction of the noncommunist leadership appealed to the American unions for support. They received it. Although by today's standards the sums delivered were not large, they were quite significant in the immediate postwar period. Organizers could be hired, paper and mimeograph machines purchased, and tracts distributed.

The AFL also played an organizational role. At first this meant serving as a rallying point for those trade unionists who refused to work with Communist unions in their own countries and to involve themselves in the World Federation of Trade Unions (WFTU), the international organization of national trade union centers. (Individual unions in a country usually belonged to a national center such as the AFL in the United States. These national centers, in turn, tended to affiliate with an international labor body such as the WFTU.) The AFL was the only major national trade union center that refused to join the new international organization—formed in 1945—mainly on the grounds that the Russians and their Communist allies would soon get control of the organization and use it throughout the world as an instrument of Russian foreign policy.[3] The AFL also urged European and American affiliates of the international trade secretariats— industry-based federations such as the International Transport Workers' Federation—not to affiliate with the WFTU, lest the secretariats, too, fall under Russian domination.

Although many national centers ignored AFL overtures and joined the WFTU anyway, the AFL's efforts were a significant factor in preventing the secretariats from falling under WFTU control. By 1948, moreover—as Russian attempts to use the national centers and the WFTU to thwart the Marshall Plan, European recovery, and political stability became more overt—disillusionment set in among the noncommunist WFTU affiliates. At this point, the AFL played a major role in helping to bring together those elements that had refused to work with Communists from the beginning with those that had given coexistence a flyer until then. New national centers were created in France and Italy, and a new international organization was established (in early 1949) with AFL assistance. The International Confederation of Free Trade Unions (ICFTU) and the trade secretariats, together with the AFL, served as a counterforce to Russian attempts to use the WFTU and the Communist unions in France, Italy, and also Germany for disruptive political ends.

Each year from 1947 through 1950, Communist labor organizations (in France and Italy particularly) organized political strikes, engaged in espionage and sabotage, and may have tried to foment revolutions and coups d'état—all presumably at Moscow's direction. The democratic labor organizations fought back. On the docks, ships, and barges and in the factories and streets of Europe, a political war was fought. Some battles consisted only of an exchange of bulletins and ballots; others involved bullets and blows. Enormous daring and courage were displayed, sometimes openly but more often in the day-to-day resistance of men and women who continued going to work in spite of bribes, threats, and intimidation. When the battle was over, Western Europe was on the way to

---

[3]The AFL briefly was affiliated with the major interwar international labor body, the International Federation of Trade Unions, in the early 1920s. It withdrew from this organization after a few years, mainly because it did not want to get involved in the ideological struggles of the European unions, but it reaffiliated in 1937. The Europeans, however, dissolved the organization at the end of World War II and created the WFTU.

economic and political stability and progress. The internal balance of power within a number of European countries was no longer seriously threatened. The global balance of power, which had broken down even before World War II, also was finally restored.

These conclusions do not, of course, go unchallenged. Many commentators, most of whom have altogether ignored the role of nongovernmental organizations in postwar European and world politics, believe that labor's international involvement was not especially significant at this particular historical juncture. Others assert that the AFL on its own, as a nongovernmental force, was unimportant, but that as a tool of United States foreign policy it did play a significant role in quashing genuine "revolutionary" movements in Europe and elsewhere.

At the other end of the spectrum, some participants in these postwar events have exaggerated the AFL's role. They maintain that the AFL, virtually alone, was able decisively to affect the European labor movement and European politics. But reality was more complex. As will be demonstrated, the AFL was never able to impose its preferences on European labor. Instead it was necessary that European and American trade unions share, to some substantial degree, the same values, attitudes, and objectives. The greater the coincidence, the greater was the AFL's ability to influence events in Europe.

In fact, the case of the AFL in postwar Europe suggests that a number of conditions may have to be present for unions in any one country—acting alone or in concert with others—to be able to influence world politics. Indeed, this study describes a number of conditions or "the context" that enabled the AFL to play a significant role in world affairs at a particular time and place. If enough of these conditions can be delineated correctly and if, based on much more research, they can be matched up with conditions in other times and places, it may be possible to suggest other occasions when unions—in the United States or elsewhere—may have been or may become significant forces in world affairs. The formulation of a set of such preconditions, which in the future may be generally applicable as a tool of analysis, will run through this study as a continuous thread.

As a first precondition, the fate of postwar Europe was crucial to the restoration of the global balance of power. Europe had been at the center of world politics for centuries. What happened there affected politics everywhere. At the end of World War II, Western Europe may no longer have been the single most important center of world power, but it remained of critical importance. If one of the postwar superpowers could obtain control of Europe's resources, it could, if it chose to, impose its will on the rest of the world. This was, after all, one of the major underlying reasons that the United States went to war in 1917 and again in 1941—to prevent one state from overturning the global balance of power. The United States could not allow what it regarded as an expansionist power to gain control of both Europe and Western Russia, lest that power be tempted to impose its will on the Western Hemisphere.

The same was true after World War II. The United States could not allow the Stalinists to control both areas without risking that, sooner or later, this combined might would be brought to bear against the United States itself. Thus, at the end of the war, any actor that was able to influence power relations in Western Europe was in a position not only to affect events on the Continent but also to help restore a global balance of power. The AFL, as this study attempts to show, was one such actor. American trade unions were able to influence events in a crucial area at a crucial time in world history.

Second, referring still to preconditions, the Soviet Union was bent on establishing its hegemony over Western Europe and intended to use Western European labor unions for this purpose. Whether the Soviet Union wanted to do this for offensive reasons (to obtain Western Europe's resources so that it could dominate the world) or defensive reasons (to prevent any power or combination of powers from again attacking Russia) is uncertain. What is fairly clear is that the Soviet Union wanted United States power removed from the Continent and regimes either subservient or friendly to itself in power. Moreover, Stalin had the ability to use European unions for this purpose.

The political use of organized labor was a key element in Russia's postwar strategy. Whether it was for the purpose of themselves dominating Western Europe or of precluding a United States alliance with a powerful Western Europe, the Russians were determined to obstruct postwar European recovery, impede the effectiveness of NATO, and perhaps even encourage their local allies, the French and Italian Communist parties, to seize power. Unions were an obvious vehicle for this strategy, particularly in such strategic industries as communications, transportation, and energy. Moscow-oriented European Communists had begun to pursue these tactics even before the war. After the war they came close to success, particularly in France and Italy.

In the face of what they regarded as a common enemy, anticommunist American and European unionists coalesced. The transatlantic labor allies worked together to prevent the Communists from increasing their control of the European labor movement. First, from late 1945 until late 1947, only militantly anticommunist European trade unionists welcomed AFL involvement. After 1947, however, when the Russians began using their control of European labor to sabotage the Marshall Plan and NATO, many union leaders who previously had rejected American criticism of the WFTU and had favored working with the Communists abandoned this policy; they, too, sought the AFL's cooperation and assistance.

As a third precondition, a number of political and economic factors that existed in postwar Europe had much to do with the AFL's ability to influence events on the scale it did. Both economically and politically, the Continent was very weak and, in many instances, almost in ruins. Morale was low, and most people were struggling just to get enough to eat. Much of industry and the bulk of the institutions that European workers had built up to protect their interests had been destroyed in the war. In this situation, it was relatively easy for foreigners to become involved in the rebuilding of the European labor movement.

Furthermore, at the end of the war many European unionists were interested in the American style of unionism. The AFL placed much greater stress on collective bargaining to achieve its objectives than it did on partisan political action—quite the opposite of the prewar European model. The postwar environment gave the Americans an opportunity to put their stamp on European unionism. In countries such as Germany and Austria, which were occupied in part by United States forces, the AFL and other American organizations could be very influential in shaping the institutions of the reviving labor movement. By pressuring the United States government—particularly the military occupation authorities—the AFL was in a position to shape the new union structures that were gradually established in the Western Zones of Germany and Austria. The AFL's influence extended to the new industrial relations laws, the officials who carried them out, and the kinds of labor organizations that would be allowed to exist and thrive.

Because many of the characteristics of today's non-Western, less-developed states existed in such European countries as France and Italy, the Americans were in a position to be influential even outside the zones of occupation. Although the French and the Italians had created industrial infrastructures and work forces in the first few decades of the twentieth century, major sectors of the economies of France and Italy had failed to respond to the dynamics of industrialization. Prewar labor organizations were weak or "underdeveloped." For a variety of political and economic reasons, they had never become genuinely established. Instead of relying on their own strength to improve the conditions of workers through collective bargaining, French and Italian unions had fallen back on pressuring their respective governments to impose their demands on employers. Thus, although the AFL did not have the opportunities for direct influence that existed in the American Occupation Zones, those French and Italian unionists who believed neither in working with Communists nor in engaging in direct political action tended naturally toward the major national center that shunned this kind of unionism. Indeed, the new union structure that was created in France and to some extent in Italy was modeled, in many ways, on what has been called the "business unionism" of the AFL.

In France particularly, trade unionists of various political shades—socialists, Trotskyists, anarcho-syndicalists, and independents—joined forces under the umbrella of a new organization. Refusing to align themselves with any political

party, these groupings in 1947 formed the Confédération Générale du Travail–
Force Ouvrière (CGT-FO).[4] This new body strove to improve the conditions of
French workers primarily by negotiating with employers and consulting with
government agencies rather than by trying to change the government or, at the
extreme, the very system of government.

Another characteristic of French unionism enabled the American unions to
play a key role. Because French workers did not have a tradition of paying dues,
FO, like other trade union centers in France, had to rely on outside support. But
by refusing to ally itself with a political party or the church, FO had cut itself
off from these traditional sources. This situation meant that this fledgling organization was anxious to receive material assistance from an apolitical trade union
source. Thus the AFL, a dynamic center of apolitical unionism, by helping to
finance FO was able to affect the situation in France even without having the
opportunities offered by control of the government in the occupation zones of
Germany and Austria.

Another factor—a fourth precondition—that enabled the American labor
movement to become involved was the active encouragement of certain European trade unionists. Only when American labor leaders were able to ally themselves with powerful forces inside the European trade union movement were
they able to be truly influential. When they tried to secure the adoption of
policies that did not have the approval of the Europeans—for example, merging
of French Catholic and non-Catholic unions—they failed. The history of the
early postwar period indicates that American unions, to be influential, had to
develop coalitions with indigenous labor forces in Western Europe.

A fifth precondition that enabled American unions to influence European
developments was the toleration of the United States and European governments. As far as can be determined, there was never a formal agreement that
allowed the AFL to involve itself in European trade union affairs. The European
governments, however, did not oppose such activities. If they had, it is difficult
to see how the AFL could have operated effectively. After 1947, when the
Communists were expelled from the governments of France and Italy, some of
the European governments did more than passively tolerate the American-
European labor coalition: in France, Italy, and elsewhere, they openly encouraged and supported the efforts of trade union forces to contain the Communist
unions.

The attitude of the United States government also was important to the
AFL. Like its European counterparts, the United States government initially

[4]Not to be confused with the Confédération Générale du Travail (CGT) proper, the
long-standing principal national center of French trade unionism, or with Amis de Force
Ouvrière, formed shortly after World War II by former members of Résistance Ouvrière, a
noncommunist trade union body that participated in the Resistance. However, Amis de
Force Ouvrière militants became the core of CGT–Force Ouvrière in December 1947.

neither impeded nor supported the AFL's activities. Some United States officials privately encouraged the American unionists to develop transatlantic coalitions, but it was not until after 1947 that most senior United States officials believed that AFL's concerns about Soviet intentions and capabilities in the European labor movement were justified. After that time, as official United States involvement deepened with the beginning of the Marshall Plan in 1948, the transatlantic coalitions were actively supported. The AFL remained an independent entity, however—tolerated and even supported but never, so far as one can discover, the outright instrument of official policy.[5]

Last but certainly not least, the AFL was able to affect European affairs because it was a special type of private organization. Its leaders were highly motivated. The AFL had been concerned with international affairs since the 1880s, and the AFL policy makers believed that it was essential to assist noncommunist unionism in the postwar period. They were, of course, at odds with much of the conventional wisdom of the day. They were scorned, but they remained firm in their convictions. Moreover, they were not sure they could do very much, but they were willing to take the chance. As World War II drew to a close, they were determined to prevent the Soviet Union from using the European labor movement to dominate the Continent and believed that they knew how to do it. Moreover, the AFL leadership could send significant resources to Europe and other parts of the world. Food, propaganda, and money were essential parts of this campaign. But the AFL leaders also found talented American organizers who could use these material resources effectively. Without this combination of human and material resources, the efforts of American unions might have turned out quite differently.

Even with the advantage of hindsight, it is difficult to tell which of these conditions were most important—the shattered state of postwar Europe, the Russians' use of organized labor as a policy weapon, the Occupation, the underdeveloped institutions, the groups inside the European labor movement seeking American allies, the tolerance of the United States and European governments, or the existence of a highly motivated American nongovernmental organization that was able to mobilize its resources effectively—or whether the combination of all of them was essential. These were, in any case, a number of the conditions that enabled the AFL to influence European—particularly French—developments. If in the future American labor is again to play a significant world role, it would seem that at least some of these conditions ought to be present.

ORGANIZATION OF THE STUDY

First, in Chapter 2, the context of AFL activities will be examined. What was the nature of the world of which the AFL was a part? What were the major characteristics of the postwar period? Who were the major governmental and

---

[5] But see Chapters 3 and 8 for discussion of conflicting allegations.

nongovernmental actors, and what were their policies? What were the major socioeconomic forces at work? How were the actors and socioeconomic forces on both sides of the Atlantic and both sides of the Elbe related to one another? How did the AFL fit in?

To answer these questions briefly, the author will summarize a number of standard secondary sources. It should be noted that revisionist or New Left authors, in addition to Communist scholars, are unhappy with these sources and have attempted to reinterpret the history of the early postwar period. In particular, they have suggested that at the end of World War II if not before, the United States government, on behalf of American capitalists, was seeking to dominate Europe and that the United States and not the Soviet Union was in large part responsible for initiating the cold war. While this writer does not accept the revisionist thesis, this study will not refute it directly. Doing this would require one or more major works; several scholars cited in Chapter 4 have begun this task. However, a number of specific points raised by the revisionists, particularly those pertaining to labor, will be discussed and refuted in various parts of the text.

After the scene is set, in Chapter 3 the salient features of the AFL will be described. Was it really a nongovernmental actor as it claims, or was it subservient to the United States government as revisionist critics have maintained? As a means of answering this question, the AFL decision-making process will be analyzed. How did the AFL obtain information on developments abroad? Who received it and formulated the Federation's options? Where did the Federation obtain its resources for its foreign policy activities? How were the final policy choices made? The answers suggest that the AFL was indeed a nongovernmental organization. A small group of leaders and staff gathered the requisite information, defined the Federation's choices, and secured the approval of their colleagues for the mobilization of the Federation's resources.

In Chapter 4, the foreign policy perspectives of this leadership group will be analyzed—with the suggestion being made that AFL policy makers were motivated primarily by political rather than economic considerations.[6] This conclusion may come as a surprise to some observers. Union leaders, particularly American union leaders, are not supposed to have a developed political perspective or ideology. Their main concerns are assumed to be economic, or what some students of the field call "business unionism." While economic considerations were not completely absent from the international concerns of AFL leaders, to be sure, an examination of their objectives and their views of the forces at work in the postwar period reveals that political concerns were paramount. Specifically, the study demonstrates that they believed that peace, free trade unionism, and

---

[6] It is assumed that political behavior is rooted in an individual's values, identification, and expectations; see Harold Lasswell and Abraham Kaplan, *Power and Society* (New Haven: Yale University Press, 1950) and William T. R. Fox, *The American Study of International Relations* (Columbia, S.C.: Institute of International Studies, University of South Carolina, 1968).

economic and social justice throughout the world could be jeopardized by developments in the international labor movement and in a few key countries, particularly Germany and France and, to a lesser extent, Italy. If the Russians were able to control the labor movements in these countries, they concluded, sooner or later American unions and American workers would suffer both economically and politically.

To substantiate these conclusions, heavy reliance will be placed on the public and private statements, as well as previous actions, of the leaders. The burden of this descriptive analysis, plus the AFL's subsequent actions in the postwar period (which will be described in later chapters), supports the view that political perspectives were uppermost in the minds of the AFL leadership and were the determinants of action.

Examination of their public pronouncements and private documents also indicates that this group of men had similar values and expectations about world politics. The statements and actions of individual AFL leaders can be interchanged almost at will. Moreover, systematic examination of the Federation's archives indicates that it is difficult to determine precisely who wrote each speech or published statement.[7] The AFL files indicate that speeches and published articles frequently were drafted by the staff and, on occasion, amended by the ostensible author or speaker, thus further demonstrating the close harmony among the policy-making group. To avoid repetition, however, the words of only one or two leaders will be taken to delineate the views of all.

Once the AFL leaders concluded that developments in the international labor movement and in a few countries could decisively affect their interests, they began to study the situation more closely. A great deal of time, energy, and resources were devoted to this effort. Detailed reports were made on international labor politics as well as on the governmental and nongovernmental actors in a number of countries. The strengths, strategies, and tactics of these actors were analyzed in an effort to determine what precisely the AFL should do.

In Chapters 5 and 6, then, these perceptions will be described, and in Chapter 7, AFL policy in postwar Europe will be outlined. The emphasis, however, will be on the international labor movement overall and on developments in one country. France. AFL perceptions and activities pertaining to France have been selected for detailed study for a number of reasons. First, France was and remains one of the important countries on the European continent. Developments in France tend to have a decisive impact on the rest of the Continent. A study of the forces affecting developments in France is, in effect, a study of the forces affecting the entire European continent. Second, although Germany's role

---

[7]See Appendix A for discussion of documentation.

in Western Europe was as decisive as that of France, if not more so, Germany at the end of the war was very atypical of the countries of the world. Postwar Germany was completely occupied by the Allies. In these circumstances, Allied nongovernmental organizations had unusual opportunities to influence developments in Germany, opportunities that were not available at most other times and places. A case study of nongovernmental involvement in France, then, is more revealing than a study of this situation in early postwar Germany. Third, as has been noted, France had some of the characteristics of a non-Western, or less-developed, country in the early postwar period. France in some ways was a "school for developing countries." An understanding of the forces at work in France and of how the AFL was able to affect developments there may tell us something about other countries with non-Western characteristics.

After the AFL's postwar objectives and methods have been described, in Chapter 8 the impact of the AFL's activities will be assessed. It will be demonstrated that the AFL, initially as part of an international nongovernmental coalition and later as part of a coalition of both governmental and nongovernmental actors, was able to affect postwar world politics.

The validity of these conclusions is reinforced considerably if the AFL leaders were correct in their belief that the Russians, through the European Communist parties, had not only the intention but also the ability to use large segments of the European labor movement for their political objectives. This belief also is held by many scholars of postwar European Communism and labor who are cited in the text. Declassified and sanitized United States intelligence reports, which are discussed and several of which are reproduced in Appendix C, also lend a measure of support to this perspective.

In the final chapter, the conditions that enabled this role playing to take place will be summarized and these findings related to the contemporary scene. It is interesting to note that some of the conditions of the early postwar period may now be reappearing. In particular, some elements of the European labor movement are again seeking American assistance to prevent the Soviet Union from gaining control of European labor and seeking to dominate the Continent. Although Europe no longer is in ruins—industry and the noncommunist labor movement are standing on their own feet—a number of European countries are facing serious economic difficulties. In this context, can we expect American labor to demonstrate once again that nongovernmental organizations can be important actors on the international scene?

Getting at answers to these questions is not easy. For the most part, books dealing with the postwar period either have completely ignored the political role of organized labor or have mentioned it only in passing. Moreover, not all of the necessary documentation is available. Although this writer is the first to study the files of the key information-gathering and policy-implementing segment of the AFL—the Free Trade Union Committee—other important files are unavailable, lost, or even destroyed.[8] Other relevant perceptions may never have been committed to paper. The politically sensitive nature of the relationship between the AFL, French unions, and the United States and French governments probably resulted in frequent reliance on oral commitments.

Finally, for obvious reasons, it was impossible to obtain access to all the classified files of the United States, Russian, and European governments. Insofar as these governments may have been intimately involved in labor politics on the Continent, this is a serious, if unavoidable, limitation. However, it should be noted that a number of heretofore classified United States government documents have been incorporated into the study. Responding to the author's requests under the Freedom of Information Act, the U.S. Central Intelligence Agency released a number of highly relevant declassified and sanitized documents. The author also was able to utilize the previously classified State Department files available up through 1947 in the National Archives. As is discussed in the Appendix A, however, many relevant CIA and State Department documents either have been lost, stolen, or misplaced or remain classified.

In an effort to overcome these limitations, this writer conducted over 60 personal interviews. Between 1968 and 1970, he traveled to small and large towns, visiting mines, factories, and dockyards in France, Italy, and England to meet with many of the participants in the events described here or those who, for one reason or another, possessed a special knowledge of these events. People with all major perspectives were interviewed—Communists, Socialists, Catholics, and independents; those who were pro and anti American involvement. For the most part, these interviews were flexibly structured. They frequently took place over a drink or a meal; sometimes in a bar or café, other times in private homes. Most of the participants, whether former dock workers, miners, union leaders, cabinet ministers, police chiefs, or diplomats, were happy to recount the events of the period as they remembered them. In many cases, they supplied the author with newspaper clippings, minutes of meetings, and tabulations of voting records to substantiate their accounts of the period. Usually they preferred not to talk for a tape recorder; sometimes they specifically asked not to be quoted directly; as a rule, fortunately, they did not object to the author's taking notes as the conversation proceeded. The author, however, is responsible for all interpretations of the interviews and any errors that may be found in the text.[9]

[8]See Appendix A.
[9]See Appendix B for a list of the dates, places, and former positions of those interviewed, during the period covered by this study.

Chapter 2

Postwar World Politics

Prior to World War II, Europe was the center of world affairs. Russia, a semi-European state, was involved to some extent, but the governments and non-governmental actors in France, England, and Germany made the major decisions for Europe and for much of the world.

Europeans also made the rules. They established a pattern of domestic and international behavior, known as "the balance of power," that, with some interruptions, guaranteed the survival of indigenous nongovernmental forces and the independence of large and small states for nearly a century. Obviously, the internal power balance—as an analytic concept—did not apply equally to every European state. Nor did the pattern apply everywhere at the same point in time. Yet there was an identifiable pattern, and this balance of power was designed to bring adequate pressure to bear against any domestic or international actor that might try to achieve dominance.

Within the European states, the balance of power enabled the various political groupings from left to right to coexist and compete for electoral success. When conservative forces gained control of the government, they either did not

15

seek to or they were unable to destroy the liberal or socialist forces, and vice versa. On the international level, when any one state or a combination of states tried to dominate and possibly eliminate the others, the potential victims banded together. And they had the will and sufficient political, economic, and military strength to prevent the balance of power from being tipped against them.

By the end of World War II, however, everything changed. Europe and Europeans were no longer the center of world affairs. Now the peripheral areas became central. (The United States and the Soviet Union were the world's super-powers, in terms of military power both in being and potential as well as in political power.) This is not to say that Europe was no longer significant in global politics. On the contrary, in spite of wartime devastation and the decline in the power of individual states, Europe was of great strategic significance. If either of the superpowers was able to mobilize and harness Europe's military-industrial potential, the new alignment would become the dominant force in world politics. On their own, however, the Europeans were no longer the major actors on the world scene.[1]

In addition, the balance of power that the Europeans had devised to protect their domestic and international interests had broken down. Within European states, there was a fundamental realignment. The internal balance of power shifted to the Left. The Communists, extreme Left actors, were in a position to exploit the new alignment and, in the context of wretched postwar socio-economic conditions, possibly to undermine the whole precarious balance within a number of European countries. Externally, the Europeans were no longer able to protect themselves against any power that threatened to dominate the Continent. They were too divided politically and too weak economically to maintain their own collective independence.

Once the richest continent in the world, Europe was a shambles after the war.[2] The populous European workshops from the Irish Sea to the Alps had been battlegrounds. Some cities—Rotterdam, Le Havre, Cologne, Frankfurt, Düsseldorf—had been almost completely destroyed; others, like London, Coventry, St. Nazaire, Toulon, Vienna, Trieste, and Lubeck, had large areas in ruins. Also, communications among the devastated areas were limited. Roads and bridges in many parts of the Continent had been demolished. Huge numbers of vehicles had been requisitioned or destroyed. (Nine-tenths of the trucks in France, for example, were out of action.) Railways, too, had been destroyed.

[1] For a discussion of the rise of the peripheral powers see Hajo Holborn, *The Political Collapse of Europe* (New York: Knopf, 1951) and Raymond Aron, *The Century of Total War* (Boston: Beacon Press, 1954).

[2] For brief descriptions of the immediate postwar political and economic conditions prevailing in Europe see Walter Laqueur, *Europe since Hitler* (Baltimore: Penguin, 1972); Richard Mayne, *The Recovery of Europe 1945–1973*, rev. ed. (Garden City, N.Y.: Doubleday, 1973); Roger Morgan, *West European Politics since 1945* (New York: Capricorn, 1973); Franz Borkenau, *European Communism* (London: Faber and Faber, 1953).

Long stretches of track and numerous viaducts, locomotives, and wagons were out of commission. Europe's waterways, an integral part of the Continent's economy, also were paralyzed. At the time of liberation, only 509 out of the 8,460 kilometers that normally bore traffic were navigable. About half the barge fleet in Germany had been destroyed; many barges, together with bridges that had been blown up, blocked such major arteries as the Rhine. Of all the great harbors of Europe, only Antwerp and Bordeaux were functioning almost normally.

Industry, too, had been badly damaged. There were shortages of just about everything. Coal production, providing the major source of Europe's energy, was down to two-fifths of its prewar level. Other key raw materials, rubber, for example, simply were not available. Machinery also was in short supply. As a result, industrial production suffered. In such areas as southern Germany, where 90 percent of the plants were out of action, industrial output was barely 5 percent of normal prewar capacity.

Nor was agriculture in any better shape. Immense tracts of land had been laid waste. Countless farm buildings and approximately 40 percent of Europe's livestock were gone. The land still under cultivation suffered from shortages of seeds, pesticides, machinery, and manure. In France, Belgium, and Italy in 1945–1946, agricultural production was about 50 percent below its prewar average.

Hunger was the order of the day. Some countries, such as Denmark, and certain rural areas were better off than others. But according to UN reports, even some two to three years after the war 140 million Europeans were receiving fewer than 2000 calories daily; 100 million, fewer than 1500. (A man who does not engage in physical labor consumes 2500 calories per day, while a physically active person needs 3000 to 5000 calories on average.)

The war had also spawned millions of sick, wounded, and homeless people. By one count, at least 60 million Europeans had been forced to leave their homes. In addition to all of these people who had to be fed and housed, there were 7 million prisoners of war in Allied hands in Western Europe—outside the productive mainstream.

Although economic reconstruction proceeded quite rapidly in some places, for the most part the Continent did not soon return to normal. Before the war, Western Europe imported much of its food and raw materials and paid for them largely by exporting industrial goods. As a result of the devastation, however, both industrial and agricultural production fell off, and traditional supplies of food and raw materials from Eastern Europe and the non-Western world were disrupted. To restore economic equilibrium, the Europeans had to buy food, raw materials, and machinery from the only place they were available in quantity, the United States; but this required vast cash assets that the Europeans had used up in the war.

To make matters worse, the summers of 1946 and 1947 and the winter of 1946–1947 were disastrous for the European economy. For two years, summer droughts caused major crop failures. Moreover, the freezing winter temperatures simultaneously increased consumer demand for energy and, in some areas, physically prevented the mining of coal, just at the time that energy was required for industrial production.

The result—a mounting and vicious cycle of hardship and shortage. Undernourishment limited output per man-hour. Shortages of raw materials, machinery, and transportation limited production and employment but increased inflation. Unemployment, limited output, and inflation impeded exports. Without the cash from exports, the purchase of additional raw materials, food, and machinery was next to impossible. This, in turn, produced an ever-mounting cycle of hardship, unemployment, and inflation and began to touch off major strikes. The strikes, of course, further increased hardship and further undermined the return to anything approaching economic normalcy.

The prewar economies, however, were not all that had to be restored. The political structure of most of the Continent had to be rebuilt as well. The war had brought down the Right. The totalitarian Nazi and Fascist governments in Germany, Austria, Italy, and the rest of occupied Europe were, of course, destroyed. The political forces, usually conservative, that had collaborated with the Axis Powers were purged—sometimes with due process, often without. Conservative and centrist politicians and many politicians who had been part of the prewar establishment were discredited. After all, many voters felt, was it not precisely these people who had led Europe down the road to the humiliation and disaster of World War II?

The result was a shift to the Left. The extent of the shift varied from country to country, but the balance of internal power moved to the Left immediately after the war. In Britain, the voters rejected Churchill's Conservatives and gave Atlee's Labor party a landslide victory. On the Continent, the Communists and Socialists emerged as the major political forces, and the Communists in particular were greatly strengthened. Their late entry into the Resistance, their knowledge of clandestine organization, their central direction, and their identification with the popular causes of liberation and renewal served them well. In addition, the wartime Allied spirit of unity of action carried over into the postwar honeymoon period. In this atmosphere, prewar fears and anticommunist impulses were sublimated.

As the Allied armies fought their way into Germany, the Communist hierarchy initially ordered its partisan units in France and Italy to gain control of key institutions in liberated areas. Collaborationists and sometimes simply political enemies were jailed or shot. With the end of the war in the spring of 1945, Communist parties were well entrenched in various regions, although the Communist partisans did agree to be disarmed and diverted their energies to electoral politics. Urging the Left to remain united, the Communists polled more votes in

France and Italy than ever before and joined the government in France, Italy, Belgium, and Denmark. In the first few years after the war, they won control of approximately one-third of the French Assembly, and in the November 1946 election, they took a number of seats from the Socialists and won more seats than any other party. Not surprisingly, it was widely believed that the Communists would become not just one of the ruling parties but eventually *the* ruling party.

(Also in occupied Germany, the Communists began to play an important role.) Just as in the other liberated areas, they had a head start. Even before the fighting had ended in Berlin, former Communist leaders who had fled to Moscow in the 1930s were flown back to Germany and began organizing what was to become an effective political instrument.

Judged by early postwar election returns, they were a small minority even in the Soviet Zone. But they had the backing of the occupying power. Despite the fact that most rank-and-file of the reviving Social Democratic party (SPD) were opposed, the Communists in the Soviet Zone secured the approval of the SPD leadership for a merger. Gradually the Socialists were forced out. Within a few months, the Communists emerged as sole leaders of the new Socialist Unity party.

In the Western Zones, the Communists had some initial success in rebuilding their movement. The Western occupation powers did little to stop them and did not provide noncommunist parties with the material means (e.g., printing presses, paper, transportation) that the Russians supplied to their political allies. In fact, the Western governments were frequently at odds with the reviving Social Democratic party. Kurt Schumacher, the new radical SPD leader, had his work cut out rebuilding the party, pursuing radical socialist programs, and at the same time trying to prevent the Communists from becoming a major political force in the Western Zones.

Elsewhere in Europe, the Socialists also emerged as a major political force. But except in the Western Zones of Germany, the democratic Socialists gradually lost ground to the Communists. In France and Italy, the Socialists won approximately one-third of the seats in Parliament. Nonetheless, during the early postwar years, a pattern appeared that was to become even more prevalent later: the Communists began to win more seats and the Socialists, fewer.

It is not easy to explain why this happened. Probably a number of factors were at work—among them the split in the Socialist camp over precisely the question of future cooperation with the Communists. Some Socialists maintained that continuation of the wartime alliance with the Communists would increase the strength of the Left and that the Socialists could contain the Communists in the coalition. Others rejected this alternative as suicidal, arguing that continued cooperation would make the Communists respectable political partners and pave the way for Communist control of the coalition. This split not only weakened the Socialist parties internally but also, because the debate was acrimonious, created the impression that the Socialists were not able to deal with the urgent problems of postwar reconstruction. Another factor that helps explain the decline in Socialist strength was the well-known French and Italian reluctance to support centralized party activities. As a result of this "anarchical" preference, the Socialist parties in these countries never developed tightly knit organizations that could compete effectively with the relatively well-financed and well-organized Communists. Thus, in both France and Italy, the Communists appeared increasingly to be the major party of the working class.

Another feature common throughout Western Europe during this period was the emergence of moderate-to-conservative church-oriented parties. In France, it was the Movement Républican Populaire; in Italy and Germany, the Christian Democrats. With the eclipse of the more conservative and authoritarian forces, these parties pulled in the right-wing and centrist voters. Appealing to a vague religiosity, they stressed that they were something new, that they had no connection with the political formations of the past. As opposed to prewar Christian parties, which had been antisocialist and antiliberal in orientation, postwar Christian democracy was democratic and left-leaning in its economic and social welfare policies. Moreover, it attracted considerable support from the working and peasant classes. In fact, the Christian Democrats emerged as the major party in both Germany and Italy in the early postwar period and lagged only a little behind the Communists and Socialists in France.

The result was a precariously balanced democratic political system, particularly in France and Italy. The center of the system was the moderate left. The Communists were pulling from an extreme antidemocratic Left position, the Christian Democrats from the moderate or centrist Right. As long as the moderate Left coalition could solve the economic problems of postwar recovery, there was little danger that the system would be pulled further to the Left. If the moderates did not come up with pragmatic solutions, however, and the economy continued to deteriorate, the extreme Left would appear to be a much more promising alternative. In the face of continued inflation, shortages, strikes, hunger, and fear, the discredited moderate coalition might very well fall apart and the Communists might appear as the only alternative to economic stagnation and chaos.

One of the key institutions that could either undermine or assist the moderates in this effort was organized labor. Because trade unions could influence the behavior of workers in key industries, they were in a position to exercise decisive influence over the economy. If they wanted to, they could help hold down wage costs and, as a result, keep exports up and inflation down; conversely, they could stimulate greater wage demands, push export sales down, and send prices and inflation up. Looked at another way, they could help ensure an efficient production process by smoothing out grievances and securing working conditions that did not lead to slowdowns, strikes, and sabotage or they could reduce productivity by encouraging industrial strife and sometimes could disrupt or even destroy an industry.

Whichever way they played their cards, the unions were in a position to affect the political balance indirectly. Moreover, because of their mass membership and control of important industries, they were also in a position to affect the political system by direct means. By supporting electoral candidates with their organizational and material resources, and possibly even by seizing control of essential services, they could help determine the balance of internal power.

Historically, European unions most often played a political role, whether direct or indirect. Unlike American unions, they did not, as a rule, develop into strong industrial organizations that could improve the conditions of their members through head-to-head bargaining with employers.[3] Instead, European unions early on turned to politics. Their goals tended to be very broad and ideological. They saw their mission as changing the whole social system, which they believed had led to their weakness, rather than as just improving wages and working conditions. Usually, they were split along ideological lines. Political and religious movements created their own unions or tried to mold other unions to their image. This situation produced a blend of Christian, Communist, Socialist, and independent organizations each of which had some penchant for political action. Because of their weakness at the bargaining table, the European unions preferred direct action in the streets and factories. To achieve even modest improvements in working conditions, the unions tended to rely on direct action to pressure the government to impose their demands on employers rather than relying on their own bargaining strength in the work place.

With the end of the war, it looked as if the unions might break out of their prewar mold. Moved by the spirit of wartime Allied unity and the ideology of renewal that pervaded the ranks of many of the Resistance units, the unions in a number of countries came together. In Italy and France, the Communist and Socialist unions merged even before the war ended. In Holland, the Socialist, Protestant, and Catholic unions set up a system of formal rules for joint cooperation. In East Germany, various groupings were fused, and in the Western Zones, Christians and Socialists began working together in what was to become one of the most powerful union centers in the world, the DGB.

Unity of action and the mergers of various trade union centers strengthened both unions and unionism. Now they had the potential for greater reliance on collective bargaining as well as for political action if they chose it. But for the mergers and cooperative ventures to achieve this potential, ideological goals had to be buried. If they were not, the unions would be inclined to fall back into

---

[3]For a brief discussion of some of the major differences between European and American unions see Everett M. Kassalow, *Trade Unions and Industrial Relations: An International Comparison* (New York: Random House, 1969) and Eric Jacobs, *European Trade Unionism* (New York: Holmes and Meier, 1973).

their traditional ideological splits and reliance on political as opposed to industrial action.

It was not long before the traditional pattern began to reemerge, particularly
in France and Italy. The early postwar unity among the unions mirrored the
complexities of French and Italian political life. In both countries, the Communists gained considerable influence in union affairs, just as they did in working-
class politics. They soon, to all appearances, became the dominant faction in the
merged national trade union centers.[4] In 1946 and early 1947, they consolidated their position. Following Communist party direction, they sought to make
themselves respectable and respected political partners in the new Europe. By
late 1947, however, there was a change in political direction. As far as can be
determined, Communist party objectives were then to prevent economic recovery, ensure political instability, and perhaps even to seize power, in varying
orders of priority. Disruption of the Atlantic Alliance was added to the list in
due course.

Capitalizing on the miserable economic conditions prevailing in postwar
Europe and the pent-up demands of the workers, Communist parties and the
trade unions under their control went on the offensive. Communist ministers
withdrew or were expelled from the governments of France and Italy. Communist union leaders replaced their early postwar cooperation with slowdowns,
strikes, and sabotage. The fragile postwar economies, already in trouble, were
now faced with collapse. If domestic economic disruption were to continue,
United States economic assistance would be next to useless. To avoid economic
and political chaos, the democratic parties of the Left and center would have to
bring the Communists back into the government. But this time, as it was in
Prague in 1948, it would have to be on the Communists' own terms.

World War II not only undermined the internal balance of power in many
European states, it also destroyed the remnants of the balance of power among
the European nations. It left Russia the only superpower on the Continent and
brought Russian troops into the heart of Central Europe.

At the end of the war, the Russians could have followed a soft line of

---

[4] Almost all noncommunist observers believe that the major trade union centers in
France and Italy fell under the control of Communist parties subservient to Moscow. See
Georges Lefranc, *Les Expériences Syndicales en France, 1939–1950* (Paris: Montaigne,
1950); Alain Bergounioux, *Force Ouvrière,* (Paris: Seuil, 1975); Borkenau, op. cit.; Annie
Kriegel, *The French Communists* (Chicago: University of Chicago Press, 1972); Ronald
Tiersky, *French Communism 1920–1972* (New York: Columbia University Press, 1974);
Alfred T. Rieber, *Stalin and the French Communist Party, 1941–1947* (New York: Colum-
bia University Press, 1962); Val Lorwin, *The French Labor Movement* (Cambridge: Harvard
University Press, 1954); Donald M. Blackmer and Sidney Tarrow, eds., *Communism in Italy
and France* (Princeton: Princeton University Press, 1975); Donald L. M. Blackmer and
Annie Kriegel, *The International Role of the Communist Parties of Italy and France* (Cam-
bridge: Center for International Studies, Harvard University, 1975); Daniel Horowitz, *The
Italian Labor Movement* (Cambridge: Harvard University Press, 1963).

indirect control and merely "Finlandized" Eastern Europe. Instead they were tough. They gradually turned the area into a zone of satellites. The Russians also sought to expand their direct control over other adjacent areas, particularly Iran as well as Turkey and Greece.

What were the Russian objectives in Western Europe? Did they intend to seize control of the entire Continent? If so, would the Russian army march to the English Channel, or would the Communist parties of Europe be assigned the task of imposing Communist rule?

Even with the advantage of hindsight, it is difficult to answer these questions definitively. Little is known about Russian thinking during this period—even less than about other critical periods, both earlier and later. Divining Russian strategic thinking is always at best a chancy undertaking, of course. Nevertheless, on the basis of probable perspectives and overt behavior, it is possible to deduce a range of Russian objectives and outline the strategy that was used to achieve them.[5]

The maximum objective for Western Europe was a continent ruled by Communist governments subservient to the U.S.S.R. Attaining this would have considerably reduced the danger to the war-torn Russian regime itself. By enabling the Soviet Union to harness the industrial resources of the Continent, it would also have enabled that country ultimately to tip the balance of power against the only other superpower in the world, the United States.

The minimum Russian objective was ensuring that Western Europe, and particularly Germany, did not again become a threat. This also meant ensuring that a revived Western Europe and the United States did not form an alliance to threaten Russian control of Eastern Europe and ultimately Russia itself.

At first, while they consolidated their control over Eastern Europe, the Russians must have waited for the United States forces to leave Western Europe, as Roosevelt had apparently told Stalin at Yalta they would. The departure of United States troops would have been very much in the tradition of America's prevailing isolationism. Moreover, the United States, according to Russian forecasts, was about to experience a serious depression; and President Truman was under attack by the Henry Wallaceite Left for failing to pursue postwar cooperation with the Soviet Union.

Stalin took various steps to hasten this promised withdrawal. The Soviet Union engaged in a major demobilization and encouraged its allies in France and Italy, the Communist parties, to disarm themselves. Even in the face of sharp objections within the Communist Resistance movement, French and Italian partisans handed in their arms. In the first few years after the war, the Russians also

---

[5] Among the most useful secondary sources on Russia's postwar behavior are Adam Ulam, *Expansion and Coexistence*, 2nd ed. (New York: Praeger, 1974); Thomas W. Wolfe, *Soviet Power and Europe 1945–1970* (Baltimore: Johns Hopkins, 1970); Philip Mosely, *The Kremlin and World Politics* (New York: Vintage Books, 1960).

tried to give the impression that conflicts with their former allies were not irreconcilable. Skirmishes over Iran, developments in Eastern Europe, and conflict about the future of Germany were smoothed over by Russian disengagement and by foreign ministers' conferences and other forms of diplomatic accommodation and gestures of moderation. Moreover, the major Communist parties of Western Europe were behaving like respectable political organizations. Communist ministers cooperated with their colleagues. Communist elements in the unions and in other organizations encouraged their followers to work hard and to continue their sacrifices in the interests of postwar recovery and renewal.

But by mid-1947, the Russians changed direction. They may have feared that the Truman Doctrine and the Marshall Plan were designed to rebuild the military potential of Western Europe with a view to wresting away their wartime gains. Or they may simply have wanted to ensure that the Continent would remain weak, unstable, and susceptible to their influence. In any event, the Russians apparently did not believe that military conflict was likely. Instead, they mobilized their political allies in Western Europe and launched a major offensive, first against the Marshall Plan and later against NATO, Western control of Berlin, and similar Western initiatives.

The formation of the Communist Information Bureau (Cominform) in the early fall of 1947 may have been a response in part to the internal needs of the Communist bloc and not an instrument of an attempted takeover of Western Europe and other parts of the world. Nevertheless, at the founding meeting in October, the French and Italian-Communist parties in particular were told to subordinate all other activities to the struggle against the Marshall Plan.

Both Communist parties already had withdrawn from their respective governments, for one reason or another. But both probably could hope that the coming parliamentary elections would strengthen their position and, with the assistance of the Socialists, bring Communist governments to power through almost legal means. Now, in the fall of 1947, they were told to abandon any hope of electoral success. Instead, they were to use their formidable party and trade union apparatus to exploit the prevailing economic misery and to obstruct the Marshall Plan. Through strikes and riots, they were to dislocate the entire society and ensure that European economies were not put on the road to recovery.

Also, the leaders of the French and Italian parties were subjected to savage criticism for actually having followed early postwar Russian instructions. They were accused of virtually capitulating to bourgeois legalism after the war, disarming their Resistance forces, and enabling the bourgeoisie to return to power.

But while the new marching orders were to disrupt the Western economies, the French and Italian parties apparently were not to attempt to seize power by illegal means. They were—initially anyway—only to prevent Western European recovery and, as the French party loudly proclaimed, to sabotage the military efforts of their governments should there be an outbreak of hostilities with the Soviet Union.

The United States was slow to understand and respond to Russian strategy in postwar Europe.[6] The new and inexperienced United States president was constrained initially by a combination of internal and external political forces. At home, there was a prevailing belief that the Great Crusade of 1939–1945 had solved all problems of war and the underlying economic and social causes of war. It was further assumed that once the problems of world peace had been solved—through the UN in the main—the "boys" would come home and America could turn inward to its own problems. The pressures for withdrawal were underlined in demobilization riots and later in the congressional elections of 1946. As in 1918, these elections produced a Republican majority committed to reducing taxes in general and military expenditures in particular.

Within the Democratic party itself, powerful forces insisted that the United States should do nothing to increase tension with the Soviet Union. Some Democrats were ridden with guilt. They believed that United States intervention in the Russian civil war of 1917–1919 and ostracism of the Bolshevik regime in the 1920s had been responsible for unnecessary enmity. They were determined to maintain Roosevelt's spirit of cooperation with the Soviet Union.

Others within the Democrats' extended family were further to the left. Some were Communists or fellow travelers and were responsive to party discipline. Others believed that the Soviet Union was a "progressive" country with much to offer in the postwar world. Moreover, the liberals and leftists had been critical of Truman since he was placed on the 1944 ticket. They regarded him as a Midwestern conservative and no internationalist.

Almost immediately upon the war's end, Truman was under fire within his party for turning away from Roosevelt's foreign and domestic policy. In May 1946, three liberal-leftist organizations created a national alliance, in part to lobby for continued United States–Russian cooperation. There also was much talk of creating a third party, which eventually emerged as the Progressive party in 1948. In these domestic circumstances, it would have been difficult for

[6]The literature on early postwar United States policy is voluminous and is becoming more so. Among major first-hand accounts are Harry Truman, *Memoirs*, vol. I (New York: Doubleday, 1955); James Byrnes, *Speaking Frankly* (New York: Harper and Row, 1948); Dean Acheson, *Present at the Creation* (New York: Signet Books, 1970); Walter Millis, ed., *The Forrestal Diaries* (New York: Viking, 1951). Important secondary sources include Herbert Feis, *Between War and Peace* (Princeton: Princeton University Press, 1960); Seyom Brown, *The Faces of Power* (New York: Columbia University Press, 1968); Louis Halle, *The Cold War as History* (New York: Harper and Row, 1967); Adam Ulam, *The Rivals* (New York: Viking, 1971). Revisionist writers who do not share these views are cited in Chapter 4, footnote 34.

Truman to respond to Russian strategy even if he were sure about the direction to take. As it was, however, Truman also inherited much of the thinking and most of the expectations of his predecessor.

Between 1941 and 1945, the United States moved from a very narrow concept of its responsibilities to the exercise of leadership over the more productive half of Europe and over Japan. But this expansion of America's interests and responsibilities had been unforeseen and was largely unplanned—and largely unassimilated. As late as 1946, United States policy makers assumed that they would be able to set up an international system that would leave the United States free, once again, to limit drastically its commitments in other continents.

The overriding American postwar objective was to ensure that there would be no future aggression. Peace and security were to be maintained by continued cooperation among the Allies, and among all other "peace-loving states" through the United Nations, after the peace treaties were signed. Occupied Europe and Japan were to have democratic governments, and the non-Western areas formerly controlled by the European colonial powers were to be granted national self-determination. Restrictive trade practices, which many observers believed had been responsible in part for depression and the rise of aggressive dictatorships, were to be done away with and the world opened to free trade.

Although, even before hostilities had ceased, some elements within the War and State Departments warned the president that postwar cooperation with the Soviet Union could not be assumed, Washington was reluctant to alter its strategy.[7] The United States continued to emphasize diplomatic negotiations and the establishment of the UN system as the best method of ensuring peace, security, and the global balance of power. Some emphasis was placed on economic relief and reconstruction aid, particularly to Western Europe, but the United States de-emphasized military and other political instruments of policy. There was a major demobilization, and military appropriations were cut drastically. By 1947, United States forces were down from their wartime peak of about 12 million to approximately 1.5 million, scattered over Europe, the United States, and the Far East. Military appropriations were down from a wartime peak of $81 billion to $14 billion. Only small numbers of atomic bombs were produced.

Similarly, the United States cut back its ability to influence developments

---

[7]Among the few who were concerned about Soviet ambitions in Western Europe were the United States ambassador to Moscow, Averell Harriman; his chargé, George Kennan; the United States Ambassador to France, Jefferson Caffery; and the special assistant to the director, Office of European Affairs, Raymond Murphy. See for example U.S. Department of State, *Foreign Relations of the U.S., 1945*, vol. V, pp. 818, 821, and 841; General Records of the Department of State, Record Group 59, Box 6107, Decimal File 1945–1949, Dispatches nos. 2363, 2586, and 2683; Memorandum from Special Assistant Raymond Murphy to the director, Office of European Affairs, May 21, 1945. The revisionists of course maintain that these exceptions were representative of United States thinking during this period.

abroad through political operations. In the fall of 1945, the Office of Strategic Services (OSS) was closed down. Some of its analytical functions were passed on to the State Department and later to the Central Intelligence Group located in the Executive Office of the President. Intelligence, counterintelligence, and operational activities were transferred to the War Department's Strategic Services Unit. But the unit was basically a caretaker body that presided over the liquidation of most of the OSS espionage and operational network.[8]

By late 1946, however, United States policy began to change. Until then, intelligence and United States embassy reports and a few internal State Department reports warning that the Russians and their local European allies might exploit Europe's weakness were largely ignored. But during 1946, United States policy makers gradually came to doubt that peace and security could be maintained through negotiations with the Soviet Union directly and within the UN. And limited economic assistance to Western Europe would not be sufficient. The Soviet Union was, they began to conclude, attempting to expand its control around its borders whenever the opportunity arose. As Western European recovery was proceeding slowly at best, the Russians might soon be tempted to take advantage of Europe's weakness.

Moreover, as United States Chargé George Kennan wrote from Moscow in February 1946, the Russians could be expected to use official state-to-state relations as well as unofficial "front" organizations to pursue their expansionist aims. In a long telegram, which was widely read, Kennan warned that a variety of national and international nongovernmental organizations were being penetrated by Moscow-oriented Communists and that

> particular, almost vital, importance is attached in this connection to the international labor movement. In this Moscow sees the possibility of side-tracking Western governments in world affairs and building up an international lobby capable of compelling governments to take actions favorable to Soviet interests in various countries and of paralyzing actions disagreeable to the USSR.[9]

In midsummer 1946, White House aide Clark Clifford, at the president's request, completed a lengthy synthesis of advice and information available within the government on relations with Russia. In general, he noted, "Beyond the borders now under her control the Soviet Union is striving to penetrate strategic areas and everywhere agents of the Soviet government work to weaken the governments of other nations and to achieve their ultimate isolation and

[8]The fullest, but by no means complete, account of these events can be found in R. Harris Smith, *OSS: The Secret History of America's First Central Intelligence Agency* (Berkeley, University of California Press, 1972).

[9]George Kennan, *Memoirs 1925–1950* (New York: Bantam, 1969), p. 592.

destruction." In France, the Russians had hoped to "gain political control" through the Communist party in the June 1946 elections but, in spite of their inability to do this, "exercise disproportionate influence through the control of organized labor. That influence will be used to shape French policy in the manner most suitable for Soviet purposes and to prepare for a renewal of the Soviet attempt to gain France by political means."[10]

Until the winter of 1946–1947, the president took no decisive action. With the '46 congressional elections behind him, however, disturbing signals that European economic recovery was faltering and the British withdrawal from Greece in February 1947 impelled him to articulate the so-called Truman Doctrine. Although he did not mention the Soviet Union, his meaning was clear. In a broadcast speech in March before a joint session of Congress, Truman portrayed the Communist insurrection in Greece and Russian pressure on Turkey as elements of a worldwide struggle between free peoples and those resisting subjugation by armed minorities, on the one side, and outside pressures on the other. He asked what up until then had been a none too friendly Congress to appropriate modest amounts of economic and military aid for Greece and Turkey. He said if the aid was not granted and Greece and Turkey fell, the Middle East would be thrown into confusion. Other countries in Europe and elsewhere whose peoples were struggling "to maintain their freedoms and independence while they repair the damages of war" would be adversely affected. The Truman Doctrine received prompt, bipartisan support.

In the late spring, United States Secretary of State Marshall went the next logical step and announced a massive economic assistance plan to aid European recovery and help reduce political instability on the Continent. The United States would remedy the immediate shortages of essential agricultural and industrial equipment to reduce Europe's inflation and unemployment and get Europeans back on their feet. The embattled president encouraged Secretary of State Marshall to sponsor the program to help ensure congressional approval.

Thus, in 1947, the United States shifted its strategy from one of relying, in large measure, on postwar cooperation with the Soviet Union to one of containing Russian influence and preventing European Communists from coming to power. Economic and to some extent military assistance were the major means that were used early on. As 1947 drew to a close, however, the United States began to employ other instruments. When, for example, the success of the Marshall Plan appeared to be jeopardized by the actions of European Communist parties and their controlled labor organizations after the Cominform meeting in October 1947, the president approved the use of covert political operations. In early 1948, the Office of Policy Coordination, under former OSS operator Frank

---

[10] Arthur Krock, *Memoirs, Sixty Years on the Firing Line* (New York: Funk and Wagnalls, 1968), pp. 431–432.

Wisner, was established in the Central Intelligence Agency (itself an outgrowth of the Central Intelligence Group.)[11] Later, when as a result of the Prague coup and the Berlin blockade it appeared that Russian military might threatened the independence of Europe, the United States proposed treating an attack on Western Europe as an attack on itself. This commitment was embodied in the North Atlantic Treaty, and the protocols were signed in early 1949.

Thus, even as the European Communists and the Russian government coalesced in an effort to alter the internal and external political balance in Europe, the Europeans were able to turn to the United States. And the United States government responded with a growing commitment. No longer could European developments be explained without an understanding of parallel developments in Washington. The United States government slowly but inexorably added its weight to help prevent a tilt to the extreme left within a number of European countries and to prevent the Continent from falling under the domination of the Soviet Union.

The United States government, however, was not the only American actor that was called upon to help maintain the internal and external power balances in Europe. Europe was threatened not simply by a national power but by a combination of the Russian government and European nongovernmental forces, specifically Communist parties and their labor organizations. The United States and European governments could do much to resist Russian pressure and alleviate the economic misery that facilitated the Communist coalition's efforts. On their own, however, the Western governments were hard pressed to counter Western labor organizations sympathetic to Russian aims.

If Western governments were to attempt to destroy these organizations in order to maintain the balance of internal power, they would at the same time undermine that balance. Governmental efforts to destroy the Communist parties and their trade union apparatus would split the democratic center. The socialists and many independents, fearing that this might be a prelude to another right-wing takeover, might very well side with the Communists. By the reverse token, many other centrists would accept the suppression of the unions and move to the right. This would have had the effect of polarizing the countries involved and opening the way to civil war. In these circumstances, it would have been next to impossible to rebuild a stable Western Europe, and the Russians would have achieved their minimum objective without much effort.

Yet what could the Western governments have done if the unions had remained hostile to their efforts to rebuild the Continent? Because of their strategic position in the economy and political system, the unions were in a position decisively to affect the outcome of events on the Continent.

[11]Smith, op. cit., p. 366 and Victor Marchetti and John D. Marks, *The CIA and the Cult of Intelligence* (New York: Knopf, 1974), p. 22.

Thus, the noncommunist unions of the West were in a crucial position.[12] If they went along with the Communists, they would, of course, have jeopardized European recovery and undermined the balance of internal and external power. If they did not, if they broke definitively with the Communists, they would have been in a position to neutralize the Russians and their labor allies in Western Europe. By keeping the economy running, by unloading Marshall Plan imports and loading manufactured exports, and by providing their governments with reliable trade unions in defense-related industries, noncommunist unions would enable society to operate even if major segments of the labor movement remained in Communist hands.

In the middle and late forties, however, it was not at all clear that noncommunist European union leaders would be able to prevent the Soviet Union from using European unions for its political-military purposes. The unions' strength had diminished greatly during the war. In Germany the unions had to be rebuilt completely. Just who would emerge as the leader of the new labor organizations was far from certain. In the Russian Zone, the Communists were on their way to complete control, and the Russians and the WFTU were seeking to influence the new union organizations in Berlin and the Western Zones. In the reviving organizations in France and Italy, the power of the noncommunists was considerably reduced compared with their predominant prewar position. Indeed, as noted before, the Communists emerged from the Liberation much stronger than they had ever been, and most observers credited them with being the major faction in the revived unions.

Moreover, the noncommunists who had succeeded in regaining significant positions of leadership were now divided. For many of the same reasons as the Socialists had, some noncommunists favored remaining in the main union organizations, capitalizing on Communist strength and, at the same time, keeping the organization from being used by the Communist party. Other noncommunist leaders believed that this course of action would not succeed, that it was in fact suicidal, and that new trade union structures completely free from Communist control were necessary.

In the first few years after the war, however, those who favored the second strategy were not, on their own, able to counter Communist hegemony in the labor movement for the reasons described previously. The Communists at that time were highly respectable. They had fought alongside the Allies against the Nazis. They did not encourage strikes and riots. Quite the opposite: they urged hard work and sacrifice in the name of postwar recovery. Although this opened them to the charge that they were following party and government dictates

[12]For a general survey of the European labor movement at the end of World War II see Lewis Lorwin, *The International Labor Movement* (New York: Harper Bros., 1953). For a discussion of labor in Italy and France see Daniel L. Horowitz, op. cit. and Val R. Lorwin, op. cit.

rather than promoting the interests of the workers, it was difficult for the noncommunists to articulate any reasonable basis for splitting the unions so shortly after the war. The noncommunists who favored the split did not believe that large numbers of workers would follow them. Moreover, the noncommunist leaders realized that without liberal financial assistance, they would be unable to sustain a new union structure. Unlike American, British, and German workers, French and Italian workers did not as a rule pay regular dues even when they were members of a union. Thus, without some source of external assistance, it would have been impossible in postwar Europe to finance completely new national union structures.

In these immediate postwar years, the Communists effectively dominated the major labor organizations in France and Italy and were seeking to gain a foothold in the recreated German unions. The European governments on their own could do little about it. Unless some major nongovernmental force could act as a counterweight, the noncommunist European unions would not be able to prevent organized labor from being used to upset the internal balance of power in France, Italy, and Germany and then to upset the entire European balance of power. As it turned out, however, there was one such available nongovernmental counterweight. Enter, at this critical juncture, the American Federation of Labor.

Chapter 3

The Foreign Policy Making of a Nongovernmental Organization

The AFL was a substantial organization at the end of World War II. Although it was never more than a loosely knit federation of 90 separate unions, its membership during the depression and the war had grown from approximately 2 million to 7 million workers. Its annual expenditures had grown to approximately $3 million. Its leaders, partly because of their involvement in wartime government agencies, enjoyed a legitimacy and prestige they had never had before. Nevertheless, the outlook for its future was uncertain.

AFL leaders were concerned principally about demobilization and reconversion to a peacetime economy. The labor market and working conditions would, of course, be very different with 12 million men and women returning from the armed forces. Jobs would have to be found for them, as well as for another 8 million workers who had been directly employed by wartime defense industries. As the AFL saw it, the conversion from war to peace could best be accomplished through an increase in the purchasing power of the workers, whose demands for goods and services would create more jobs. Postwar prosperity would be assured, the AFL leaders argued, if wartime government controls on the economy, particularly on wages, were lifted and if management engaged in collective bargaining with labor.

This approach assumed that unions would continue operating and would perhaps even increase their strength, so that collective bargaining would be meaningful. However, a strong antiunion tide swept the country in the first few years after the war. In response to militant labor actions, such as strikes, sit-downs, and demonstrations, the president, the Congress, and many state governments took a number of actions to weaken the power of organized labor. President Truman did shift his position by the end of 1946, but the antiunion feeling continued and culminated in what AFL leaders exaggeratedly called the "slave labor" Taft-Hartley Act of 1947. In spite of President Truman's veto and the considerable resources the AFL and the CIO devoted to fighting the act, the Republican Congress overrode the veto and thus reversed some of the gains organized labor had made since the passage of the Wagner Act in 1935.

Aside from the antilabor mood in government, the AFL leaders had other problems to face. The reconversion of the economy was not being effected without serious difficulties. Although jobs were found for most returning veterans, unemployment continued to rise. By early 1946, it was up to 2.5 million—approximately a 4.6 percent rate. When wartime price-controls legislation expired in June 1946, the cost of living began to shoot up. Between June and December 1946, consumer prices rose 15 percent with food prices rising 28 percent.

The AFL leaders also faced another challenge. By the end of the war the rival Congress of Industrial Organizations, only 10 years after its founding, had attracted a membership of 4.5 million and was growing. Its leaders were welcome in government and in liberal and intellectual circles generally, and it was the American affiliate in the main international labor body, the WFTU. Many senior AFL leaders found this intolerable. AFL President Green, for example, was censured by his colleagues in May 1945 for cosigning a report with CIO officials because, it was argued, that action gave official AFL recognition to the CIO. In the early postwar period, the AFL was still trying to contain CIO influence within the American house of labor.

In spite of their domestic preoccupations, however, the majority of AFL leaders decided that they would have to concern themselves also with international affairs. Without prompting from the United States or any other government, the AFL sought to become a major actor on the world scene. The AFL created its own institutions to deal with foreign policy and international affairs. An information-gathering apparatus was established to report on conditions abroad. A special committee evaluated the information, defined the AFL's options, and recommended choices among various courses of action. The entire organization then ratified these decisions, and the leadership raised the money and hired the people to carry them out.

The AFL foreign affairs machinery appears to have operated independently of the United States government or any other external organization. Although several AFL officials held government positions during the war and the AFL exchanged information with United States officials on some projects in the postwar period, there is little evidence to indicate that the government played a significant role, or much of any role, in the AFL policy-making process.

THE AFL'S DECISION-MAKING STRUCTURE

The AFL constitution, which remained basically unaltered from 1945 through 1955, established the broad parameters within which decision making took place. This structure reflected the main interests and alignments in the loosely knit federation and the absence of any formal relationship with such external institutions as the Democratic party or the United States government.

The AFL constitution stipulated that the annual convention was the Federation's major policy-making body. The constitution's preamble stated that "every Trade and Labor organization in America" should be united "in convention assembled, to adopt such measures and disseminate such principles . . . as will permanently unite them to secure recognition of rights to which they are justly entitled."[1]

The chief policy-making functions of the convention as defined by the constitution and its order and rules of business were to (1) review the preceding year's policies and administration of the Federation's officers, (2) determine the next year's policies, and (3) elect the officers—a president, 13 vice-presidents, and a secretary-treasurer, who together would constitute the Federation's Executive Council. As a first order of business, the reports of the Executive Council and the secretary-treasurer were presented to the convention. The reports were reviewed by relevant committees appointed by the president. Finally, the convention discussed and voted on the committees' recommendations. The Federation used a similar process in adopting new legislation. Resolutions, which normally had to be received by the secretary-treasurer at least 30 days before the convention, were assigned either to the Resolutions Committee or to another relevant committee. After the committees' reports, the full convention voted on the resolutions. The final task of the convention, the election of officers, was

---

[1]*Report of the Proceedings of the Sixty-Fourth Annual Convention of the American Federation of Labor, November 20–30, 1944*, p. xxxi. AFL convention proceedings will be cited hereafter as *Proceedings*. The following analysis will be drawn from the AFL constitution, which is found at the beginning of each annual convention report. (The AFL held an annual convention in the autumn of each year covered by this study, with the exception of 1945.) Examination of the convention reports reveals that there were no basic changes in the constitution which affected foreign policy making during this period. Similarly, the order and rules of business remained basically unaltered.

straightforward. The officers were nominated and quickly elected on the last day of the convention.

Although the constitution gave the convention the power to review and set AFL policy, it also left major policy-making power in the hands of the Federation's officers. The president was to preside over the convention and appoint the leaders and members of the convention's legislative committees; he was also to supervise the activities of the Federation and inform the convention through the Executive Council report. The secretary-treasurer's duties primarily concerned collecting and disbursing the Federation's funds and helping to administer the organization.

The Executive Council was to execute the mandates of the convention and "to initiate, whenever necessary, such legislative action as the convention may direct." The council was "to authorize the sending out of trade union speakers from place to place in the interests of the Federation." Finally, the council was "to take further actions and render such further decisions during the interim of conventions as may become necessary to safeguard and promote the best interests of the Federation and of all its affiliated unions."

Formally at least, the AFL, unlike the national trade union centers in many countries, was autonomous. Unlike the unions in totalitarian or authoritarian systems, such as the Soviet Union, Nazi Germany, Franco's Spain, or Salazar's Portugal, the AFL had no constitutional provisions that allowed the government or a political party to become involved in the labor organization's decision-making processes.[2] Indeed, even in a number of democratic political systems, national trade union centers and political parties (even when a political party is in control of the government) formally permit each other to play a role in their respective policy-making processes.[3] This has never been the case in the AFL. Neither the Democratic, Republican, nor Socialist parties nor the United States government has ever had any formal role in the AFL policy-making structure.

Within this structure, the Free Trade Union Committee (FTUC) was one of the most important policy-making institutions. Its origins are to be found in the Jewish Labor Committee (JLC), the Labor League for Human Rights, and the wartime committee of emigré trade union leaders, most of whom resided in New York.

---

[2]For the legal and constitutional provisions that enabled the state or party to play a formal role in the decision-making processes of "trade unions," see for example on the U.S.S.R., Edwin Morrell, "Communist Unionism: Organized Labor and the Soviet State," unpublished Ph.D. thesis, Harvard University, 1965 and Jay B. Sorenson, *The Life and Death of Soviet Trade Unions, 1917–1928* (New York: Atherton, 1967). On Nazi Germany, see International Labor Organization, *Legislative Series*, Germany 6, Geneva, 1933 and ILO, *Legislative Series*, Germany 1, Geneva, 1934. On Spain, see ILO, *Legislative Series*, Spain 1, Geneva, 1938; *United Nations Yearbook of Human Rights for 1947* (New York: 1949), pp. 286–288; Fred Whitney, *Labor Policy and Practices in Spain* (New York: Praeger, 1965).

[3]Everett M. Kassalow, *Trade Union and Industrial Relations: An International Comparison* (New York: Random House, 1969), especially pp. 29–65.

As early as the late 1930s, two important AFL leaders, David Dubinsky and Matthew Woll, became concerned about the fate of democratic European trade union and political leaders who, they feared, would fall into the hands of the Nazis and the Fascists. The American labor leaders feared that if the democratic leadership of Eastern and Western Europe were destroyed, it would be difficult to rebuild Europe's democratic institutions in the aftermath of an Axis defeat. They believed that in the ensuing political vacuum, the Russians and the well-organized Communist underground loyal to the Soviet Union might well emerge as the new rulers of the Continent. With this in mind, Woll and Dubinsky enlisted the support of AFL President William Green and Secretary-Treasurer George Meany in the Jewish Labor Committee's effort to rescue hundreds of democratic labor leaders, politicians, and intellectuals from the Nazis and Fascists in occupied Europe.

During the war, these exiles served as a liaison group between the Labor League for Human Rights, a political and relief organization headed by Woll, and the underground organizations in occupied Europe. Working ties with Allied governments were established to enable relief aid and supplies to be dropped to the underground organizations. As D-Day approached, the exiles and the American labor leaders began to discuss ways of assisting the Europeans after the Axis had been defeated and the Western Allies had disengaged themselves from the underground groups.

In the fall of 1944, the AFL leaders asked the annual convention to pass a resolution creating a fund to support noncommunist and democratic elements throughout the world. At the convention, Luigi Antonini, an ILGWU vice-president, reported on his recent trip to liberated parts of Italy. He noted that labor elements were reviving after the breakdown of fascism, and he urged that moral and material support be given to these groups: "For while it is being reported at the moment that a truce prevails between the democratic and totalitarian groups in the central body of Italian labor, it is certain that this truce may last only until the Communists find it opportune to make a bid for domination and the overpowering of all democratic opposition."[4]

Although several important AFL leaders favored the Federation's withdrawal from international involvement,[5] the convention approved the resolution introduced by Woll observing that liberation from Nazi Germany and Japan did not offer "automatic assurance that freedom and democracy will be restored, or that workers in each country will regain or be secure in their rights as free men." To assure these results, the resolution called for the creation of a Free Trade Union Committee and a $1 million Free Trade Union Fund.[6]

[4]*Proceedings*, 1944, pp. 625–626.
[5]Interviews, Abraham Bluestein, former executive director of the Labor League for Human Rights and the first executive secretary of the FTUC; David Dubinsky; and Harry Lang, former editor of the *Jewish Daily Forward* and an intimate of Green and Dubinsky.
[6]*Proceedings*, 1944, pp. 556–557.

The committee's purpose was to secure the assistance of American trade unions in rebuilding "free and democratic trade unions" in Europe, Asia, and Central and South America. The committee was to be a new, distinct entity in the AFL structure. Its scope was limited in that it was responsible only for building free trade unions. Officially, it was not to be concerned with other international labor affairs.[7] Moreover, it was to some extent separated from the traditional policy-making machinery. Although the FTUC was to report on financial matters to "a committee nominated by the President" of the AFL,[8] the FTUC was not obligated to submit all its activities to the Executive Council for review. It was understood that the FTUC was, to some undefined extent, an independent body, albeit sponsored by the AFL.

OBTAINING AND DISSEMINATING INFORMATION

The FTUC discharged two major functions in the AFL foreign policy-making process. First, it was the primary information-gathering body. Although AFL leaders received official communications from foreign labor organizations, and occasionally the mass media reported on international labor affairs, the AFL leaders did not feel that they were sufficiently well informed about developments abroad and concluded that they needed their own, independent information-gathering apparatus. At considerable expense, the FTUC engaged a staff to prepare detailed reports on various countries in Europe, Asia, and Latin America. These reports, circulated selectively, were the AFL's primary source of information on labor developments abroad.

The FTUC's role in gathering information, particularly on developments in Europe, was greatly strengthened when Irving Brown was appointed the FTUC representative in Europe.[9] Although only in his early thirties, Brown had had considerable experience in ideological and labor politics. He had been associated with Jay Lovestone's Communist opposition group in the 1930s and also had been an AFL organizer prior to the war, a minor official in the War Production Board, and a participant in planning the United States government's postwar labor policy in areas freed from the Nazis. In the fall of 1945, he was asked by the FTUC to go to Europe for six months. His specific assignment was to gather detailed information on the international and European trade union movements and to formulate recommendations for rebuilding democratic trade unionism.[10]

Brown arrived in Europe in October 1945 in the company of ILGWU Vice-President Charles Zimmerman, who had been selected by the Jewish Labor

---

[7]Matters relating to the International Labor Organization and the exchange of fraternal delegates were generally considered beyond the purview of the FTUC.

[8]*Proceedings*, 1944, p. 557.

[9]Interviews, David Dubinsky, George Harrison, Charles Zimmerman, and Jay Lovestone and *Proceedings*, 1946, p. 73.

[10]Interviews, Abraham Bluestein and Irving Brown.

Committee to travel through Europe to receive the formal recognition and thanks of the European labor movement for the JCL's wartime assistance. Traveling with Zimmerman helped to identify Brown as an intimate associate of the principal AFL leaders concerned with international affairs. Indeed, Zimmerman and Brown were received and honored by leading trade unionists (several of whom had been rescued from the Nazis by the Jewish Labor Committee) and by high government officials (many of whom had been former trade unionists), as well as by high-ranking United States military officials and diplomats. During his first months in Europe, Brown reported occasionally by letter to Matthew Woll and often sent blind copies of his reports to Jay Lovestone, the ILGWU's director of international affairs.[11]

In the spring of 1946, the FTUC decided to retain Brown as its representative in Europe. At the end of the year, the AFL leaders decided to open a European office. When French Communists made it clear that an office in Paris was unwelcome and Brown would be physically harassed,[12] Brussels was chosen as the location of the office. Mrs. Brown, Jay Lovestone's former secretary, now joined her husband as his unpaid administrative assistant. At about the same time, Lovestone took over as executive secretary of the FTUC. With Lovestone in New York and Mrs. Brown holding down the office in Brussels, reports to the FTUC were more frequent and comprehensive.

In the years following, Brown traveled throughout Europe and occasionally to Asia and frequently returned to the United States. He knew almost every important noncommunist European trade union leader, met frequently with cabinet ministers and Socialist party leaders in most Western European countries and with the exiled leaders of Eastern Europe, and had ready access to Generals Clay and Eisenhower and every Marshall Plan administrator and United States ambassador in Europe. Indeed, if it was necessary, he was apparently able to meet with anyone west of the Iron Curtain.

In Latin America, Serafino Romualdi was the AFL's representative. Romualdi, a former Italian socialist who had left his native country when Mussolini came to power, had joined the publications department of the ILGWU in 1933. During the war, he worked for the State Department in Latin America and for the Office of Strategic Services in liberated Italy.[13] Mainly because of the Federation's long-standing involvement in Central and South America, Dubinsky and Woll, in early 1946, were able to secure the AFL Executive

[11]Free Trade Union Committee Archives, hereafter referred to as "FTUC archives." The papers of AFL President Green and other AFL records will be referred to as "AFL archives." See Appendix A.
[12]Minutes of the International Relations Committee Meeting, November 13, 1946.
[13]Serafino Romualdi, *Presidents and Peons: Recollections of a Labor Ambassador* (New York: Funk and Wagnalls, 1967), p. 609.

Council's approval of Romualdi's appointment on the AFL's and not the FTUC's payroll.[14] Nevertheless, Romualdi continued to work out of the ILGWU's headquarters in New York City, where the FTUC was located.

In Asia, the FTUC for several years had two international representatives. Richard Deverell, who had served with MacArthur's forces in Japan and had become dissatisfied with aspects of the United States government's occupation policies, was hired in the late 1940s and worked for the FTUC until he joined the staff of the International Confederation of Free Trade Unions in the early 1950s. Harry Goldberg, who, like Brown, had been associated with Lovestone since the 1930s, became the second international representative of the FTUC in Asia. In March 1951, he was sent to India, and from there he went to Indonesia in 1952. In 1953, Goldberg was assigned to Italy, where he remained an FTUC representative for five years.

Henry Rutz, a former member of the International Typographical Union who was stationed in Germany as the Executive Officer of the United States Army, Manpower Division, was also hired by the AFL when he left government service. Although the FTUC succeeded in having Rutz placed on the AFL payroll to avoid having to pay the salary and expenses of another man in the field, the detailed information he sent back on developments inside Germany and Austria were passed on to the FTUC.

The FTUC also received information on labor movements and general economic and political conditions from the AFL international representative, Robert Watt, who had had a great deal of experience in foreign labor affairs and was well known in Europe. After his death in 1947, Watt's place was filled by Frank Fenton, who, on his death in 1949, was succeeded, in turn, by George Delaney. These men attended international labor conferences and ILO meetings but, with rare exceptions, did not possess detailed information on the labor movements of specific countries. The FTUC also, on occasion, hired young academics, men such as Robert Alexander and Norman Palmer, to prepare special reports on topics of interest to the committee.

Another source of FTUC information was contacts in the United States government. During the war, a number of former trade union leaders and employees worked for the government in one capacity or another (mostly as members of the armed forces). Several of these men remained in government service for some months after the war, and one or two chose government service as a career.[15] The FTUC was also in contact with the State Department Bureau

---

[14]Interview, Jay Lovestone.

[15]Joseph Keenan, for example, a secretary of the Chicago Federation of Labor, spent two years as labor advisor to General Lucius Clay, the military governor of Germany; and James Killen of the Pulp and Sulphite Workers was an advisor to General Douglas MacArthur's headquarters in Japan.

EUR-X, a small unit charged with keeping tabs on the international Communist movement.[16]

Once the Marshall Plan was under way, a number of AFL union leaders and staff became Economic Cooperation Administration (ECA) officials. For example, Boris Shishkin, who had been AFL research director, became head of the ECA Labor Division. William Green's files and the FTUC archives are studded with information exchanged with these and other contacts in the United States government.

There are no indications in the AFL's files, however, that the AFL was dependent upon the United States government for information. Frequently, the AFL–United States government correspondence concerned small pieces of information that served to confirm or expand on an AFL conviction about a given labor leader, organization, or program. Also, it was a two-way street: on occasion, the AFL leaders attempted to draw sympathetic United States officials' attention to a problem, organization, or personality.[17]

Another source of information was the visits of American labor leaders to Europe and vice versa. ILGWU Vice-President Luigi Antonini made several trips between 1945 and 1952. Vice-President Zimmerman's trip has already been mentioned. Beginning in 1948, Dubinsky himself traveled through Europe several times. George Harrison and other leaders of the transport unions made several visits to attend meetings of the International Transport Workers' Federation. And in 1949, Green, Woll, Meany, Dubinsky, and Lovestone journeyed to Europe to attend the founding conference of the ICFTU.

Also, key European trade unionists and Socialist party leaders visited the United States and consulted extensively with members of the FTUC. For example, French trade union leaders Léon Jouhaux and Louis Saillant, who also headed the WFTU, made several visits in relation to their roles in the WFTU and the ILO. French Socialist party leader Léon Blum made a lengthy visit to the United States in the spring of 1946—one of many such visits by prominent labor leaders and politicians in the early postwar period, frequently as guests of the AFL.

---

[16]FTUC archives. Moreover, one of Murphy's EUR-X researchers, Benjamin Mandel, had corresponded with Lovestone since their days together in the Communist party in the 1920s.

[17]AFL-CIO archives and FTUC archives. For examples of the AFL efforts to inform United States officials about important labor developments see the *White House Daily Summary, 1946–50*, July 3, 1947 and November 28, 1947, General Records of the Department of State, R.G. 59, N.A. (The White House Summary was prepared daily for the president by the State Department.) See also the recently declassified embassy report on Communist strikes in the maritime industry designed to cripple the Marshall Plan, "Possible Cominform Strike Action among Dock Workers of the World," U.S. Embassy, Rome, August 12, 1949. The report was based in part on the views of the AFL's European representative, Irving Brown.

Finally, the FTUC obtained information from European exiles, mainly from Eastern Europe and Russia, and from wartime refugees from Germany, Austria, and Italy who resided in New York. Many of these exiles and refugees still maintained direct or indirect contacts with their homelands and conveyed information thus acquired to Dubinsky and Lovestone among others.[18]

From interviews with members of the FTUC and examination of archival material, it is possible to discern the processes by which members of the FTUC assimilated the information they received and engaged in policy formulation and implementation. A predominant pattern was established, particularly after Jay Lovestone succeeded Abraham Bluestein as executive secretary of the FTUC.

Lovestone possessed an encyclopedic knowledge of labor movements and politics abroad. As a former national secretary of the American Communist party in the 1920s and the leader of a Communist opposition group—the "Lovestoneites"—he had traveled extensively in Europe in the 1920s and 1930s and had well-placed contacts in almost every European country. After the Nazis came to power, he was instrumental in setting up Anti-Nazi Leagues and the International Rescue Committee to save social democratic leaders, intellectuals, and other potential victims of nazism in Germany and, later, in other parts of Europe. Anticommunist and anti-Nazi activities drew Lovestone to David Dubinsky. During the 1930s and during the war, they worked together on a number of projects, and in 1944, Dubinsky appointed Lovestone to handle ILGWU international affairs. Woll, at that time the AFL's senior vice-president and director of the Labor League for Human Rights, had begun to share Dubinsky's confidence in Lovestone. In the spring of 1946, Lovestone was engaged to administer the FTUC's activities from ILGWU headquarters.

Reports from the FTUC representatives and contacts in Europe, Asia, Latin America, and the United States government were collated and circulated to FTUC members by Lovestone. Although the men in the field frequently had their own particular views of the tactics they wished to see employed, Lovestone usually agreed with their broad interpretation of events in their region. When he did not, Lovestone would circulate his correspondent's reports and generally attach a memorandum stating his own views on the subject.[19] Thus, with the exception of occasional visits of foreign trade union and political leaders to the United States and occasional visits of AFL leaders to Europe, most of the

[18]Interviews, Lang, Brown, and Lovestone. The Jewish Labor Committee, for example, continued to maintain contact with its wartime representatives in bothWestern and Eastern Europe. Many of the prominent intellectuals, social democrats, and trade unionists it rescued from the Nazis and Russians also maintained contact with their homelands and passed information to the JLC, the ILGWU, and the FTUC.

[19]See for example memorandum from Lovestone to Dubinsky, July 5, 1946, FTUC files. Memoranda and letters between AFL leaders hereafter will be cited simply by reference to the last names of the correspondents. Unless otherwise specified, all correspondence between AFL leaders is in the FTUC archives.

FTUC's information came from the oral and written reports of Lovestone and his correspondents.

The principal recipients of the information were the members of the FTUC, especially Woll, the chairman, and Dubinsky, the vice-chairman.[20] The committee's honorary chairman, AFL President William Green, and honorary secretary, AFL Secretary-Treasurer George Meany (who in 1952 became the AFL president), also received regular reports or excerpts from the committee's representatives and contacts.[21] Members of the AFL International Labor Relations Committee were occasionally sent FTUC reports, and confidential reports were sometimes sent to members of the Executive Council and other leaders of national and international unions.[22] In addition, excerpts from these reports were published, in the form of signed articles, in the AFL's monthly magazine, *American Federationist*, as well as in the FTUC's monthly, *International Free Trade Union News*.[23] Finally, the FTUC's representatives and many of its contacts in the United States government and abroad attended and spoke at the AFL's annual convention.

MAKING DECISIONS

The second major function of the FTUC was decision making. In this, Woll and Dubinsky appear to have been the principals. Woll, to begin with, was highly respected by the AFL leadership. He was president of the Union Labor Life Insurance Company and vice-president of the Photo-Engravers Union of North America, a small craft union but one with members in almost every city in the United States. The son of Catholic immigrants from the Benelux countries, he had risen to the top level of the Executive Council, and in 1925, he had been expected to succeed Samuel Gompers as president of the AFL. Woll had been interested in international affairs for many years, and after the United Mine Workers blocked his assumption of the AFL presidency, he turned his attention increasingly in that direction.[24] In the 1930s, Woll was active in organizing the AFL's anti-Nazi boycotts. In 1937, he was dispatched to Europe to ensure the AFL's readmission into the main prewar labor body, the International Federation of Trade Unions, from which the AFL had withdrawn in the 1920s. In 1938, he was chosen to head the Labor League for Human Rights, and through-

[20] Interview, Lovestone, and FTUC archives.

[21] See William Green's files, AFL-CIO archives.

[22] See for example "Confidential Reports to All International Presidents of the American Federation of Labor," nos. 1–20, 1949–1950, AFL-CIO archives.

[23] The articles in *American Federationist* and the *International Free Trade Union News* are the best sources on the AFL's information about and interpretation of postwar international politics.

[24] See for example Charles A. Madison, *American Labor Leaders* (New York: Harper, 1950), p. 108.

out the war, he coordinated organized labor's role in multi-million-dollar relief activities. By the end of the war, Woll was highly regarded in leading labor circles as a capable administrator knowledgeable in international affairs.

Dubinsky's interest in and knowledge of international affairs also gave him a preeminent role in FTUC and AFL policy making. Dubinsky had maintained contact with the European socialist and trade union movements since his youth in Tsarist Russia.[25] In the 1930s, he was a member of the AFL's first delegation to the ILO. While in Europe, he met with a number of leading trade unionists and social democrats. After Hitler's rise to power, he was instrumental in organizing anti-Nazi boycotts and in founding organizations, including the Jewish Labor Committee,[26] with contacts in almost every European country.

Unlike Woll, however, Dubinsky did not have the confidence of most AFL leaders. First, as noted, he came out of the Socialist tradition, and the other AFL leaders were suspicious of his contacts with European Socialists as well as his association with Lovestone.[27] Second, he was not a longtime intimate of the AFL's leaders. Throughout the 1930s, the ILGWU and the AFL's Executive Council did not always share the same perspectives, particularly in regard to the fledgling CIO.[28] Third, Dubinsky maintained that he recalled overhearing unfavorable remarks by several other AFL leaders about his ethnic origin—he and many of his associates were Jewish—coupled with his identification with socialist circles.[29]

But he did have an important independent base of support in the ILGWU. The presidency of a large, well-organized union gave him power both inside and outside the AFL hierarchy. The ILGWU had its own financial base, and Dubinsky could commit the union's funds to FTUC programs almost on his own motion. An examination of ILGWU convention proceedings and interviews with senior ILGWU leaders and several of their staff indicate that Dubinsky faced little opposition in his 34 years in office. Although there were occasional attempts at the convention to change the course of the ILGWU's foreign policy position, these efforts never got off the ground.[30] Similarly, the General Executive Board almost always approved of Dubinsky's proposals and financial

[25]There are numerous books and articles on the early life and career of David Dubinsky. One of the best sources is the articles and selected bibliography in the Special Supplement, "David Dubinsky, the I.L.G.W.U., and the American Labor Movement," *Labor History*, Spring 1968. Another useful source is Melech Epstein, *Jewish Labor in the U.S.A., 1914–1952* (New York: Trade Union Sponsoring Committee, 1953).

[26]See for example Epstein, op. cit. passim.

[27]Interviews, Meany and Lovestone.

[28]Taft, *The AFL from the Death of Gompers to the Merger* (New York: Harper, 1959), pp. 140–203.

[29]Interview, Dubinsky.

[30]See for example *Report and Proceedings of the Twenty-Fifth Convention of the ILGWU, May 29–June 9, 1944* pp. 502–503 and *Report and Proceedings of the Twenty-Sixth Congress of the ILGWU, June 16–26, 1947*, pp. 473–489. These documents are hereafter referred to as *ILGWU Convention Proceedings*.

commitments.[31] Dubinsky was thus in a position to play an important role in FTUC policy making.

AFL President Green had been interested in foreign affairs since he traveled to Paris with Gompers in 1919, but as a number of authors have pointed out, he was not an innovator in AFL foreign—or, for that matter, domestic—policy making.[32] Indeed, most of the AFL leaders and staff concerned with foreign policy making recall that Green did not initiate policy and almost always accepted Woll's recommendations.[33]

Secretary-Treasurer Meany, as a result of his New York background and his association with Woll and Dubinsky, had become interested in international affairs in the mid-1930s.[34] Meany lived in Washington, however, and, compared with Woll in the early postwar period, did not possess detailed knowledge of labor developments abroad. By the time Meany assumed the AFL presidency, to be sure, he was well versed in labor's role in international affairs; and he gradually was to overshadow both Woll and Dubinsky as the principal AFL and later AFL-CIO policy maker.

The contrast between Woll and Dubinsky (and later Meany) and most of the other AFL leaders was even more striking. For a variety of reasons, the AFL leaders had become concerned enough about the international environment to reenter the IFTU in 1937 and to participate in World War II relief activities; yet, on the whole, the AFL leadership had little interest in and was relatively ill-informed about international affairs.[35] Indeed, Abraham Bluestein recalls that in conversation with Woll at the 1944 convention, Daniel Tobin, the Teamster president and a member of the AFL's inner circle, maintained that the AFL had done enough for the Europeans in the war, principally through the Labor League for Human Rights, and that that constituted a sufficient commitment.[36] The

[31] Interviews, Dubinsky and Zimmerman.

[32] See for example Walter Galenson, *The CIO Challenge to the AFL* (Cambridge: Harvard University Press, 1960), p. 8 and Madison, op. cit., pp. 113 and 134–135.

[33] Interviews, Meany, Harrison, Dubinsky, Bluestein, and Lovestone.

[34] In an interview, Meany recalled that in 1935, Woll and Dubinsky had stimulated his interest by inviting him to attend a conference at the Aldine Club in New York to set up the nonsecretarian Anti-Nazi League. In his biography, *Meany, The Unchallenged Strong Man of American Labor* (New York: Atheneum, 1972), the journalist Joseph Goulden suggests that Meany was the dominant policy maker (pp. 118–123). Although Meany did play a significant role in the early postwar period and a dominant role in the later period, there is little evidence to confirm the role attributed to him by Goulden in the early postwar period. Lovestone, for example, did not write the 1944 AFL resolution creating the FTUC "at Meany's behest." Meany did not formulate the AFL alternatives and persuade Dubinsky and Woll to adopt them. He was consulted by Woll and Dubinsky, and he played a role in the FTUC's decision-making process; but the evidence does not suggest that he was *the* dominant policy maker.

[35] Interviews, Dubinsky, Zimmerman, Harrison, Bluestein, and Lovestone.

[36] Interview, Bluestein, Another indication of Tobin's lack of interest in, or ignorance of, international affairs can be found in his union magazine, which was allowed to print an article suggesting that the AFL adopt a foreign policy posture that the AFL Executive Council, including Tobin himself, had opposed. See *The New Leader*, September 1, 1945.

AFL's first vice-president, William Hutcheson of the Carpenters Union, and John L. Lewis of the Mine Workers—both anti-FDR—also appeared to believe that the AFL should return to its comfortable prewar isolationism.[37]

A major exception to this general pattern was George Harrison, president of the Brotherhood of Railway Clerks. Harrison had become interested in international affairs in the 1930s, had traveled to ILO meetings, and had met many leading European trade unionists. During World War II, he kept himself informed of developments in Europe and made radio broadcasts to the occupied countries. In the immediate postwar period, he occasionally attended meetings of the FTUC and received its reports.[38]

Thus, with the exception of Green, Meany, Harrison, and one or two others, AFL leaders were, as a general rule, either uninterested in or ill-informed about developments abroad. Even those who were interested in international affairs lacked the knowledge and experience of a Woll or a Dubinsky. The contrast between the highly respected Woll and the independently powerful Dubinsky, on the one hand, and the run of AFL leaders on the other gave the New Yorkers in the FTUC and the AFL a preeminent role in foreign policy making.

Another factor that explains Woll's and Dubinsky's ability to formulate the Federation's foreign policy was their sensitivity to avoiding impinging on the values of other important AFL leaders. To make Woll's and Dubinsky's task easier, most AFL leaders shared similar if not identical perspectives. They had goals, values, and broad expectations in common. In particular, since its inception, the Federation had openly opposed systems of government that prohibited the rights of workers to organize unions and to strike. Although these were considered relative rather than absolute rights in the democracies, the Federation since the time of Gompers had condemned the Soviet Union and later Nazi Germany, Fascist Italy, and Falangist Spain for denying these rights and had furnished limited assistance to forces opposed to both the communists and the fascists.[39]

After World War II, there was a basic consensus about the desirability of maintaining democratic pluralism and free trade unions worldwide. Although many top union leaders were not enthusiastic about continued international

[37]Interviews, Dubinsky, Bluestein, and Lang. A number of writers have also supported the view that Lewis was an "isolationist," e.g., John Windmuller, *American Labor and the International Labor Movement 1940–1953* (Ithaca, N.Y.: Cornell University, 1954), p. 29. It should be noted, however, that mainly as a result of his daughter's influence, Lewis secured a $50,000 contribution from the United Mine Workers for the FTUC and, in 1947, became a member of the ILRC. Interview, Lovestone.

[38]Interviews, Harrison, Lovestone, and Bluestein.

[39]Philip Taft, *The AFL In The Time of Gompers* (New York: Harper, 1957), pp. 437–438 and 449–450; *Proceedings*, 1922, pp. 457–465; *Proceedings*, 1934. For a complete listing of the AFL's World War II activities, see Labor League for Human Rights, "Memorandum to International and National Unions, State Federations of Labor, Central Labor Unions," December 31, 1946.

involvement and did not wish to become intimately engaged in the formulation of international objectives and strategies, Dubinsky and Woll and the FTUC operated in an essentially friendly environment. If, for example, the basic principle of free trade unionism had ever been questioned by key AFL leaders, it is difficult to imagine that Dubinsky and Woll would have been able, as they were, to operate the AFL's foreign policy establishment with such a minimum of supervision.

The one major issue that might have led to dissension was the question of whether or not to work openly with the CIO, especially if both organizations were awarded equal status in the same international labor body. Once the AFL decided not to join the WFTU, the issue was not pressing. Occasional maverick convention resolutions requesting official AFL and CIO international cooperation were promptly voted down.[40] Only when a decision had to be made concerning the creation of a new international entity to rival the WFTU did foreign and domestic policy become intimately interrelated. By 1948–1949, however, the domestic situation had changed to such an extent—which is to say, the AFL had accommodated itself to coexistence with a CIO that had purged CP unions— that the issue did not become divisive.[41] Thus, without too much difficulty, Woll and Dubinsky were able to accommodate themselves to the relatively light constraints imposed by the organizational environment within which they had to operate. And they ran the show, largely unfettered.

MOBILIZING RESOURCES

Woll and Dubinsky realized that to be effective, the FTUC needed not only the AFL's mantle but also the financial support of the Federation and its international and national affiliates.[42] They knew, however, that although the AFL leadership was willing (under Woll's prodding) to sanction the creation of the FTUC, it was reluctant if not completely unwilling to divert the AFL's financial resources to international affairs. Although, during the war, the Labor League for Human Rights was able to raise several million dollars for relief activities, some of which was later administered by the FTUC, the FTUC itself was never able to raise enough money from American unions to achieve all its purposes. From 1945 through 1947, American trade union organizations contributed approximately $170,000 to the committee.[43] Over half of this money came from the ILGWU, the Boilermakers, the Hatters, the Machinists, the Pulp and

---

[40]*Proceedings*, 1946, p. 540.

[41]See Windmuller, op. cit., especially pp. 151–156.

[42]It was hoped also that, through the semiautonomous FTUC, unions that were unaffiliated with the AFL (e.g., the International Association of Machinists) would in effect contribute to the AFL's activities. Interviews, Lovestone and Bluestein.

[43]FTUC archives.

Sulphite Workers, the Teamsters, and the United Mine Workers. In addition, from 1945 through 1947 and, indeed, until 1955, the ILGWU provided the committee with office space and paid the salary of the FTUC executive secretary.

The AFL itself, in addition to making a $6,200 contribution in 1947, paid the salaries and expenses of Rutz and Romualdi as well as the international representative. In a 1948 International Labor Relations Committee report to the Executive Council, Woll noted that the AFL had provided "scores of thousands of dollars for relief, but that the FTUC's shoestring budget was completely worn out and that a recent appeal to various international presidents for support had raised only a few thousand dollars." Woll then asked the Executive Council for financial assistance.[44] Thus, although Woll and Dubinsky could formulate FTUC policy virtually on their own, effective implementation required the cooperation of other AFL leaders. And while these leaders did not prevent the FTUC from using the AFL mantle to foster free trade unionism abroad, their lack of enthusiasm for international involvement imposed a major constraint on FTUC policy makers. Woll and Dubinsky were careful not to disregard this constraint. Only after the FTUC had been functioning for several years and only when they believed that the situation abroad had become critical did they request sizable appropriations from the Executive Council.

In connection with the availability of resources to pursue the Federation's foreign policy objectives, it should be noted that neither in the archives nor in interviews with United States government officials[45] are there any indications that the government offered or that the AFL accepted government money during these years. Indeed, a controversial and unsubstantiated *Saturday Evening Post* article by Tom Braden, a former CIA official, tended to confirm this apparent absence of United States government–AFL financial ties. Braden asserted that although CIA financed AFL international operations at a later time, the AFL operated with its own funds until at least December 1947. Sometime thereafter, according to Braden, when they "ran out of money," the AFL leaders "appealed to the CIA" and "thus began the secret subsidy." Braden then went on to observe that although the AFL leadership received CIA funds, it refused to be guided by the United States government in their disbursement; consequently, the CIA "cut down" its subsidy and set up "new networks in other international labor organizations."[46]

It is virtually impossible to substantiate or definitively refute Braden's contentions. In an interview with Meany's biographer, former FTUC staffer Richard

[44] International Labor Relations Department, "Report to the Executive Council," undated (but subject matter indicates Spring 1948).

[45] Interviews with former Ambassadors Averell Harriman and Jefferson Caffery.

[46] Tom Braden, "I'm Glad the CIA Is 'Immoral'" *Saturday Evening Post*, May 20, 1967, pp. 13–15. Braden does not mention the FTUC in his article. Apparently he considered the AFL, the FTUC, and "Dubinsky's Union" as one and the same. He also notes that

Deverell lent a measure of support to Braden's assertions.[47] AFL leaders, however, have insisted that AFL or FTUC employees never received CIA funds at
this time or at any other time.[48] Without access to all the relevant classified files
of the United States government, it is, of course, impossible to verify either the
AFL's or Braden's assertions.

Nevertheless, even if one accepts Braden's assertion that at some point after
1947 the AFL used CIA funds, it still appears that AFL policy makers retained
their autonomy. The AFL and the FTUC, even on Braden's showing, had been
supporting noncommunist trade unionists in Europe for years. When they
needed additional support, they requested it of the United States government.
Yet, having received this assistance for their own freely determined policy, they
refused to explain how the money was being spent or to permit the CIA to
participate in their deliberations. Undoubtedly, if Braden is correct, the AFL
leaders were aware of the government's views, and these opinions on occasion
may have had some influence; but it seems clear that the CIA never had a major
role in the AFL policy-making process. Indeed, if the Agency was kept substantially in the dark about the use of whatever funds it may have allocated, it is
difficult to see how the CIA could have played even a minor role in the process.

This is not to say that the AFL and the United States government did not
support similar specific objectives. Often they did. But often they did not. In the
early postwar period, for example, when the United States government and the
AFL leaders varied in their perspectives about Russian objectives and the danger
of Communist control of organized labor in Western Europe and elsewhere, the
AFL went its own way. With the onset of the Marshall Plan and the United
States government's much more vigorous efforts to oppose Communist influence
in European and other trade unions, however, the United States government
began to change its policy and there was substantial agreement between the two
autonomous institutions which may have led to a greater degree of cooperation.

At any rate, the AFL's internal foreign policy-making process went forward
according to its own rules and its own values, with the FTUC in a central role.

---

the CIA appealed to a "high and responsible labor leader" when the Agency became dissatisfied with what Braden considered "Lovestone's" failure to consult the agency about the
disbursement of funds. According to Braden, the labor leader rebuffed the appeal.

In an interview, George Harrison also said that in 1950 or 1951, the director of the
CIA, Walter Bedell Smith, complained to the AFL president about the Federation's, and
particularly Lovestone's, activities in general. Green sent a delegation that included Harrison, Dubinsky, Woll, Meany, and Lovestone to meet with the director. According to
Harrison, the AFL leaders believed that CIA operatives simply did not understand international labor politics. They rejected Smith's complaints, Harrison said, and the AFL continued its activities abroad.

[47]Goulden, op. cit., p. 130.

[48]AFL-CIO President Meany's press conference, May 8, 1967, as quoted in John
Herling's *Labor Letter*, May 13, 1967. Meany also told Goulden that "Braden is a damned
liar." Goulden, op. cit., p. 129.

Although many decisions were made informally by Woll and Dubinsky, the FTUC met officially about once a month. The agenda was usually drawn up by Woll and the executive secretary, and both were almost always in attendance. Green and Meany occasionally attended the meetings, as did several other prominent labor leaders. At the meetings, Woll and Dubinsky were usually in agreement and decisions were usually unanimous. The minutes of the meeting were then circulated to members who had been unable to attend.[49]

To secure the cooperation of the other AFL leaders and preserve the AFL mantle over FTUC activities, the FTUC leaders took their reports and decisions to the International Labor Relations Committee (ILRC), whose jurisdiction extended over all the AFL's international affairs. The committee's functions in the policy-making area consisted of recommending policy to the Executive Council and formulating policy between council sessions.

The 16-member committee, a secretary, the ILRC international representative, and, on occasion, the executive secretary of the FTUC met every few months, frequently at the quarterly meetings of the AFL Executive Council. Like those of the FTUC, many ILRC decisions were made prior to the formal meetings. The agenda usually consisted of topics dealing with the ILO and other international labor affairs. There was, typically, little disagreement on major issues. The ILRC minutes reveal that the FTUC's decisions were frequently put in the form of motions and adopted with other minor alterations. Resolutions and reports of the committee were then forwarded periodically to the full Executive Council.[50]

The consensus within the committee and its adoption of FTUC policy recommendations were primarily functions of the permanent membership of four committee members and their dual membership in the ILRC and the FTUC. Woll was the chairman of both committees from 1945 to 1955. Woll, Dubinsky, Green, and Meany were also "permanent" members of both committees during this period. The other members of the ILRC were, of course, interested in international affairs, but with rare exceptions they did not oppose the views of the permanent membership. Their information on the complex and ambiguous issues of postwar international politics came primarily from the mass media and the FTUC. Moreover, with the exception of Harrison, they were not well informed and their transient tenure on the ILRC did not lead to the development of expertise. Finally, the permanent members carefully refrained from imposing too many potentially controversial decisions on the committee—

[49]Interviews, Dubinsky, Lovestone, and Bluestein and minutes of the Free Trade Union Committee, FTUC archives.

[50]The complete set of ILRC minutes appears to have been lost, destroyed, or misplaced. Some are available in the AFL-CIO archives. Others can be found in the FTUC archives. Interviews with Lovestone, Dubinsky, Meany, and Harrison lead to the conclusion that the process described here remained basically unaltered throughout the period under consideration.

decisions, that is to say, outside the parameters of the broad leadership consensus. After all, these decisions would have to undergo the scrutiny of the Executive Council and obtain the support of the AFL's international and national union presidents.

Foreign policy making in the Executive Council was apparently similar to that of the ILRC.[51] Throughout the period under consideration, the council discussed resolutions and reports presented by the ILRC which had first been discussed in the FTUC. There tended to be little disagreement and little discussion. The few motions that were formulated were usually carried unanimously.

In this period, Green began as the AFL president and Meany was at first secretary-treasurer and later (from 1953) president. Woll and Harrison served continuously as members of the council, and in 1946 Dubinsky was elected to membership. Thus, 5 of the 15 council members were "internationalists," well informed and well placed in the AFL leadership. The other members of the council, sharing the value of free trade unionism but less interested in and less well informed about international affairs, were naturally inclined to follow the leadership of the five as long as it did not conflict with domestic concerns and did not involve major commitments. The internationalists were careful in the early postwar years not to request large financial allocations for international activities. As the council members became more familiar with international affairs and as the need for support appeared more urgent, however, the internationalists gradually stepped up their requests. In 1947 the Executive Council had allocated $6,200 to the FTUC[52]; in 1948, the council allocated $24,965[53] and in 1949, $32,400.[54]

The functions of the convention, as already noted, were to review and formulate AFL policy and to elect the Federation's officers. Because the key foreign policy makers of the Executive Council were almost all elected prior to 1945 and continued to serve in these capacities until at least 1955, attention will be focused here on the convention's legislative process.

At the beginning of each convention, the Executive Council's and secretary-treasurer's reports, as well as previously submitted resolutions, were divided into sections and assigned by the president, as appropriate, to either the Resolutions Committee or the convention's International Labor Relations Committee (which is not to be confused with the permanent ILRC).[55] There was usually little

---

[51] This account of Executive Council foreign policy making is based on interviews with Harrison, Dubinsky, Meany, and Lovestone.

[52] *Proceedings*, 1947, p. 145.

[53] *Proceedings*, 1948, p. 26.

[54] *Proceedings*, 1949, p. 79. At the same time, the FTUC received additional financial support from individual unions, such as the ILGWU.

[55] This account of the convention's policy-making process is derived from an examination of *Proceedings*, 1945–1955 and interviews with Dubinsky, Harrison, Zimmerman, and Harry Lang, one-time editor of the *Jewish Daily Forward*. Lang, a confidant of Dubinsky

dissension in either committee. Green and later Meany determined their composition and selected the committee leaders.

During the period under consideration, Woll was always chairman of the Resolutions Committee, and Charles Zimmerman and 25 high-ranking union leaders were members. The convention's International Labor Relations Committee was continuously chaired by William McSorley, who was a regular member of the permanent ILRC for several years between 1945 and 1955. Woll, Green, and Meany also were permanent members of the convention's ILRC. The remaining 15 to 20 members of that committee were usually international presidents who, because of their presumed interest in international affairs, had been fraternal delegates at the British Trades Union Congress. At the same time, Green added one or two men to the committee who had had no previous contact with international affairs, in the hope of stimulating their interest in and support for the Federation's foreign policies.

The members of the FTUC, ILRC, and Executive Council assured their colleagues that the newest resolutions were only logical extensions of previous policies. With rare exceptions, the establishment did not ask for more than general approval of its actions. Although the Executive Council reports reveal that the Federation was financing some of the FTUC's and ILRC's activities, the resolutions always left the international presidents and the Executive Council free to limit their commitments the following year. Usually, the committees unanimously recommended nonconcurrence with the few resolutions that were inconsistent with establishment policy.[56]

From 1945 to 1955, there were no fights over foreign policy on the convention floor. The foreign policy makers were able to secure the adoption of their recommendations by a combination of their knowledge and political skills and the consensus within the Federation. Reference has already been made to the long-standing support the Federation's leaders and members had given to free trade unionism. But beyond this broad consensus, it appears that most rank-and-file, middle-level and upper-level union leaders were as a rule uninterested and ill-informed about international affairs in general and international labor affairs in particular.

An examination of the records of leading international unions confirms this conclusion. Even the convention proceedings and labor press of the ILGWU, one of the most internationally minded unions, contain little discussion of foreign policy alternatives. Although the ILGWU establishment was occasionally challenged, its resolutions were carried with only two or three dissenting votes. The delegates approved general resolutions and financial reports indicating that the

---

and Green, attended most AFL conventions during this period and occasionally sat in on the closed meetings of the International Labor Relations Committee.

[56]See for example *Proceedings*, 1946, p. 540.

union was spending thousands of dollars each year on foreign policy with only the most cursory knowledge of how this money was used and what effect it was having in the recipient countries.[57] Even so, compared with other international unions, the ILGWU was exceptional. Most unions rarely donated more than token amounts ($500 to $1,000 per year) to the FTUC,[58] and foreign policy was rarely discussed in the trade union press[59] or at national-union conventions. Indeed, the only major sources of information on foreign policy questions easily available to most AFL leaders were the outlets of the AFL foreign policy estab-lishment, articles in the *American Federationist* and the FTUC's *International Free Trade Union News*, and the short speeches of the Federation's international representatives at AFL conventions.

The absence of any opposition elite, any considerable group of leaders who felt that the Federation's foreign policy impinged on other values they held, also helps explain the apparent lack of direct involvement of most of the convention delegates. The convention speakers who addressed themselves to foreign affairs were either FTUC and AFL representatives or foreign trade union leaders and politicians brought to the convention by the establishment. In the absence of knowledgeable leaders defining alternatives and organizing opposition coalitions, it would have been fruitless for less powerful delegates to oppose the foreign policy elite even if they had wanted to do so.[60]

It should be noted in passing that the Democratic party appears to have played no role in AFL foreign policy making. Although the AFL began to develop close ties with the Democratic party during the New Deal period,[61] there is no evidence to indicate that the party was able significantly to influence the AFL, particularly AFL foreign policy making, during the years under consid-eration. The AFL remained politically neutral in the presidential races of 1940, 1944, and 1948. In a number of elections, some AFL leaders lined up publicly with one party and some with the other party. Moreover, it is especially signifi-cant that the AFL never rated political candidates according to their views and votes on foreign policy. Voting records and work on behalf of labor's domestic programs were the decisive factors in the AFL's support of a candidate.

In sum, on the basis of this analysis, it appears that a handful of AFL leaders, assisted by several of their staff, constituted the AFL foreign policy-

[57]*ILGWU Convention Proceedings*, 1944, 1947, and 1950. See also the ILGWU paper, *Justice*, 1945–1950.

[58]FTUC archives, 1945–1955.

[59]Martin M. Perline, "The Trade Union Press: An Historical Analysis," *Labor History*, Winter 1969, pp. 110 and 112–114.

[60]Throughout the AFL's history, there were few floor fights over foreign policy. Even when a dispute was brought to the convention floor, the views of the foreign policy estab-lishment prevailed. For one of the few examples see *Proceedings*, 1922, pp. 420–437 and 457–465.

[61]For a discussion of this relationship see J. David Greenstone, *Labor in American Politics* (New York: Knopf, 1969).

making elite. Woll and Dubinsky, with the cooperation of Green and Meany and the assistance of Lovestone, Brown, Romualdi, and one or two others, gathered the requisite information and defined the Federation's alternatives.

Nevertheless, AFL foreign policy makers were aware that they were acting in an environment constricted by the AFL's constitutional structure and the need to win the support of important AFL leaders. Because of their political skill, the separation of domestic and foreign policy, the shared value consensus within the Federation, and the relative lack of interest in and knowledge about foreign affairs of most AFL leaders, the policy-making group was able to secure the moral and material support of the Federation for their policies.

It also appears that these policy makers were, for all principal purposes, autonomous. In fact, as the following chapters reveal, the AFL and the United States government did not always have the same views or adopt identical policies.

Chapter 4

Perspectives of the AFL Policy Makers

To understand why many AFL leaders have devoted so much of their energy and resources to international affairs and why the AFL has behaved as it did, it is essential to understand the leaders' objectives and underlying values—in sum, their perspective about world politics. What have these men seeked to accomplish? What have been their theories of domestic and international politics?

This guiding philosophy has not been well understood. Many liberal writers and commentators have argued that the AFL leadership has not had a coherent perspective at all and that American labor, as a general rule, has been merely "opportunistic." George Meany's only biographer has stated that the foreign policy goals of American labor have been "pragmatic" and have led American trade unions to support "conservative—even reactionary allies."[1] Another writer has argued that labor has given the United States government "unswerving

[1] Joseph C. Goulden, *Meany: The Unchallenged Strong Man of American Labor* (New York: Atheneum, 1972), p. 137.

loyalty" and has supported "any type of anti-communist regime."[2] A closer examination of the labor leadership's perspectives, however, leads one to question these assertions—at any rate, to qualify them in major respects. American labor appears to have been far from opportunistic or pragmatic. As a result of markedly idealistic principles and a systematic set of theories, American labor leaders have never supported "reactionary" or just "any type of anti-communist regime"; often, and on key issues of policy, the AFL has found itself sharply at odds with the United States government.

Since the creation of the AFL in the 1880s, American trade union leaders have been seeking an amalgam of what they have regarded as worldwide democracy and free trade unionism, peace and stability, and economic and social justice. For them, free trade unionism and democracy are inextricably linked. Democratic societies need trade unions to remain stable and progressive, and trade unions need democracies to promote economic and social justice in a context of tranquillity. Dictatorships cannot tolerate free trade unions and inevitably seek to undermine and destroy them. In the continuing world struggle between democracy and dictatorship, American labor has sided with democracy whether the dictatorial regimes might be totalitarian, authoritarian, colonialist, or racist, whether of the Left or the Right.

For American trade union leaders, the crucial struggle in the post–World War II period was between democrats and Communists, first for control of the strategic area of Western Europe and then for control over the future of the European colonies and other non-Western areas. The AFL leadership believed that if the Communists could gain complete control of these areas by gaining control of the labor movement, the United States would be isolated. The United States government then would be faced with the choice either of submitting to the domination of the Soviet Union and its allies or of going to war to assure American national security.

THE LEADERSHIP'S ULTIMATE GOALS

Since the time of Samuel Gompers, the American labor movement has been grounded in the belief that democracy is the best method of government and democratic societies the only ones in which free trade unions can exist, function, and grow. As George Meany, following in this tradition, stated in an address to the British Trades Union Congress at the end of World War II:

> You and we have the same fundamental love for democracy as a way of life. You and we believe that every man and woman irrespective of race or creed

[2] Ronald Radosh, *American Labor and U.S. Foreign Policy* (New York: Random House, 1969), especially Introduction.

or economic status, has a right to equal voice and vote with all others as to how and in what way we will be governed. You and we alike have a deep rooted hatred of tyranny. You and we both feel that it is a right—not a privilege—for the governed to speak out aloud in criticism of those chosen to govern whenever and wherever they so desire.[3]

The AFL leaders, however, with one or two exceptions, have not been socialists. Unlike many of their European counterparts, they have not believed that the government should own or control the major sources of wealth. Rather, the AFL has supported, in Meany's phrase, a "total system of free enterprise." The Federation has been content to let control of United States industry remain in private hands as long as the employers and the government respected workers' right to organize and engage in political activities—as long, that is to say, as free trade unionism was permitted.

These values have not been restricted to American society. The AFL leadership has subscribed to the principle that all workers should, if they wanted to, enjoy the opportunities offered to them by democracy and free trade unionism. That many workers and union leaders in other democracies were socialists has not bothered the AFL leadership. That many of them wanted to eliminate the private ownership of major industries, as the British and the French did, has not concerned them either. What has concerned them has been the continued existence of democracy and free trade unionism. That has been basic and non-negotiable.

The AFL also has viewed the maintenance of peace, or the absence of war, as a fundamental objective. War not only has resulted in death and destruction for combattants and innocent civilians, of whom large numbers were workers, but also, in wartime, the rights of labor have been almost inevitably curtailed, production has been disrupted, and resource priorities have been skewed to support the war effort and not the producer or the consumer. For these reasons, although the AFL leaders have supported the goal of helping to extend democracy to those who desired it, they have not regarded war as an appropriate means to this end. Only when it has appeared that the United States or its vital interests were threatened has the AFL leadership supported war. Thus they have been frequently at odds with the administration of the day. In 1912, for example, the AFL convention opposed armed intervention in Mexico. Samuel Gompers, then president of the organization, personally became involved in trying to avoid war between Germany and the United States prior to 1917. In 1919, Gompers insisted that United States troops be withdrawn from the Dominican Republic. Later, although both the AFL and the CIO condemned the Nazis, Fascists, and Communists for their suppression of democracy and their use of force against

[3]George Meany, "Address to the British Trades Union Congress," September 1945. FTUC archives.

other states (e.g., Poland, Ethiopia, Spain, Finland), American labor organizations did not favor United States military involvement in World War II until the United States was attacked. And after the war, when some people in the United States suggested driving the Russians out of Eastern Europe and the Falangists out of Spain, the AFL opposed the use of force to overthrow either right-wing or left-wing dictatorships.

Another primary goal of the AFL leadership has been the improvement of economic and social conditions throughout the world. The labor leadership has not been motivated, however, solely by the self-interest of American workers—i.e., improving economic and social conditions abroad so that foreigners might buy from the United States and not undercut wage gains by working for lower wages than Americans did. The AFL unions have maintained that all human beings are entitled to "more" as a matter of principle. As President William Green once put it:

> Social security is indispensable to peace security. It means economic security to those who work. It means that every human being should be guaranteed, by the community of which he is a member, an income sufficient to sustain him, an income sufficient at least to meet the living requirements, the minimum requirements of decency and health. The principle of social security is one which should be and I am confident, will be universally applied. . . .[4]

THE LEADERSHIP'S VIEWS OF DOMESTIC POLITICS

Democracy and free trade unionism have been very closely linked in this view. Genuinely free trade unions, those free from government or employer control, cannot long exist without democracy, and the AFL leaders have believed that democratic societies need trade unions to remain stable and progressive.[5] By representing the interests of the work force in the economic and political spheres, trade unions help ensure that major discontents do not go unattended and erupt into violent upheaval. At the same time, by promoting the interests of their members, unions help ensure that the profits and benefits of modern industrial life are more equitably shared.

The AFL leaders have believed that by helping workers achieve increased purchasing power for domestic-market expansion, unions contribute to economic growth and ensure better living conditions for everyone. In this view, unionism has exercised a profound influence on the course of economic and

[4]William Green, "American Labor and World Affairs," *American Federationist*, July 1943, pp. 10–11.
[5]For a more detailed statement of this point see William Green, *Labor and Democracy* (Princeton: Princeton University Press, 1939), passim.

political history in the West by persuading or forcing management to pay higher wages. Without union organization, without collective bargaining or other means of exerting pressure, the balance of economic power necessary for continued growth and stability would never have been achieved.

Similarly, in the political sphere, the AFL leaders have believed that the work force needs its own organizations to promote its interests. For democracy to progress, they have argued, neither employers nor government should command a highly disproportionate amount of power. The ability to limit the excesses of other social and economic groups cannot exist in the absence of a free and independent trade union movement.

For the American labor leaders, the reverse is also true. Genuine trade unions cannot long survive the absence of democracy. A totalitarian government would inevitably establish the rules for economic growth as a means of strengthening its power base. For economic growth to proceed at a projected rate, the program as established by the state would have to be rigidly adhered to. If other groups had different opinions about how best to achieve economic growth, they would be forced into line. Strikes, for example, would halt production and prevent the attainment of the established goal; thus, strikes would have to be outlawed—as, indeed, they were in Soviet Russia and Falangist Spain, for example. Free collective bargaining—which affects labor distribution, wages, and prices—would also have to be a casualty of rigid adherence to state-fixed production schedules.

To prove this point, the AFL leaders have often cited the cases of Nazi Germany and Soviet Russia. In Germany, with the establishment of the Weimar Republic in 1919, organized labor was accorded full recognition within the provisions of the democratic constitution and became one of the largest free associations of workers in the world. In the late 1920s, Nazi leaders initially made overtures to the trade union movement and promised workers even greater benefits if the Nazis came to power. In spite of Hitler's apparently friendly attitude to the trade union movement, however, the workers remained firm in their hostility to nazism. In 1933, even after Hitler became chancellor, Nazi candidates in elections for shop steward committeemen won only 7.7 percent of the total vote throughout Germany. This blow to Hitler's prestige triggered the onslaught that destroyed the free trade union movement in Germany.[6] Union offices and buildings were occupied by storm troopers. Prominent labor leaders were murdered and others were sent to concentration camps. Hundreds of thousands of suspected anti-Nazi workers were forced out of their jobs, and union treasuries were seized. Labor's right to organize was abolished, collective bargaining was eliminated, and other benefits that had accrued to labor since the establishment of the Weimar Republic were wiped out. The destruction of the free

[6] Joseph Mire, "Labor under Hitler," *American Federationist*, April 1943, pp. 15 and 28–31.

trade union movement paralleled the destruction of German democracy. As Woll concluded, "We know it is impossible for a free trade union movement to exist in a dictatorship and that no dictatorship can exist so long as there is a free trade union movement."[7]

The experience of the Russian trade unions after the Bolsheviks came to power also helped convince American labor that free trade unions could not exist for long in totalitarian societies. As Meany put it in 1945, referring to the government-controlled labor organizations in the Soviet Union:

> We believe that only through trade unions can the ideals, aspirations, and collective desires of workers anywhere on earth be implemented into constructive action for the improvement of the standards of labor. We believe in political freedom as well as economic freedom . . . how can the representatives of a government controlled and dominated [trade union] movement speak for the workers? How can they know what workers are thinking about . . . what they desire . . . just what ideals and principles they would have their representatives espouse and uphold? Where there is no freedom of the press, where there is no free speech . . . just how and by what method can the workers make known their ideals, aspirations, policies to individuals who are supposed to represent them?[8]

Thus, for the Federation's leaders, it has been a demonstrated fact that free trade unions cannot survive in a climate of totalitarianism. Although they might grant that there have been cases in which trade unions have been able to exist in less than total forms of dictatorship, the AFL leaders have believed that in the long run a free trade union movement can survive and flourish only in a democratic environment.

THE LEADERSHIP'S PERSPECTIVES ON INTERNAL THREATS TO DEMOCRACY AND FREE TRADE UNIONISM

Within democratic states, of course, antidemocratic groups can and do exist. The AFL leadership believed that in the twentieth century, domestic Communists and other totalitarian groups, such as Nazis, Fascists, and Falangists, would attempt to win control of and ultimately destroy democratic government. Such movements began as small, militant, well-organized groups united by a common ideology and a hierarchical party structure. They operated in a democratic environment in which most workers, although opposed to totalitarianism, were

---

[7]Matthew Woll, "A Reply," *Labor and the World Crisis* (New York: Workers Education Bureau Press, 1940), p. 13.

[8]Meany, op. cit.

disunited. Moreover, the inability of some democratic societies to solve social and economic problems, or at least to alleviate miserable social and economic conditions, facilitated totalitarian takeover. Most AFL foreign policy leaders believed to some extent in the "stomach theory" of authoritarian or totalitarian takeover. As defined by President Green in testimony before the U.S. Senate,

> Communism thrives on poverty and distress. It gains strength at the lower levels because workers don't stop to think many times what causes the distress and poverty from which they suffer, and when there is some new method offered with a guarantee that "if you accept this method you will never go down to this position of poverty and distress again," they respond.[9]

The post–World War II Communist movement seemed particularly menacing to the AFL leadership. The defeat of Nazi Germany left Moscow-directed communism as the principal threat to democracy and world peace.[10] Furthermore, American labor leaders concluded that it was much more difficult to combat communism than nazism and fascism, because communism pretended to be the champion of labor and posed as a higher form of democracy, to which it tirelessly paid homage. In this very hypocrisy lay the key to the appeal of Communist fifth columns and their many fronts; it was the key to their possible success where the Nazis and the fascists had failed.[11]

To American labor leaders, Communist parties operating in democratic countries under normal peacetime conditions had two available strategies—one overt, the other covert. The overt tactic was to seek power by attempting to bring about violent revolution. Alternatively, they could camouflage their aims, infiltrate the major groups and institutions of state and society, and maneuver themselves into power, either through the electoral process or through what would appear to be noncommunist violence. The AFL leaders have believed that the Communists usually adopted covert tactics, and necessarily so. They were too few in number and their aims had insufficient popular appeal for them to use overt methods.[12]

The Communists employed the "boring from within" approach to obtain control of such strategic institutions as trade unions. A well-coordinated anti-democratic minority then used these institutions to destroy democracy. AFL

---

[9] U.S., Congress, Senate, *U.S. Assistance to European Recovery*, pts. 1 and 2, 80th Cong. 2d sess., 8 January 1948, p. 837. For the prewar views of the AFL, see Green, *Labor and Democracy*, pp. 186–187. See also article by Irving Brown, *New Leader*, January 22, 1952. Dubinsky, Harrison, and Meany, in interviews, also expressed the view that miserable economic and social conditions lend themselves to totalitarian takeover.

[10] David Dubinsky, "World Labor's New Weapon," *Foreign Affairs*, April 1950. Interviews with Dubinsky, Meany, Lovestone, and Brown.

[11] Dubinsky, op. cit.

[12] Interview, Lovestone. He maintained that Lenin discovered this in the early 1920s.

leaders had been conscious of this strategy since the 1920s; they had personal experience of Communist attempts to take over American trade unions.[13]

As ILGWU President David Dubinsky put it, defending the United States government's program of loyalty tests,

> Our government is perfectly justified in defending itself—just as every other democratic institution is against the penetration by communist and other totalitarian termites. When communists enter government employment, they are entering not for the sake of serving the government of the American people, but only for the sake of utilizing positions of confidence and trust in the interests of another—a foreign power.[14]

The AFL leaders believed that the Communists, if they could, would use trade unions for a variety of political purposes. First, by disseminating Communist propaganda in campaign contexts, they might secure the election of Communist candidates to national office or at least neutralize the effectiveness of anticommunist candidates. The organizational talent and muscle and the financial resources of labor could be influential and even decisive in shaping the political attitudes of workers. Second, unions could be used to infiltrate the government of a modern industrial state. Many high-ranking union officials serve on government industrial and economic commissions as nominees of their own movement. A Communist-controlled labor movement would presumably place communists in such influential positions.[15]

The political as opposed to the economic strike was a third weapon, the AFL leaders believed, that could be utilized by Communist-controlled unions. "Economic strikes" might be defined as those called to improve the wages and conditions of union members, simply and directly. Such strikes, of course, often have political as well as economic effects. An increase in wages may lead to an inflationary spiral, thus creating political repercussions and undermining a government's popular standing. An economic strike, however, is not called to create such political repercussions. They are unintended side effects, and unions engaging in economic strikes will frequently try to hold political fallout to a minimum.

Political strikes, conversely, are called not to improve the lot of the workers but rather to produce desired political consequences—inflation, political and economic instability, or the removal of uncooperative officials. They turn the strike weapon on its head. Improvements in the conditions of union members, if

---

[13] Green, *Labor and Democracy*, p. 91.

[14] Dubinsky, answers to questions by Eve Curie, June 10, 1947. FTUC archives.

[15] Dubinsky, in his previously cited defense of government loyalty oaths, also referred to the disastrous effects of the infiltration of Nazi sympathizers into the French government in 1939–1940. FTUC archives.

such should result from a political strike, are strictly incidental. AFL leaders understood this use of trade union power. David Dubinsky, George Harrison, and Jay Lovestone all had visited Europe in the 1930s, when this technique was common.

By the end of the 1930s, many American labor leaders were familiar with the use of trade unions to support candidates and causes as well as with the political strike. But with the exception of Lovestone, a former leader of the American Communist party, they were less well informed about other important political uses of trade unions. During World War II and the first few postwar years, however, they began to realize that unions could be used for a considerable range of political purposes.

One of the most influential confirmations of this idea came from German Communist Richard Krebs, who settled in the United States in 1940 after 20 years as a Communist organizer. In 1941, Krebs, under the pseudonym of Jan Valtin, published a sensational and flamboyant autobiography, *Out of the Night*,[16] which became a best seller. Krebs described his travels as a paid and dedicated Communist organizer, his capture and torture by the Gestapo, and finally his escape from both the Gestapo and the Russian secret police. Two-thirds of the book is devoted to describing Krebs's training and his organizing of trade unions for purposes of spying, staging coups d'état, and creating paramilitary organizations to serve Russian foreign and military policy.

Experiences in World War II also made the AFL leaders sensitive to the use of trade unions for subversion. European trade unions played an important part in the Resistance. Although few trade unionists have written about their experiences, many were involved in anti-Nazi espionage and sabotage. The head of the Belgian Seamen's Officers Union, Omer Becu, for example, worked for both British Intelligence and the American OSS. He supplied the Allies with trusted contacts in occupied Europe and, on the basis of information supplied by other trade union leaders, suggested improvements in Allied military operations. Based in London, he frequently visited the United States to consult with Arthur Goldberg, head of the OSS Labor Division. On these visits, he also made a point of meeting with AFL officials who were aware of the true nature of his work.[17]

In addition, Dubinsky, Lovestone, and Woll had their own contacts with the underground in Europe. The AFL-supported Jewish Labor Committee was in almost daily contact with the underground in Poland and elsewhere. The Labor League for Human Rights, cosponsored by the AFL and the CIO, raised money

[16] Jan Valtin, *Out of the Night* (New York: Alliance Books, 1941).
[17] Interview, Becu. See also A. E. Jolis, "The OSS and the Labor Movement," *The New Leader*, August 31, 1946; Carey Ford, *Donovan of the OSS* (Boston: Little, Brown, 1970), pp. 240–243; R. Harris Smith, *OSS: The Secret History of America's First Central Intelligence Agency* (Berkeley: University of California Press, 1972), passim.

for trade union victims of nazism and reported on the exploits of their contacts in occupied Europe.[18]

Although *Out of the Night* increased their appreciation of the role unions could play in a coup d'état, it was not until the events in Czechoslovakia early in 1948 that all the AFL leaders realized just how important unions could be. The Czech coup and contacts with exiled Eastern European trade union and socialist leaders indicated that control of key industries could be decisive.

As Meany explained,

> They get the machinery, that is all they want. They had less than fifteen percent in the Parliament; they did not have a newspaper; they did not own any industries. But they got control of a country where freedom is valued as highly as in this country . . . they tied up the city of Prague for twenty-four hours. No telephone, no bus, no radio, no hospital services, no milk, no mail service or anything else. Then they went to the politicians in charge and they said, "Have we proved that we have the workers in this city with us—that we control the workers?" They wanted in and they got in. They only wanted one position, Minister of Internal Security . . . Within seven days they had the entire country. Masaryk and Beneš were dead. . . .[19]

The principal targets were transportation, communications, electricity, and printing. Once these industries were controlled, they could be used in two ways. Political strikes could be employed to secure the entry of Communist ministers into a coalition government. The Communists would then insist on being given responsibility for the police and armed forces. If their demands were denied, they could insist at least that determined anticommunists not control these strategic ministries. Then, during the critical period of actual takeover, control of the key industries could be used to facilitate the putschists or impede the government's efforts to maintain itself. In some circumstances, denying the government access to printing presses in order to mobilize workers, or to transportation in order to mobilize armed forces, could be decisive.

The AFL leaders have known also that trade unions can be important for consolidating and maintaining power in the aftermath of a coup, revolution, or invasion. The Nazis attempted at once to win control of the trade unions in 1933; failing that, they immediately destroyed them.[20] The Nazis, Communists, Fascists, and Falangists set up labor fronts to help ensure their control and domination of the work force.[21]

[18] See for example *Labor League News*, I, no. 1, June 1945.
[19] Goulden, op. cit., p. 137.
[20] Mire, op. cit.
[21] ILRC, "What Happened to the Trade Unions behind the Iron Curtain," FTUC, New York, 1947. See also Philip Selznick, *The Organizational Weapon* (New York: McGraw-Hill, 1952), p. 227.

To AFL leaders, there appeared to be only two major methods of preventing the Communists from seizing control of democratic institutions and governments from within. Alleviation of the unbearable social and economic conditions that totalitarian groups exploited was the most important method. As William Green maintained in discussing the depression of the 1930s, "Our insistence upon equal opportunity for labor has been a bulwark against the fascist or communist tendencies."[22] After World War II, Dubinsky told a French interviewer that in the United States, the "increasingly progressive role of the trade unionists is one of the main reasons for recent loss of ground by the communists,"[23] and Green testified to a Senate committee that the AFL supported the Marshall Plan because it would help rectify the economic conditions that furthered totalitarianism.[24]

The second method of preventing the Communists from gaining control of democratic institutions was to prevent them from joining and participating in the activities of these institutions. Every attempt by the AFL to cooperate with the Communists, or even to work alongside them, failed. In the view of the AFL leadership, the Communists were fanatics whose ideology and codes were the reverse of and incompatible with their own. The AFL leaders concluded that once the Communists were in control of an institution, particularly a trade union, it was almost impossible to dislodge them by democratic means.[25] The human and material resources available to the Communists were, as a rule, superior to those of the disunited democratic forces. Moreover, the Communists used tactics such as terror and intimidation, unavailable to those who lived by democratic values. Democratic elements, therefore, could only try to prevent takeover by exposing and expelling active Communists.[26]

THE LEADERSHIP'S VIEW OF WORLD POLITICS

American labor leaders identified the major actors in international politics as nation-states, international organizations, and national and international labor groupings. Nation-state are, of course, the basic units of the international system; but international organizations, both governmental and nongovernmental, also can be powerful. As Green observed, the AFL had always been interested in international organizations' involvement in social and economic problems because "without the attainment of economic justice for workers of all

---

[22] Green, *Labor and Democracy*, p. 194.

[23] Dubinsky, answers to questions by Eve Curie, op. cit.

[24] U.S., Congress, Senate, *U.S. Assistance to European Recovery*, op. cit., p. 837.

[25] Woll, "World Issues and the AFL," p. 11. See also Green, *Labor and Democracy*, p. 93.

[26] The AFL leaders in interviews all vigorously expressed these views. They repeatedly pointed to the inability of democratic forces to regain control of Communist-dominated unions.

countries, there can be no true reciprocity in international trade and there can be no fair standard in international relations."[27]

International labor organizations, the AFL leaders have known, can engage in many of the same political activities open to national trade unions. First, although they usually cannot contribute directly to the election of candidates for national office, international labor bodies are a valuable source of propaganda in national elections. A national trade union or party citing the resolutions of an international labor body can claim, for example, that it was speaking on behalf of the world's workers.[28] Second, international labor organizations can play a lobbying role in other international bodies. While the international labor organizations usually cannot place labor leaders in the principal offices of such bodies, the AFL did attempt to send representatives to the Dumbarton Oaks Conference in 1944 and later sought and gained admission to the United Nations Economic and Social Council.[29] Third, international labor organizations can be used to put pressure on national governments and trade union centers.[30] They can issue propaganda, organize international political strikes and boycotts, and intervene in local trade union disputes, as the World Federation of Trade Unions tried to do in Spain immediately after World War II. Finally, international labor organizations can play the same important role in espionage and paramilitary activities as local unions can.[31]

The AFL leadership has viewed the main struggle in the world as the conflict between totalitarianism and democracy. In the 1930s, this struggle took the form of a struggle between the Nazi-Fascist Axis and the democratic states.[32] After World War II, the decisive international confrontation for the AFL was the struggle between the Soviet Union and the democracies. In 1951, Matthew Woll felt that "the present acute 'world crisis' was not to be attributed to any conflict between different forms of property ownership or of economic systems." Nor was it a matter of conflict over boundaries and territories between two nations or two blocs of nations. Rather, on Woll's showing, the conflict had its source in the Soviet Union's "reckless destruction of the critical spirit, the most systematic and thoroughgoing abuse and anihilation of all human rights. Russia today is the model of twentieth century slavery. Forced labor has become an integral part and organized phase of the entire Societ economy." He concluded

[27] Green, "American Labor in World Affairs," op. cit., p. 10.

[28] Indeed, one reason why the AFL withdrew from the IFTU in the 1920s was its disinclination to become involved in the political maneuvers of the European Socialists. See Lewis Lorwin, *The International Labor Movement* (New York: Harper & Row, 1953) pp. 78–84.

[29] For elaboration, see the Executive Council reports, *Proceedings*, 1946, pp. 57–69.

[30] AFL leaders were familiar with the use of these techniques in the 1930s. See Lorwin, op. cit., especially pp. 165–194.

[31] See Valtin, op. cit., Jolis, op. cit., C. L. Sulzberger, *A Long Row of Candles* (New York: Macmillan, 1969), p. 385.

[32] Green, *Labor and Democracy*, especially pp. 185–194.

that "clearly the roots of the present crisis are deeply embedded in the challenge of Soviet slavery to human freedom. . . . In this crisis, Communist totalitarianism has the initiative. It is the aggressor, just as Nazi totalitarianism had been before."[33]

THE LEADERSHIP'S VIEW OF RUSSIAN POLICY

AFL policy makers believed that Russian leaders had one primary goal: the establishment and maintenance of communism throughout the world. The Russians may have had other values, such as nationalism and peace, but these were strictly subordinate to the overriding objectives of the destruction of the noncommunists and the furtherance of "world revolution."

Even before the United States entered World War II, American labor leaders were concerned about Russia's global ambitions. They feared that the Nazis' success would result in the elimination of most of Europe's noncommunist political and labor leadership and that it would be almost impossible to restore democratic government in Europe even if the Nazis were eventually defeated. The Russians and the Communist undergrounds would become the new rulers of the Continent. The AFL leaders did not oppose allying with the Soviet Union during the war. But contrary to prevailing United States official opinion,[34] they

[33] Matthew Woll, "American Labor and the World Struggle for Freedom," address at the Economic Club of Detroit, Michigan, February 26, 1951. FTUC archives.

[34] Most senior United States officials were fairly sanguine about Russian intentions. As Philip Mosely, Herbert Feis, and Arthur Schlesinger have pointed out, they did not believe that the Russians intended to dominate Eastern, let alone Western, Europe. Major revisionist historians, who believe that United States government officials were very suspicious of Russian intentions in Eastern Europe, confirm that these officials, with some exceptions, were not worried about Russian ambitions in Western Europe or the potential roles of trade unions in achieving these ambitions. See Herbert Feis, *Churchill, Roosevelt and Stalin* (Princeton: Princeton University Press, 1967), pp. 596–599. See also his *Between War and Peace* (Princeton: Princeton University Press, 1960); Arthur Schlesinger, Jr., "Origins of the Cold War," *Foreign Affairs*, October 1967, pp. 23–53; Philip Mosely, *The Kremlin and World Politics* (New York: Vintage, 1960), p. 219. For first-hand American accounts of the period see for example Harry S. Truman, *Memoirs* vol. I (Garden City, N.Y.: Doubleday, 1955), p. 552 and James Byrnes, *Speaking Frankly* (New York: Harper & Row, 1948). For examples of revisionist writings see Gar Alperovitz, *Atomic Diplomacy: Hiroshima and Potsdam* (New York: Simon and Schuster, 1965) and Martin F. Herz, *Beginnings of the Cold War* (Bloomington: Indiana University Press, 1966). Gabriel Kolko, in *The Politics of War* (New York: Random House, 1968), pp. 428–456, however, maintains that United States officials became worried about Russian threats to Western Europe in 1945. For refutations of the revisionist thesis see Eugene Rostow, *Peace in the Balance* (New York: Simon and Schuster, 1972); Robert James Maddox, *The New Left and the Origins of the Cold War* (Princeton: Princeton University Press, 1973); Michael Harrington, *Socialism* (New York: Saturday Review Press, 1972); Walter Laqueur, "Rewriting History," *Commentary*, March 1973, pp. 53–64. On the reaction of academic historians to these refutations see Oscar Handlin "Failure of the Historians," *Freedom at Issue*, September–October 1975, pp. 3-6.

did not believe that the worldwide struggle between democratic elements and Russian-controlled Communists would cease once the war began to wind down; rather, in their view, the Russians would attempt to gain control of Western and Eastern Europe.

Control of Europe would protect the Russian government by acting as a buffer zone or *cordon sanitaire*; and control of the European industrial heartland would lead to preponderant Russian power and thus, eventually, to global hegemony. This analysis seemed correct to the AFL leadership. Woll had pointed out in 1940 that if Hitler could subjugate the working people of Europe and control the resources of the continent of Africa, it would be impossible for the United States to compete against this monolith of production.[35] The prospect of Russian domination of the Continent, added to the vast natural resources of the homeland, would face the United States with a far more formidable antagonist.

Immediately after the war, the AFL leadership concluded that the Kremlin's strategy was to refrain from provocative action in Western Europe so that the United States would be unlikely to attack the Soviet Union or interfere with its consolidation in Eastern Europe. Indeed, if sufficiently lulled, the United States might even withdraw its forces from Western Europe. On this strategic projection—following the imposition of Russian control over Eastern Europe and a possible United States troop withdrawal—Western Europe would be acutely vulnerable to Communist takeover. The Russians, however, would not move directly against Western Europe unless they were ready to risk armed conflict with the United States.

The short-range Russian objective in Western Europe was not to seize power, according to this scenario, but to maintain political and economic instability. As Dubinsky wrote: "The Communist hope for the future lies in the collapse of the European economy. The hope of the people on the continent lies in the rebuilding and expansion of their economies. The prospects of totalitarian communist domination of Europe depend on a divided continent—with each nation undercutting the other, with one country at the throat of another." However, he continued, "the prospects of a free and democratic Europe are bright only to the extent that its people can cooperate in a spirit of mutual aid, in continental endeavor, in helping one another so that all can be strong enough to repel and smash any attempt at imperialist domination and every attempt—from within or without—at strangulation of their democratic liberties."[36]

In the immediate postwar period, Irving Brown in particular believed that— judging by the Russians' own statements and actions—France was the key to the control of Europe. As early as March 1946, in his reports to Woll and Lovestone,

[35] Woll, "A Reply," op. cit., p. 20.
[36] David Dubinsky, "The European Scene—Highlights and Shadows," *American Federationist*, November 1948, p. 8.

he stressed this view: "France is the immediate key to the problem of Western European democracy (in the long run Germany will be the decisive question) and there can be no thought of achieving democratic objectives in Western Europe without changing the internal French situation."[37] Lovestone shared this view and wrote to Brown a few days later, "I believe France is the key to Russia's control of Western Europe. If Joe gets France he outflanks Germany and then he might allow us to go home or lend lease us the railroad fare."[38] These views were incorporated into Brown's address to the AFL's 1946 convention.[39]

The AFL leadership agreed that Communist control of the international labor movement and of European and particularly French trade unions was crucial. This view was clearly expressed in the Executive Council report, "Free Trade Unions in Europe and Our Responsibility for Free Trade Unions," adopted by the 1946 convention: "The key to the future in Europe lies with the reconstructed and slowly reviving free labor movement. The extent to which this is reorganized on truly democratic lines, will determine in large measure, which way Europe will go in terms of the basic struggle that is ensuing between democracy and Soviet totalitarianism."[40]

In summary, the AFL leadership believed that the Russian strategy would effectively serve long-range Communist objectives. If democratic forces did not respond, Western Europe would utlimately fall under Communist control. The United States would then be forced either to surrender the Continent to Russia and eventually face the preponderant power of the communist camp alone or to engage in preventive war.

American trade unionist leaders were concerned also about the considerable Russian effort to condemn and remove Western influence from the non-Western world. The Russians were attempting to capitalize on the legacy of colonialism and the emergence of authoritarian regimes in many parts of the Western and non-Western world. Colonialism, whether practiced by the United States or other nations, had always been roundly denounced. As early as the 1898 convention of the AFL, President Samuel Gompers had argued against United States annexation of the Philippines and Cuba. In his view,

> The policy of imperialism is a declaration that self-government has failed, and that the people cannot be trusted, that the dollar is of more consequence than man, and plutocracy and militarism nobler than humanity. . . . The institutions of our republic have taken root too deeply in the

[37] Brown to Woll, March 14, 1946. FTUC archives. See also Irving Brown, "The Fight against Communism in Western European Countries," speech delivered at the State Department, November 9, 1948, p. 6. FTUC archives.

[38] Lovestone to Brown, March 18, 1946.

[39] *Proceedings*, 1946, pp. 438–439.

[40] Ibid. p. 433.

minds and hearts of our people to permit us to become a nation of con-
querors, or to dominate by force or arms, a people struggling for liberty and
independence.[41]

After World War II, when colonialism again became one of the primary
concerns of the AFL, the AFL leadership felt that the subjugation of native
Africans and Asians by the European colonial powers was unjust. Moreover, it
could lead only to violence and ultimately to totalitarianism. In this early postwar period, American labor continuously criticized the United States government because it continued to countenance the European colonial powers.

Similarly, the AFL leadership has believed that right-wing dictatorships deny
their citizens economic and social justice and undermine the health and vitality
of democracy and trade unionism everywhere. Right-wing dictatorships maintain
power by eliminating those institutions that interfere with the ruling elite. This
suppression, which is frequently brutal in practice, also affords a well-organized
Communist minority the opportunity to rally the opposition forces, propose
far-reaching democratic reforms, enter into alliances over a broad front—even
with anticommunist groups—and eventually assume control of the coalition. By
exploiting their anticolonialist, antidictatorial credentials and the organizations
thus created, the Communists are then able to pose as the champions of
democracy. The Third World is not as vulnerable as highly industrialized states
to the interruption of essential services. Nevertheless, American labor leaders
have believed that in the postindependence period or in the aftermath of a coup
or revolution against a right-wing dictator, such as Franco, Batista, or Duvalier,
there will be a danger that the Communists will emerge as the only "respectable"
and organized force, controlling significant institutions such as the trade unions,
and will fill the power vacuum. Once they obtain sufficient support, the Communists will substitute their brand of totalitarianism for the old.[42]

THE STRATEGIC IMPORTANCE OF ORGANIZED LABOR

In the post—World War II period, American labor leaders were concerned about
the strategic potential of trade unions. The AFL leadership was convinced that
the Russians were devoting considerable effort to gaining control of all trade
unions and particularly those in Western Europe. The Russians would attempt to
establish hegemony over the Continent by using the labor movement to keep
conditions unstable until, should it come to direct action, they were ready to

[41] *Proceedings*, 1898, p. 27.
[42] The clearest statement of this thesis can be found in Irving Brown, "Alternatives to
Attrition: The Role of Democratic Forces in a Political Solution," National Strategy Information Center, New York, 1970. A revised version of this paper is printed in *Labor and
International Affairs* (Washington, D.C.: Georgetown University International Labor Program, 1976).

risk military confrontation with the Western powers. The successful implementation of this strategy, the AFL leaders believed, would be disastrous for peace, democracy, and free trade unionism—everywhere.

France, in their view, was the key. Organized labor there might very well play a decisive role in the success or failure of Russian policy and, indeed, in the future of liberal democracy.

But what actions could the United States government take in the face of this situation, particularly if the trade unions in France and other countries of the West fell into the hands of the Communists? The United States and other Western governments could hardly destroy the entire trade union movement. If they did so, the Communists would maintain that democracy itself was at stake—which, perversely, would have had a germ of truth to it. They would be able to rally many noncommunists fearful that the destruction of the labor movement was the first step toward dictatorial power. Many such noncommunists would find it preferable to stand firm at that point, even if it meant civil war and revolution, rather than wait until the unions had been destroyed.

The AFL leaders believed that early nongovernmental involvement in European, and particularly French, affairs would be far less dangerous than governmental involvement at a later stage. American nongovernmental aid, even if the United States government contributed in some measure, also would be far less costly to working taxpayers than United States military assistance when all of Europe might be at the brink.

The AFL leaders believed that although it meant a major diversion of their resources and energy, they had to play a heightened role in world politics if they were to achieve their ultimate objectives. Democratic governments could lend them support. But governments should not, and probably could not, do an effective job of organizing workers on their own.

American labor did not wait for the United States government to come around to its view that all types of dictatorships and antidemocratic elements had to be opposed and that prodemocratic trade union forces needed assistance. But before the AFL took action, it engaged in a detailed analysis of the international and French trade union movements.

Chapter 5

AFL Perceptions of Communist Strength in the International, European, and French Labor Movements

Even before Germany surrendered in May 1945, the AFL leadership was coming to the conclusion that large segments of the international and European labor movements were falling under Communist control. Within a few months after the war, they were convinced that the WFTU, the major international trade union body, was completely dominated by the Russian All-Union Central Council of Trade Unions, that Eastern European labor also was rapidly falling under Russian control, and that unions throughout Central and Southern Europe were similarly threatened. By early 1946, the AFL leaders believed that the main national centers and key unions in strategically important France were Communist controlled. The same they believed was true in Italy. Moreover, as the AFL leadership viewed the situation, the Communists were expending considerable efforts to gain control of the reviving unions in the Western Zones of Germany and Berlin.

THE INTERNATIONAL LABOR MOVEMENT

The AFL had been suspicious of the WFTU since the British and Russians suggested its creation in 1943.[1] The AFL had supported wartime planning to reconstruct the shattered European unions by working through the International Federation of Trade Unions (IFTU).[2] However, the AFL leadership believed that the CIO and the Russians saw the creation of a new organization, the WFTU, as a way for them to acquire full stature in the international labor movement. The British apparently saw the creation of the new organization as a method of securing the postwar international cooperation of the Russians and the CIO.[3]

In 1945, the AFL refused to participate in the WFTU. There were several reasons for this, but probably the most important was the participation of the Russian "trade unions." As AFL President Green wrote to British union leader Walter (later Lord) Citrine in December 1944, the AFL objected to the inclusion of "so-called organizations of labor that are in reality government-controlled and government-dominated."[4] This was no new AFL policy. Since the 1920s, the Federation had been one of the strongest opponents of Russian affiliation to international labor organizations.[5] By early 1946, the AFL was convinced that it had adopted the right course and that the WFTU had fallen under the domination of Communists completely subservient to the Soviet Union. This view can be found in almost every major pronouncement on international affairs of the AFL leadership. It was substantiated, the AFL leaders believed, by studies of the WFTU's organization and policy.

A 46-page study in the FTUC archives, for example, referring to the 1945 London conference creating the WFTU, maintained that "at no time in the development of the World Federation of Trade Unions was the preponderance of the Communist faction led by the Soviet Union in doubt."[6] Communist control of this group, the study continued, was based on a number of factors.

First, the Russian delegation claimed to represent 27.5 million workers out of a total of 70 million workers in all participating countries. At the London conference, the Russian delegation included 50 representatives and attachés, in

[1] See for example Green's remarks at the 1944 convention. *Proceedings*, 1944, pp. 454–455.
[2] The AFL had withdrawn from the IFTU shortly after World War I but rejoined the organization, the main interwar, noncommunist, international labor body, in the late 1930s.
[3] John Windmuller, *American Labor and the International Labor Movement 1940–1953* (Ithaca, N.Y.: Cornell University, 1954), pp. 36–67.
[4] Quoted by Meany in "American Federation of Labor's Position on the International Federation of Trade Unions," address to Central Trade and Labor Council, New York City, April 5, 1945, p. 7. FTUC archives.
[5] The major reason for this was the belief that Russian trade unions were not trade unions at all in the Western democratic sense of the term. Instead, they were instruments of the state and an organ of the Russian government. For an analysis of the AFL position, see Windmuller, op. cit., especially pp. 67–73.
[6] "Evaluation of the WFTU." Undated study in the FTUC archives.

comparison with 8 CIO delegates, and also carried with it the international prestige of the Russian government.

Second, representatives from countries under direct Russian influence could be counted on to support the Russian delegation's position at the conference. The unions of Albania, Bulgaria, Czechoslovakia, Rumania, Poland, Austria, Yugoslavia, Hungary, and Finland, which had been destroyed during the Nazi occupation, were revived under close Russian supervision. Hence, it was assumed that delegates from these unions were subservient to Russian interests.

Third, in non-European areas, which had been poorly organized prior to World War II, the forces of the international Communist movement were largely responsible for the organization of trade unions. These non-European unions furnished a major share of the WFTU membership. The principal case in point was the Latin American Federation of Labor led by Vicente Lombardo Toledano.[7]

The report rated the political tendency of each delegate. It concluded that there were 128 Communists or pro-communists present, of whom 67 were all-out supporters of communist causes. There were 101 "conservative labor" or "right-wing" socialist delegates. The sympathies of the remaining 59 delegates were unknown.[8]

The report maintained that the fairest measure of the strength of the forces making up the WFTU was their representation within the organization's leadership. Louis Saillant, who was elected secretary-general, the Federation's most important officer, had a record of "close collaboration with the French Communist Party."[9] The Executive Bureau, which consisted of the nine leading officers, included only three conservative labor leaders: the federation's president, Walter Citrine,[10] Chu Hsueh Fong of the Chinese Association of Labor, and Evert Kupers of the Dutch Federation of Labor (NVV). The Communist faction was represented by V. V. Kuznetsov of the Soviet Union; Lombardo Toledano of the Mexican and Latin American Federations of Labor; and G. Di Vittorio, general secretary of the main Italian center, the CGIL. Sidney Hillman of the American CIO and the French CGT leader, Léon Jouhaux, were considered Communist "collaborators."[11] The Communists had a similar majority in the WFTU General Council.[12]

[7]Ibid., pp. 13–15.

[8]Ibid., pp. 13–24.

[9]"Evaluation of the WFTU," op. cit.

[10]The presidency of an international labor organization, however, is considered largely symbolic compared with the post of secretary-general.

[11]Jouhaux, it was believed, was forced to collaborate with the Communists if he was to survive as leader of the CGT. After the old leader had returned from exile, he found that the CGT was predominantly controlled by the Communists. Hillman, who had a long record of collaboration with the Communists, was also surrounded by Communist sympathizers such as the lawyer John Abt. These characterizations are derived from the WFTU evaluation in the FTUC archives. They presumably reflect the perceptions of the AFL leaders.

[12]"Evaluation of the WFTU," op. cit., pp. 26–28.

Finally, in order to counteract the possible opposition of noncommunist delegates, the Communist leaders of the WFTU energetically sought to impose strict discipline on the organization's affiliates. At a meeting in Oakland, California, in May 1945, the Russians requested that the new federation be given the power to direct world trade union policy. At the insistence of the British and several other delegations, the federation was given less power. The Communists agreed to a compromise, which carried with it significant implications of compulsion, in order to preserve the unity of the conference.[13]

The WFTU, the report concluded, would be useful to the Russians in several ways. First, the affiliated "conservative" unions would be unable to prevent the organization from dispensing anti-American and anti-British propaganda. Second, through recognized WFTU representatives in the United Nations Economic and Social Council, Russian policies would be enunciated and fostered in this body as well. (The WFTU also would be a useful substitute vehicle if the Russian government were ever to decide to withdraw from the UN.) Third, the WFTU would be used to bring direct pressure to bear on noncommunist governments and labor organizations. The federation could threaten and carry out politically motivated strikes and boycotts. Indeed, the report maintained,

> There is no doubt that with the present high degree of integration of the world economy, the WFTU has sufficient strength to cause serious dislocation. . . . General strikes for political ends have already made their appearance on a minor scale in a number of countries including the United States, led by affiliates of the World Federation of Trade Unions. It may be expected that this trend will increase in intensity, scope and synchronization, within the near future.[14]

Fourth, the WFTU would also be useful in solidifying Communist control over reviving national trade union centers—in Germany, for example—and thus would further strengthen Russian power.

Finally, as the only major international labor body, the WFTU would serve as a rallying point for all unions, including noncommunist ones.[15] The appeal of unity is a powerful one in trade union circles at any time. This was especially true after the common struggle against the Nazis and Fascists. The liquidation of the IFTU had left a vacuum that the AFL feared would be filled by the WFTU. Russian and WFTU activities in Germany in 1946 and Italy in 1947 and inter-

---

[13]Ibid., pp. 34–38. Each affiliate was morally bound to carry out the WFTU's decisions. A degree of flexibility and consultation was permitted in the method of executing the Federation's decisions, but there was no provision enabling an affiliate to refuse to carry out the collective decision. In addition, an affiliate could be expelled for failure to comply with the organization's policy.

[14]"Evaluation of the WFTU," op. cit., p. 46.

[15]*Proceedings*, 1946, p. 72.

vention in the internal affairs of the CIO in 1948 all served to reinforce the fears that the AFL harbored in early 1946.[16]

THE EUROPEAN LABOR MOVEMENT

The AFL leadership did not believe that there was any imminent threat of Communist takeover in Scandinavia, the Benelux countries, or England through the leverage of union power. The Communist parties in these countries were weak and controlled only small segments of the labor movement. However, many national centers in these countries were affiliated with the WFTU; and through this organization, the AFL feared, the Russians might be able to exert some influence. But the AFL leadership believed that the principal threats to postwar stability were to be found in Germany, Italy, and France.

In Germany, the reviving trade unions were faced with a number of obstacles. For one thing, some United States military authorities were unsympathetic to the formation of any unions at all; worse, some occupying authorities were openly sympathetic to the WFTU—which was allowed to operate in the Western Zones—and, it appeared to the AFL, the Western authorities were to some extent influenced by the WFTU's judgments on how to organize the reviving unions. Similarly, AFL leaders were worried about the infiltration of American Communists and fellow travelers into the Occupation apparatus. The AFL feared that such officials as George Shaw Wheeler (who subsequently defected to Czechoslovakia) would hinder democratic unionists and facilitate Communist takeover of the reviving labor movement. In the American Zone this would take some time. The AFL leaders believed that in Berlin, however, the Russians were mounting a major effort to win control of organized labor in the Western sectors through a variety of legal and illegal methods. If successful, they would be in a position to paralyze the city.

The AFL leaders believed that the Communists already had gone beyond the threat of control in Italy and France. In Italy, they had succeeded in capturing control of the revived trade union center, the CGIL, in which Christian Democrats and Socialists also participated. In addition, they controlled unions in such key sectors as the docks and the metal industry. In France, the peril was even greater.

THE FRENCH LABOR MOVEMENT

Even before Irving Brown was dispatched to Europe in late '45, the AFL leadership feared that the major unions in France were falling under Communist

---

[16]For an elaboration of several WFTU maneuvers, see Windmuller, op. cit., pp. 135–136.

domination.[17] Lovestone in particular was dismayed when the prewar CGT leader, Léon Jouhaux, returned from incarceration in Germany and accepted equal status with Louis Saillant, the newly elected general secretary-general of the CGT. There were to be two secretaries-general of the CGT, Jouhaux and Saillant. Convinced that Saillant was a Communist or Communist supporter, Lovestone refused to meet with him when he passed through New York after attending the founding UN conference in 1945.[18] Within a month after his arrival in France in November 1945, Brown, too, was convinced that the CGT was falling under Communist domination.[19] By the late spring of 1946, the entire AFL foreign policy leadership believed the CGT to be Communist controlled.

Brown attended the CGT convention in April 1946 and reported that it was a completely dominated "Communist Party affair. It is almost safe to say," he continued, "that the C.G.T. no longer exists as a trade union. It has become so thoroughly a Stalinist organ that there are grave doubts about the possibility of internal reform."[20]

Brown reported, among other things that (1) the new CGT reorganization, as proposed by the Communist party via Henri Reynaud, one of the Communist CGT secretaries, was adopted by about 80 percent of those voting, and control of the CGT in the future would rest in the hands of 6 large federations (metal, building trades, mines, railroads, textiles, and chemicals) all of which were under Communist party domination, the power of the smaller unions in which the noncommunists had strength being virtually eliminated; (2) Saillant's international report was a "strictly Stalinite affair in defense of the Russians, an attack against Churchill";[21] (3) resolutions, actions, and the major speeches fitted into the pattern of Russian interests; and (4) there was an almost complete absence of discussion of direct trade union problems, such as wages and working conditions, except in a very general way. Instead, politics was the central issue. Brown's report formed the basis for Woll's article in the July 1946 *American Federationist*, which concluded that "France's great CGT of former years—one of the foremost trade unions in the world—exists no longer. The name is the same, but the CGT instead of being free and democratic has been captured by the communists and transformed by them into a direct instrument of Communist Party policy."[22]

[17]William Green, "The AFL and World Labor Unity," *The New Leader*, August 4, 1945, p. 16.
[18]Interview, Lovestone.
[19]Interview, Brown.
[20]Irving Brown, "Report on the 1946 CGT Convention," April 1946. FTUC archives.
[21]Ibid.
[22]Matthew Woll, "The Communists Move in on French Labor," *American Federationist*, July 1946, p. 6.

STRATEGIC SECTORS

Coal mining and transportation, the AFL leaders believed, were the immediate and most important Communist targets. When the Communists entered the French government in 1945, they took over key managerial posts in these nationalized industries. The AFL leadership concluded that if, in addition, the Communists controlled the unions in these industries—as well as perhaps in electricity, communications, and metal working—they would achieve their objectives with respect to France and, as a result, with respect to noncommunist Europe.

The mining and transport industries, Brown knew, had several qualities in common. In the first place, each was a strategic industry and each played a vital role in the French economy. If either of these industries were paralyzed, the French economy would be disrupted. Moreover, the workers in these industries, particularly the transport workers, were well placed for paramilitary activities. Furthermore, many sectors of these industries were virtually closed shops. Tradition and employment conditions made it extremely difficult to break the hold of the union over individual workers. If one of the strategic sectors within these industries could be closed down, the industry as a whole would grind to a standstill; for example, if railroad engine drivers went on strike, the railroads would cease functioning. Finally, the Communists were well represented among the workers and unions in these industries—as a result of massive investments of resources, both human and material, over a long period of time. Thus, both the AFL and, apparently, the Communists believed that the struggle for France might very well be won in the battle for control of the unions in these two sections of the economy.

Coal Mining

As early as January 1947, Brown was sure that coal mining was one of the keys to the economic and political stability of France and Europe.[23] Northern France, the center of coal production, was the critical area. Without coal from this region in particular, the French had no major source of fuel for industrial or private consumption. This was presumably a major reason why the Communists had concentrated their attention on controlling the mines, particularly those in the Pas de Calais and Nord departments.

Brown maintained that the Communists had concentrated their financial and organizational resources in the mining area of northern France and had built up a political machine even before World War II. During and immediately after the Liberation, this machine went into action with sufficient funds and personnel to

[23]Brown to Lovestone, January 27, 1947.

carry out Communist objectives. Even before the war, the party had eight organizers in the north. In 1948, Brown reported, it had 48 trade union specialists in
the mines separate and distinct from the trade union bureaucracy.

In the aftermath of the war, the Communists also gained control of the relief
and welfare agencies, which were important in mining areas, as well as major
sectors of the industry's management. High-ranking Communists, such as
Auguste Lecoeur, the mayor of Lens and a member of the Party's Central
Committee, were appointed to ministerial posts supervising the operations of the
newly nationalized mines. Not surprisingly, the new minister surrounded himself
with persons who were politically compatible.[24]

Another method of gaining control of the mines and the parallel trade union
apparatus was the purge. This instrument was used not only to eliminate wartime collaborators but also to undermine any "element ready to conduct an
open fight against Communist Party domination."[25] The symbols of unity and
the fear of a split in the ranks of the workers also helped the Communists, as did
the division and the lack of clear-cut purpose among the noncommunists.
Finally, the Communists' continuous emphasis on the fact that many of the
major CGT leaders—René Belin and George Desmoulins, for example, who were
close to Jouhaux and the "reformist" tendency—had gone over to Pétain in 1940
had considerable weight.[26]

By calling strikes and keeping them going through a combination of economic and physical force, the Communists would be able to close down the
mines and keep them closed down. However, until 1947, the Communists held
this weapon in abeyance. They were members of the government, after all, and,

---

[24] For confirmation and a discussion of Communist influence in the nationalized industries, see Mario Einaudi, Maurice Bye, and Ernesto Rossi, *Nationalization in France and
Italy* (Ithaca, N.Y.: Cornell University Press, 1955), pp. 100–105.

[25] Brown, "Report on the 1946 CGT Convention," op. cit.

[26] A number of writers have described Communist techniques in passing. There are few
published works, however, which systematically explain how the prewar Communist minority was able to gain control of many of the national federations by the time the CGT
congress met in April 1946. An exception is Thomas Hammond, "How the Communists
captured a French Trade Union," in J. S. Curtis, ed., *Essays in Russian and Soviet History*
(New York: Columbia University Press, 1963). Among the authors touching on the subject
are Alfred J. Rieber, *Stalin and the French Communist Party 1941–1947* (New York:
Columbia University Press, 1962), especially pp. 177–183; George Lefranc, *Les Expériences
Syndicales en France 1939 à 1950* (Paris: Montaigne, 1950); Seymour Chalfin, "Causes
Leading to the Communist Domination of the French Labor Movement 1944–1947" (M.A.
thesis, University of Illinois, 1949); Peter Novick, *The Resistance versus Vichy: The Purge
of Collaborators in Liberated France* (New York: Columbia University Press, 1968), pp.
131–138. Novick, while agreeing that the Communists probably used the purge to remove
noncommunist leaders, maintains, with little supporting evidence, that the trade union
purge was probably only a very "subordinate factor in the takeover of the CGT." He
explains the takeover in terms of the levels of popularity the Communists attained prior to
1939 and the same postwar developments that led to Communist electoral ascendency over
the Socialists.

far from organizing strikes, they favored imposing additional sacrifices on the workers. Indeed, as prices rose, the Communists in the government endorsed wage controls, piecework, and speedups. When they were expelled from the government in mid-1947, they jettisoned this policy and changed tactics.[27]

Brown maintained that the strikes that occurred in late 1947 and again in late 1948 were manifestations of these new tactics. The '48 strike, he pointed out, was given legal cover by holding a strike vote phrased in such a way that he himself would have voted to strike.[28] The majority of workers, Brown believed, were in fact apathetic. Many were incensed by what they felt to be unjust economic conditions, but few wanted a long strike, least of all in winter.[29] The Communist militants could last through a long strike by living off Party funds and the enormous sums contributed by Communist-controlled unions in other countries. Brown reported to Lovestone that the front page of the CP newspaper, *L'Humanité*, revealed that Russian and Eastern European "unions" contributed 600 million francs to the French miners during the '48 strike.[30]

After the '48 strike had been in progress for a week or two, many miners wanted to return to work. To prevent this, Communists in management positions, in social welfare organizations, and in the unions applied economic and physical pressure. Recalcitrant miners were threatened with losing their jobs when the strike was over. They were told that if they returned to work, their opportunities to receive dividends and food from the cooperatives controlled by the unions would be jeopardized.[31] If, in spite of these pressures, additional "incentives" were needed, the Communists applied physical force against the miners and their families. Many miners, Brown reported, were beaten. Thus, whatever the miners' lack of sympathy for maintaining the strike, few attempted to break it.

In this strike, the Communists also engaged in a tactic, Brown stated, that no trade union movement in the French coal industry had ever employed—that is,

[27]For an analysis of Communist strategy and options from 1945 to 1947 see Rieber, op. cit., passim.

[28]"The Fight against Communism in Western Europe," p. 19.

[29]Long strikes were rare in the French mines. Unlike American miners, the French miners did not have enormous strike funds to sustain them during a long strike. In the winter, long strikes were even rarer because the miners were unable to secure alternative employment. Moreover, they could not farm or live off the small plots of land they held to obtain vegetables, fruits, and other basics.

[30]Brown to Lovestone, January 2, 1949.

[31]"The Fight against Communism in Western Europe," op. cit. p. 20. These descriptions probably strongly influenced William Green. In his partially autobiographical work, *Labor and Democracy*, Green described his early recollections of the mining company's power owing to its control not only of the mines but also of local shops, housing, etc. He noted in the mining areas that the union was the only other center of real power and security. One can imagine his reaction to reports indicating that the officials of the company and the unions were under the same political management. *Labor and Democracy*, pp. 1–10.

they started to withdraw the maintenance and repair workers from the security posts, from the pumps, from the operations that keep the mines in running order even when no work is going on. Even during the Nazi occupation, he pointed out, when there had been a short strike in 1943–1944, these services were maintained to ensure the mines against being flooded or filled with gas. Their withdrawal of these security personnel, Brown concluded, made it clear that the Communists were not interested in economic redress. Instead, their orders and their policy were designed "to prevent the French mines from becoming a contributing part in the successful economic stability and reconstruction of France and of Western Europe."[32]

The strike of December 1947, Brown reported, cost the French economy 2 million tons of coal.[33] The 1948 strike amounted to a loss equivalent to almost one-quarter of the entire Marshall Plan aid to France. France's reserves of coal were completely exhausted. If there were another strike in February 1949, he told Lovestone, France would freeze and many industries would be forced to shut down. If France requested additional coal from the United States to build up a reserve, then employment in other industries (e.g., textiles) would decrease because dollars needed to buy essential raw materials would have to be diverted to the purchase of coal.[34]

Transportation

The second industry necessary for the successful operation of the French economy and the Marshall Plan was transportation. As a result of his background and wartime experience, Brown knew that transportation was essential for France's economic recovery, for the French war effort in Indo-China, and, to a lesser extent, for Western defense of France and Europe.

After the war, there were only two major means of transportation that could effectively serve France's economic and military needs. Mass transport by road and air was economically impractical. Given the primitive state of these industries at the time, they simply were unable to carry even a minor portion of the country's industrial and military traffic. This situation left overland transport by rail and marine shipping as the crucial means of transportation.

Dock Workers   The docks were one of Brown's major concerns. Particularly in the postwar period, substantial numbers of dock workers were necessary to load and unload ships.[35] If the dockers had refused to work, an attempt could

---

[32] "The Fight against Communism in Western Europe," op. cit. p. 23.
[33] Irving Brown, "Good News in France," *American Federationist*, p. 16.
[34] Brown to Lovestone, January 2, 1949.
[35] By the 1960s, the importance of dockers had been reduced by the increased mechanization of the docks. Large numbers of dockworkers are no longer needed for the successful loading and unloading of a ship.

have been made to use the military as a substitute labor force. Moreover, the army could have been used to protect dockers who did not wish to honor a strike. In addition to requiring physical strength, however, loading and unloading a ship is a skilled task. The rapid operation of the cranes and interrelation between the crane operators and manual workers require both confidence and know-how. The soldiers and nonskilled workers hired for this task would probably have found it difficult, if not impossible, to load and unload ships both rapidly and successfully. In addition, the military and those not honoring the strike would have been subject to harassment by the dockers and sailors, who would have regarded them as strikebreakers. Finally, the use of the military for civilian tasks was obviously undesirable politically.

In the event of dock strikes, an alternative would have been to load and unload at the ports of another country. But even if this was economically and physically possible, transport workers are fairly internationally minded and generally well organized. Ships circumventing strikebound ports would likely encounter hostile labor and political reactions wherever they docked.

Dockers also could sabotage ships and engage in intelligence and paramilitary operations. Troops and war materials, for example, must pass through their hands. If a docker wants to know what is in a carefully guarded crate, it is relatively simple for him to arrange for it to be dropped and smashed open. Conversely, it is possible to load and unload various types of contraband (e.g., arms) in secrecy with the cooperation of local dockers.

Finally, the AFL feared that dock strikes and the destruction of American goods[36] would create an unfortunate political reaction in France and the United States. Indeed, in congressional hearings on the European Recovery Program, several senators raised questions about strikes in recipient countries.[37] There was fear that Congress would become increasingly reluctant to fund the program if striking French workers refused to accept or utilize Marshall Plan goods.[38]

From 1947 on, Brown was concerned about Communist control of this sector. He knew from Valtin and other sources that a major Communist thrust in the interwar period had been controlling the docks. He feared that in the postwar period, they had almost achieved this goal by gaining control of the French dock workers' union and securing the cooperation of the employers. Many of the same techniques employed in the mines were used to win control of the CGT's Fédération des Ports et Docks. In 1935, when Georges Piquemal became the head of the Federation, there was only one Communist in the union's Executive Bureau. In 1944, there was a second, and by 1946, the Communists

[36]Traditionally, politically motivated actions in port cities result in the throwing of goods and personnel into the sea.

[37]See for example U.S., Congress, Senate, *U.S. Assistance to European Economic Recovery*, Pt. 1, 80th Cong., 2d sess., 8 January 1948, p. 63.

[38]Interview, Brown.

gained sufficient strength at the union's congress to dismiss Piquemal and other noncommunist leaders.

The Communists were able to secure the acquiescence of employers in the shipping industry partly through blackmail. During the war, many employers had worked with both Vichy and the Nazis. After the war, the Communists, as a result of their position in local as well as national government, were able to use police and other dossiers to blackmail compromised employers.[39]

The Communists used their control of the union and employers in at least four ways. First, they controlled the hiring of dock workers. In France after 1947, dock workers had to be certified by a local manpower bureau (Bureau Central de la Main d'Oeuvre, or BMCO) before they could be hired by one of the dozen or so companies in each port. Once they were certified, they were entitled to the privileges of professional dockers.[40] The BMCOs were composed of an equal number of representatives from the dockers' union and the employers, plus the port director or another representative from the responsible ministry in Paris. Thus, by controlling the union and securing the acquiescence of some employers, the Communists were able to control the BMCOs and the certification of dockers. This power, Brown believed, was used to ensure that Communist sympathizers or those amenable to Communist pressure received certification. Control of the union enabled the Communists at least to impede the employment of "uncooperative" workers. In February 1950, for example, approximately 100 dockers in Marseilles were expelled from the CGT union for unloading a boat bound for Indo-China.[41]

A second technique the Communists used to prevent the loading and unloading of a ship was to pay the dockers not to work. This tactic was employed, for example, in Cherbourg in January 1950. The CGT simply paid each worker 1,000 francs not to unload an American ship.[42]

The third technique was organizing a limited political strike. This was a subtle ploy involving the collusion of both the employer and the Communist party. The employer, whose consent was usually obtained by blackmail, ensured that five members of a secret Communist cell were hired to work the same gang

[39] In an interview with this writer, Georges Piquemal named two employers in Bordeaux who were blackmailed by the Communists. For occasional reference to trade unionists, employers, etc., who "whitewashed" themselves in this fashion, see Peter Novick, op. cit., pp. 38−39 and 136−137.

[40] For a detailed explanation of the official method of hiring dock workers in most French ports, and particularly Marseilles, see Vernon H. Jensen, *Hiring of Dockworkers and Employment Practices in the Ports of New York, Liverpool, London, Rotterdam and Marseilles* (Cambridge: Harvard University Press, 1964), especially pp. 265−272.

[41] For elaboration see Force Ouvrière, *Bulletin d'Information de la Manche*, February 1950.

[42] Interview, Brown. For elaboration see Force Ouvrière, *Bulletin d'Information de la Manche*, January 1950.

in a given ship's hull. The Communist gang would find some pretext (e.g., a grievance) to call a work stoppage. The other gangs, unaware of the true motivation of the Communists, would then follow suit. If one or two workers argued against the work stoppage, the Communists would have a difficult time organizing this kind of strike. It was the job of the cell to ensure that uncooperative dockers were neutralized so that a strike would result.[43]

If control of the BMCOs and the unions plus bribery and deliberate work stoppages did not prevent dockers from loading and unloading a ship, the Communists used terror as a fourth instrument. Not only are dockers prone to use violence, but also it was easy to arrange for uncooperative dockers to have "accidents" on the docks or in the narrow streets around the piers. Violence was used also to intimidate "occasional dockers"—those who fill out the ranks of the professionals in the ports. Needless to say, the injury or death of several men increased the reluctance of both occasionals and professionals to work on the piers.

Oceangoing Sailors Brown was also concerned by Communist control of other sectors of the maritime industry. Oceangoing sailors, by refusing to work, could paralyze France's shipping industry. Although they would not have had an immediate impact on the Marshall Plan and the transport of NATO's military equipment, they would have hurt France's war effort in Indo-China.[44] Sailors also were in a position to sabotage ships and, as has been pointed out, to engage in espionage and paramilitary operations.

French sailors belonged to two unions, the Fédération des Officers de la Marine Marchande and the Fédération des Syndicats Maritimes. Like mines and docks, these sectors had long been important Communist targets throughout Europe. The fact that several of the key noncommunist French maritime leaders had been either killed or deported in the war—Pierre Ferri-Pisani was one leading example of the deportees—facilitated increased Communist control in the postwar years.

Barge Workers Brown also believed that barges were an important means of transportation in France. (In the early postwar period, inland waterways accounted for approximately 15 percent of France's total transportation.) Most

---

[43]Even under normal working conditions, there is a high frequency of strikes among dock workers. As V. L. Allen has pointed out, this situation can be explained by a variety of factors, including the casual nature of the work and the culture of the dock workers. For a discussion of this point see his *Trade Union Leadership* (London: Longman, Green, 1957), pp. 191–196.

[44]France would have had to sacrifice foreign currency and hire the services of friendly neutral ships to transport men and material to Indo-China. American ships transported most of the Marshall Plan and NATO materials.

important, he knew that most of the canals and barges were located in the industrial north and east. Paralyzing the canals would have dislocated a major portion of France's coal, steel, and other heavy industries. Furthermore, because the canals crossed Europe's frontiers, the men who ran the barges had an opportunity to engage in paramilitary and intelligence operations.

Although Brown considered inland transportation important and knew that the Communists, as Valtin had pointed out, had devoted considerable attention to this sector, he did not believe that they were in a position to close down the waterways. The approximately 10,000 French inland transport workers differed considerably from other transport workers. For one thing, approximately 4,000 owned their own barges and lived on them with their families. The remaining workers were salaried and also lived and worked on the barges. Neither the owners nor the salaried employees considered themselves manual workers. They saw themselves as artisans. In the case of the owners, they had to work hard to pay off the debts for their barges and had little time for, or interest in, political affairs.

Another difference between inland and other transport workers was the nature of their "trade union." Their organization, the Secrétaire du Cartel Artisanal de la Batellerie, was an autonomous cartel. It had been created in 1945 under the leadership of an ex-Communist, Roger Blanckaert, and represented such disparate tendencies as Communist, Socialist, and Catholic. The CGT had objected to the creation of the independent cartel, maintaining that the Batellerie should be incorporated into the already existing CGT structure. To avoid CGT domination and at the same time maintain the strength of the Batellerie, Blanckaert rejected these arguments. Thus, Brown did not believe that although there were a few Communist militants among the barge owners, that the Party was in a position to close down the inland waterways.[45]

Railroad Workers   Not only was the operation of the railroads essential for France's economic life, but, as was suggested in the last chapter, the railroads could play an important role in a coup d'état or an invasion. A relatively small number of railroad workers could make a major contribution to intelligence operations and political warfare. Employees of the *Wagon-lits* (dining room and sleeping car workers), for example, were one of the few groups of people who traveled constantly across the frontiers of Europe.[46] The *Wagon-lits* were part of an international company. Frequently, when a train reached a frontier, the engineers were changed and passengers would have to go through customs. It was

[45] Interviews, Brown and Blanckaert.
[46] Many workers in the railroad industry, like those in the maritime industry, rarely remain in one place for any length of time. They pose a problem for union or political organizers in that special ways of reaching them must be devised. Nevertheless, it should also be noted that railway workers have usually been well organized.

scarcely practical, however, to search the dining room and sleeping cars top to bottom. Employees in these sections could be watched, but it would be all but impossible to prevent them from receiving intelligence information from contacts in the railroad industry in another country or from smuggling money to finance these operations. The union that controlled the *Wagon-lits* and other sectors of the railroad industry would have a decided advantage in engaging in these operations and, at the same time, in preventing others from engaging in them.

Brown was aware that the Communists controlled the major railroad workers' union, the Fédération des Cheminots. Like the mines, the railroads had long been a primary Communist target. The Communists had expended considerable time, effort, and money to implant themselves in a union whose members, because of the nature of their work, were difficult to organize.

Communications

Brown also believed that the Communists controlled the unions of the electrical workers and major sections of the communication workers, the Fédération de l'Éclairage et Forces Motrices and the Fédération des P.T.T. They would thus be able to interdict electrical current and communications, which were, of course, vital for French industry. In addition, control over these industries at critical moments could be decisive in facilitating or inhibiting paramilitary and other activities that might lead to the toppling of a government. Turning off the electrical current, for example, after Communist newspapers were printed and demonstrators were organized at strategic urban centers would give the Communists a decided advantage in controlling the streets and important political institutions. Similarly, if postal, telephone, and telegraph workers went on strike, the French economy would be thrown into chaos. If they refused to process the communications of noncommunist parties at moments of political crisis, the Communists would receive decisive advantages. Brown was also convinced that workers in the metal, printing and entertainment industries were all Communist dominated and that continued Communist control would be decisive in determining the course of French politics.

COMMUNIST USE OF ORGANIZED LABOR

A few weeks after Ramadier expelled the Communists from his government in May 1947,[47] Brown told Lovestone that the CP had begun to engage in economic

[47]During 1946 and 1947, when leaders of the Communist party were members of the French cabinet, Brown and Lovestone believed that the Communists were consolidating their control of the unions and improving their position in other sectors of the French economy. Interviews, Lovestone and Brown. Examples of Communist infiltration during this period can also be found in Rieber, op. cit., pp. 289–292.

blackmail. By suddenly claiming that the government was asking the workers to pay for postwar recovery, by demanding immediate wage increases without price increases, and by militating against wage ceilings geared to production, the Communists intensified inflationary pressures on the government. At the same time, Brown reported, the Party told workers in the shops that the Socialists were responsible for the failure to secure improved economic conditions.[48]

After the announcement of the Marshall Plan, the founding Cominform meeting in the autumn of 1947, and the general strike in the winter of 1947–1948, Brown reported that the power that French Communists wielded through the trade union movement had been "the major contributing factor to the situation in France which can best be characterized as one of rising prices and falling governments."[49] The general strike of 1947, he continued, was part of the overall effort to prevent the successful implementation of the Marshall Plan. If France remained unstable and went communist, he said, the "whole Western European offensive for the Marshall Plan . . . will fall to the ground because there will be no successful reconstruction merely with the Benelux Trade Union Movement and the Benelux countries, the Scandinavians, etc."[50]

The strike, he maintained, cost France from 137 to 200 billion francs (over $1 billion). Production and material losses also contributed to an inflationary price rise by further aggravating the shortage of goods. The inflationary pressures, he suggested, provided the Communists with a legitimate pretext to strike again at the economy.[51] The prolonged coal mine strike in the fall of 1948, in Brown's view, was not a strike for legitimate economic grievances. Rather it was a "strike organized by the militarized, totalitarianized Communist movement of France to destroy the French economy as the first step in an attempt to destroy the efforts of the European Recovery Program."[52]

At the same time, he reported, the CP organized a "quasi-military organization based on trade union militants—what in Czechoslovakia they called 'action committees,' which had been the means whereby power was seized."[53] Communist tactics in France were geared not only to Russian foreign policy but also to the "Soviet military time-table." Since 1948, Brown told the 1950 AFL convention, Communist organizations in France had been "transformed in the main, into paramilitary cadres geared to obstruct Western economic reconstruction, sabotage the production and delivery of military weapons, and act as partisan forces in the time of armed invasion."[54]

[48] Brown to Lovestone, June 20, 1947.
[49] "The Fight against Communism in Western Europe," op. cit., p. 6.
[50] Ibid.
[51] Brown, "Good News in France," op. cit., p. 17.
[52] Proceedings, 1948, p. 271.
[53] "The Fight against Communism in Western Europe," op. cit., p. 11.
[54] Proceedings. 1950, p. 147.

These perceptions narrowed the choices of the AFL leadership. If the Federation, in addition to the United States government and other nongovernmental organizations, remained aloof from the politics of the Continent, the resulting Russian takeover would lead to a catastrophic decline of Western influence throughout the world. The problem the AFL leaders faced was how to prevent the Russians from using their control of key labor organizations to establish their hegemony in Western Europe. For a possible resolution, the AFL looked to developments among the noncommunist labor groups of Europe.

Chapter 6

AFL Perception of Noncommunist Perspectives and Power

The AFL leaders perceived that there were sizable noncommunist elements within Communist-dominated union organizations which were striving to prevent the Russians from using the European labor movement as an instrument of Communist hegemony. They observed that these noncommunists were divided into two groups or factions. One group favored working within Communist-dominated organizations to prevent the Communists from having free rein and in the hope that they, the noncommunists, would be able to regain control at some future time. The other group favored boycotting and attempting to weaken the WFTU and Communist-controlled national unions. This group favored working through the international trade secretariats and groups of noncommunists in France, Italy, and other countries to prevent the Communists from using organized labor for their political purposes. The AFL leadership concluded that the strategy of the second group was potentially the more effective—but that external assistance was essential to its success.

WORKING WITH COMMUNISTS

The first group of noncommunists described above consisted of noncommunist affiliates of the WFTU (e.g., the British TUC and Dutch NVV) and important noncommunist leaders in Communist-controlled WFTU affiliates (e.g., Léon Jouhaux of the CGT). Its strategy was to develop strong labor organizations by welding Communists and noncommunists together. By virtue of the fact that noncommunists would be well represented in the union leadership, the Communists would presumably be precluded from using such organizations—the WFTU, for example—for their political purposes.

The AFL leadership, however, did not believe that these WFTU "conservatives" would be effective against the Communist *apparat*. Sooner or later the WFTU would become a vehicle of Russian political/military objectives. Indeed, as Brown reported, this opinion was held even by important officials of the TUC as well as by several key aides of Foreign Minister Bevin, himself a longtime TUC kingpin.

In France, until December 1947 at least, the conservatives consisted of the prewar leaders of the "reformist" wing of the CGT: Jouhaux and CGT secretaries Robert Bothereau and Pierre Neumayer. In common with the noncommunist affiliates of the WFTU, this group believed in working with Communists in the same organization. Like many Europeans, these older French leaders appeared to accept the "myth of unity," as Brown put it, and believed that noncommunists and Communists could work together to strengthen the French labor movement.

The myth of unity, well-grounded in working-class tradition, was particularly strong in the early postwar period. The French Communists' support of the Hitler-Stalin Pact of 1939 was forgotten because of their vigorous participation in the Resistance, and the Soviet Union enjoyed particular prestige as one of the victors in World War II. It was widely believed or hoped that Communists and noncommunists could continue to work together to ensure postwar peace and economic and social progress. Jouhaux and his associates believed that a split in the ranks of labor (they had witnessed two such fissures in their lifetimes) would gravely weaken the labor movement's power by splitting the already meager material and organizational resources of the unions.[1] Moreover, after a scission, the Communists seemed to emerge stronger than before—in the short run at least. If the split also came at a time when the Communists were relatively popular, as they were in early postwar France, this would further weaken the noncommunist forces.

The AFL leaders also realized that the old reformist leaders did not want to abdicate the moral and material assets of the CGT wholly to the Communists.

---

[1] Irving Brown, "Report on the 1946 CGT Convention," April 1946. FTUC archives.

The name "Confédération Générale du Travail" had become embedded in the tradition of the French masses. (This was, for example, a major reason that during the interwar period the Communists adopted the name "CGT-Unitaire." The material assets of the organization, built up over a 40-year period, included offices, furniture, mimeograph machines, and the like, in every city and department in France. Furthermore, the old CGT leaders were, of course, reluctant to relinquish their senior posts in the well-established organization they had spent most of their lives creating.[2] Finally, Jouhaux and Bothereau did not believe it would be possible to create a new, effective noncommunist confederation without material assistance from a source other than the dues of French workers. Yet they were reluctant, Brown knew, to put themselves in the position of seeking and receiving such assistance.[3]

The reformist leaders also believed that somehow, sometime they would be able to regain control of the CGT. They believed that they had the support in this endeavor of a group known as "Amis de Force Ouvrière"—consisting of trade unionists in all parts of France who had participated in Résistance Ouvrière, a noncommunist trade union grouping that had engaged in underground activities during the war. The reformist leaders hoped that they would be able to galvanize these noncommunists into a force capable of either retaking control of the CGT or, at the least, preventing it from being used for Communist political purposes.[4]

By the spring of 1946, the AFL leaders decided that the reformists were incapable of implementing this strategy. To begin with, they believed, it was almost impossible for democratic forces to gain or regain control of a Communist-dominated organization. The French CGT was no exception. To be sure, the environment was suitable for a noncommunist resurgence in that "the vast percentage of the workers of France are anti-communist or non-communist"[5] and their traditional dissatisfactions lent themselves to dynamic noncommunist representation. But the AFL leaders were not convinced that the reformist leadership had the skill, drive, or financial means to topple the Communist party's *apparat*. As Brown reported in April 1946, the reformists were not providing the noncommunist militants with clear central direction or a unifying program. Indeed, the workers were confused, Brown reported, by the reformists' acceptance of unity with the Communists and by Communist participation in the government, and thus they were disarmed in the internal CGT power struggle. Moreover, although the workers were disgruntled with the failure of the Communist leadership to press their economic demands, the reformists

[2] Interviews, Brown and Lovestone.
[3] Interview, Brown.
[4] Ibid.
[5] Irving Brown in *Proceedings*, 1946, p. 439.

failed to provide a unifying dynamic program "to channelize dissatisfaction into constructive, progressive leadership."[6]

BOYCOTTING COMMUNISTS AND BUILDING AN INTERNATIONAL FREE TRADE UNION MOVEMENT

The second group of noncommunists—active not just in France—consisted of many international trade secretariat (ITS) leaders as well as younger noncommunist leaders in France and Italy. During the interwar period, they either had refused to become associated with organizations that admitted Communists or Communist-controlled unions or, if they were already participating in Communist-controlled organizations, had waited for a suitable opportunity to withdraw.

During the interwar period, relations between the secretariats and the International Federation of Trade Unions (IFTU), the association of national trade union centers, had not been harmonious. The secretariats preferred to remain autonomous; the IFTU wanted them in. For the most part, during this period, the 27 secretariats, with a membership of 13 million workers, remained autonomous in their internal affairs but coordinated their activities with the IFTU.[7] The strategy of the ITS leadership in the early postwar period was to maintain or build autonomous organizations, free from WFTU control, as the best way of furthering trade union interests and preventing Communist control of the entire international labor movement.

Under the leadership of the ITF (transport workers) general secretary, J. H. Oldenbroek, the secretariats resisted their proposed incorporation into the WFTU's trade departments as a first step toward the demise of the trade secretariats as viable international labor bodies.[8] Moreover, there was a growing awareness within the secretariats that the WFTU was Russian-controlled. Incorporating the secretariats into the WFTU's trade departments would thus increase Communist control over such key sectors as transportation and coal mining. Finally, Oldenbroek believed that autonomous secretariats might provide the nucleus for a new noncommunist international labor body.[9] Indeed, in a confi-

---

[6] Brown, "Report on the 1946 CGT Convention," op. cit., pp. 5–6.

[7] For a more detailed explanation of the interwar organization and activities of the ITS and their relations with the IFTU see Lewis Lorwin, *The International Labor Movement* (New York: Harper & Row, 1953), especially pp. 122–127 and John Windmuller, *American Labor and the International Labor Movement, 1940–1953* (Ithaca, N.Y.: Cornell University, 1954), pp. 98–99.

[8] For a detailed explanation of the ITS and analysis of their relations and negotiations with the WFTU, see Windmuller, op. cit. pp. 96–117; Joseph L. Harmon, *The Public Services International* (Washington, D.C.: U.S. Department of Labor, 1962), pp. 92–106; *Proceedings of the Thirty-Fourth Miners' International Federation Congress*, 1947.

[9] Brown to Woll, December 23, 1946.

dential report, Brown wrote, "The International Trade Secretariats should be regarded as a major organizational instrument for the AFL to advance the cause of Free Trade Unionism, combat the WFTU and create the base of a future International Trade Union Federation."[10]

If the secretariats were to remain autonomous, their leaders had to command the support of the national affiliates. Many of these affiliates, however, either were Communist-controlled (e.g., the Italian transport workers) or were joined to noncommunist national centers that were already participating in the WFTU (e.g., the British Transport and General Workers Union affiliated with the TUC). In the early postwar years, quite naturally, both the noncommunist WFTU affiliates and the Communists were interested in bringing the secretariats into the WFTU. If these national centers and their unions could convince the smaller ITS affiliates that the secretariats should be incorporated into the WFTU, the secretariats would lose their identity.

To prevent this, leaders of the secretariats and the AFL agreed that American unions, which on the whole were not affiliated with the ITS, should join and take an active role. Among the most important secretariats, the AFL leaders knew, were the ITF and the IMF (International Metalworkers Federation). Perhaps the key secretariat was the ITF. Even before World War II, it had been the strongest in terms of size, solidarity, and geographic distribution of its membership. The transport workers had been among the first to organize. Their work had brought various national groupings together in ports and at international railroad crossings. They soon learned of each others' working conditions and believed that, unless they cooperated, employers would play off the workers of one country against those of another.

The ITF had also been welded into a strong organization, as a result of the dynamism of its first leader, Edo Fimmen. Fimmen, a Dutch socialist, had traveled throughout the world organizing the ITF and, at the same time, attempting to prevent Comintern infiltration of the transport industry.[11] During the course of his work, both he and his young assistant, Oldenbroek, became acquainted with many of the world's labor leaders. When Fimmen died, Oldenbroek immediately stepped into his shoes as head of the ITF.

The ITF was one of the few secretariats that had functioned throughout the war and into the immediate postwar period. Indeed, it was one of the few secretariats that was running smoothly when the question of affiliation with the WFTU was raised. In all probability, if the ITF and perhaps the IMF affiliated with the WFTU, the AFL believed, the other secretariats would follow suit. If, however, the American workers in these sectors could help sustain Oldenbroek's

[10] Report from Brown to the AFL International Labor Relations Committee, November 10, 1947, p. 6.
[11] See for example Jan Valtin, *Out of the Night* (New York: Alliance Books, 1941), p. 744.

policy of nonaffiliation, the ITF and the other secretariats would probably remain autonomous.[12]

BOYCOTTING COMMUNISTS AND BUILDING
FREE TRADE UNIONS IN FRANCE

In France, the militants opposed to working with the Communists included many disparate elements. Some of the militants had been members of the CGT until World War II and, after the war, either had been purged or had withdrawn. Others remained in the CGT but waited for a suitable opportunity to split the organization. There were also groups of anarcho-syndicalists, Trotskyists, and Catholic trade unionists. Although the AFL was aware of these numerous tendencies, its attention was focused on two main elements among the French noncommunists—Catholic trade unionists affiliated with the CFTC and non-Catholic unionists who had been, or continued to be, members of the CGT but wanted to build a new, noncommunist union structure.

The non-Catholics were convinced that it was impossible to regain control of the CGT or to prevent the organization from being used by the Communist party. Some of them had been purged by the Communists. Others had lost their elected posts to Communists. Whatever their backgrounds, they believed that the CGT as an organization would remain in Communist hands. Indeed, in April 1946, Brown reported that "the opinion is gaining ground, which I am beginning to share, that the CGT as an organization cannot be reformed since its Stalinite nature makes it impervious to democratic change."[13] This group also believed that unity and cooperation with the Communists would not necessarily increase the strength of the French labor movement or improve the lot of French workers. Rather, as the AFL tended to agree, the interests of the workers would be subjugated to those of the Communist party and, by extension, the Soviet Union.

This view was reinforced by the refusal of the Communists, when they were members of the government, to sanction any major strikes. From late 1945 until early 1947, Maurice Thorez and the Communist party, far from attempting to bring about a major redistribution of income or taking other measures to improve the conditions of French workers, appealed for greater production, not increased wages.[14] The ensuing wildcat strikes and the declining strength of the CGT in social security elections and membership also helped convince many noncommunists that cooperation with the Communists was not in the economic interest of the French workers.[15] Finally, the French Communists' sudden shift

---

[12] See for example Lovestone to Dubinsky, July 8, 1946.

[13] Brown, "Report on the 1946 CGT Convention," op. cit.

[14] These tactics caused considerable dissension within the CGT and the Communist party; see Auguste Lecoeur, *Le Partisan* (Paris: Flammarion, 1963), pp. 213–222.

in policy in the spring and summer of 1947 provided additional evidence that the CGT and the Communist party were moving to the beat of a distant drummer. The French Communists were apparently following the Russian decision to oppose the Marshall Plan and attempt to prevent the reconstruction of Europe's economies. By the late spring of 1947, the French Communists switched from exhorting the workers to self-sacrifice in the interests of increased production to demanding immediate and inflationary wage increases; in the fall of 1947, they organized a general strike.[16]

The belief that the CGT would remain Communist-controlled and that cooperation with the Communists would not necessarily benefit French workers led many noncommunist labor leaders, as well as the AFL, to the conclusion that a new union structure had to be created. Many militants, however, refused to leave the CGT until the auspicious moment arrived. They knew that they would be abandoning the moral and material assets of the organization. To reduce this disadvantage and to secure the largest possible following, the militants wanted to bring Jouhaux and the old reformists along with them. If Jouhaux and the other leaders refused to leave the CGT, this would create bewilderment and uncertainty among many workers and thus jeopardize the future of any new union structure.

A New Union Structure?

Just how this new structure was to be erected was far from clear. Indeed, the AFL was not at all certain that a new organization could successfully compete with the well-entrenched CGT.[17] Nevertheless, the Americans tended to believe that the environment at this time was not unsuitable for the effort. As has been pointed out, the AFL was convinced that most French workers were not Communists and, given a suitable opportunity, would opt for representation by noncommunist unions. And because the CGT did not appear to be fighting for the economic interests of its members during the early postwar period, the ensuing economic grievances could provide a unifying program for a rival union structure. As Brown wrote in March 1946,

> I do not claim there is any certainty about what can be done nor do I deny that the Communists have and will continue to have control of the CGT. But no one can deny that there is a movement and a restlessness that can be utilized in the ranks. There is a fundamental desire to re-establish free trade

[15] Brown to Lovestone, May 17, 1947.

[16] For a detailed analysis of Communist choices at this time see Alfred J. Rieber, *Stalin and the French Communist Party 1941–1947* (New York: Columbia University Press, 1962).

[17] Lovestone told Brown in March 1946, for example, that the AFL leaders tended to believe "that the situation is lost and that anything put into the proposition in France today is a hopeless waste because the Communists have the thing sewed up." Lovestone to Brown, March 14, 1946.

unionism. There are groups all over France ready to act and be galvanized into a force for free trade unionism.[18]

The problem, as the AFL saw it, was how to "galvanize" the natural sympathies and the discontent of the workers.

In the spring of 1946, Brown reported that a strong nucleus of noncommunist organizers existed throughout France. He reported that at the April CGT convention, he had met with practically every important opposition delegate and had noted that the "ranks are beginning to produce new and qualified leaders."[19] Brown believed that although these emerging leaders were scattered throughout various economic sectors and geographic areas, the incipient leadership in three key sectors—communications, mining, and railroads—was especially important and promising.

As early as late 1945, the emerging noncommunist leadership of the PTT (communications workers) came to the fore at the Communist-dominated PTT congress at Limoges. In early 1946, the noncommunists organized a *grèves de cotisations*, a strike on dues paying to the national federation. In midsummer, they organized one of the first major successful strikes since the Liberation under the leadership of a three-man strike committee headed by a leading "résistant," Camille Mourguès. The strike was strongly supported by communications workers in Lille, Limoges, Bordeaux, and Clermont-Ferrand in spite of opposition of the union's Communist leadership. In October, a Comité d'Action Syndicaliste des PTT was formed. (This group carried the membership cards of Force Ouvrière with a special PTT stamp costing each member 1 franc per month.) Finally, in July 1947, the comité officially became an autonomous organization under the leadership of Mourguès.[20]

Another important sector in which a noncommunist leadership was developing was the mines. As early as December 1945, as noted previously, Brown had visited the northern mining regions. He had met with the well-respected miners' leader "Pere" Mailly and with the secretary of Nord's Union Départmentale (UD), Jules Carpentier.[21] They had introduced him to numerous members of the

18 Brown to Woll, March 14, 1946.
19 Brown, "Report on the 1946 CGT Convention," op. cit.
20 Irving Brown, "Report to the International Labor Relations Committee," November 11, 1947, p. 3.
21 French trade unions have a horizontal as well as a vertical structure:

	Vertical	Horizontal
Local	Syndicat	Union Locale
Regional	Union Syndicat	Union Départmentale
National	Fédération	Confédération

Each of France's departments has a Union Départmentale (UD) roughly equivalent to a state federation of labor. For an analysis of the structure of French trade unions, see Val R. Lorwin, *The French Labor Movement*, (Cambridge: Harvard University Press, 1954), pp. 145–175.

CGT who believed that it was impossible to prevent the Communists from maintaining their control. Indeed, these miners, under the leadership of Mailly and Carpentier, by indicating that they intended in any case to secede from the CGT, played a crucial role in forcing Jouhaux and the other noncommunist CGT leaders ultimately to lead the split of the CGT.[22]

Among the railroad workers, a clear-cut de facto split developed in 1946 and early 1947. In 1946, the employees of the *Wagon-lits* were the first to break away from the Communist-controlled railroad unions. Then, in mid-1947, other railroad workers, under Socialist leadership, followed the PTT example and created a Comité d'Action Syndicaliste des Cheminots. A few months later, this organization and the autonomous *Wagon-lit* organization joined forces to become an 8,000-member Fédération Syndicaliste des Cheminots, under the leadership of André Lafond. Brown's reports from late 1946 to late 1947 contained numerous references to these developments.[23]

The AFL realized, however, that the leadership of these and other noncommunist splinter groups by themselves would probably not be able to challenge and take over the CGT's control over the labor movement. They were aware, first, that there was no central direction or unity on the part of the movement opposing Communist domination—beyond the mere fact of opposition. In June 1947, for example, Brown noted the growing likelihood of Lafond's split and the activities of the anarcho-syndicalists and the Trotskyists but maintained that "the great weakness of the whole opposition movement is their disunity while the Communist Party, in spite of all reports about internal dissension, continues to act as a solid bloc."[24] The opposition leaders, in other words, had organized small and scattered nuclei of noncommunists. To break the Communist party's control of the labor movement, however, they needed central organization and coordination.

A second major problem, AFL leaders knew, was securing and holding the support of militant noncommunist trade unionists. Although, as Brown reported, there were strong nuclei of noncommunist leaders and most workers were noncommunist, there clearly was no large number of local organizers interested in and capable of securing the support of workers in the local shops, factories, mines, and docks.

---

[22] George Lefranc, *Les Éxperiences Syndicales en France de 1939 à 1950* (Paris: Montaigne, 1950), p. 191. In an interview, Antoine Laval, a secretary of the FO, maintained that the point of view expressed by Carpentier and the other miners must have weighed heavily on Jouhaux. The miners traditionally had been one of the staunchest supports of the CGT. It must have been difficult for Jouhaux to have considered remaining in the CGT if a key federation such as the miners had seceded.

[23] See for example Brown, "Report to the International Labor Relations Committee," op. cit.

[24] Brown to Lovestone, June 18, 1947.

The AFL believed that several factors accounted for the reluctance or inability of potentially militant local leaders to engage in organizational activity. One factor was the myth of unity. Many potential militants and workers feared that splitting the CGT would lead to chaos and the inability of organized labor to further the economic, social, and political interests of the workers. Unless these militants were convinced that a new union structure could effectively represent their interests, they would be reluctant to leave the traditional and established organization.

Another factor was morale. In France, this problem had two facets. One sprang from what AFL leaders considered to be a self-fulfilling prophesy, the fear that the Communist party would come to power anyway within a few years. Many noncommunist militants and workers were reluctant to oppose the Communists openly, not only because they feared immediate economic or physical terror but also because they believed that either Russian or local Communists would soon control the French government and anyone who had openly opposed the Party would be subject to drastic sanctions.[25] The second facet of the problem was the "loneliness" of anticommunist militants. The Communists (until 1947 at least) had been embraced by the French government and the old, well-respected noncommunist trade union leadership. A militant opposing the general trend was subject to informal local pressure from skeptical noncommunists as well as from the Communists themselves. Indeed, AFL leaders knew that to be effective in the long run, the unionists who daily bore the brunt of the Communist propaganda barrage and organizational offensive would have to receive moral support and encouragement.[26]

It was difficult, however, to see how this would be done. The national noncommunist leadership, taken as a whole, did not support trade union organization outside the CGT structure. Who could provide the militants with central coordination? Who could provide them with the national and international information and analysis to counter the arguments of the Communist militants? Even if the new noncommunist leadership could obtain this information and some degree of coordination, how could they communicate with their cadres on the local level? The trade union press was predominantly under CGT control, and the noncommunist leaders did not have the financial resources to weld the cadres into one entity.

As far as one can tell, the AFL leaders did not make a systematic study of the financial requirements of a new French organization,[27] but they quickly

[25] Interviews, Brown and Lovestone.
[26] For examples of the AFL's awareness of this problem, see Irving Brown's reports and speeches, specifically his "Report to the International Labor Relations Committee," op. cit., p. 1 and the speech to the 1947 AFL convention, *Proceedings*, 1947, p. 374.
[27] Examination of the FTUC archives and interviews with Brown and Lovestone.

realized that money or its absence was the third major problem jeopardizing the success of the noncommunists. Prior to the creation of a new organization, the minority within the noncommunist faction in the CGT and the noncommunists in the autonomous organizations would have no ready source of financial support for their activities. The Communists and the majority faction of noncommunists controlled what meager CGT funds there were, and workers could hardly be expected to be generous, given the economic conditions and the distribution of incomes in postwar France.

The AFL hoped, however, that once the new union structure was created and functioning smoothly, it would be able to finance much of its own activities. AFL leaders knew, for example, that local governments directly subsidized *unions locales* by providing them with office space in the Bourse de Travail or its equivalent.[28] Furthermore, according to French law, once a union was recognized as a bargaining agent the employers of more than 10 workers were required to pay shop stewards for several hours a week spent adjudicating grievances. If these hours were aggregated, the activities of a small number of full-time militants could be financed.[29] Finally, unions in the public sector of the French economy (e.g., in communications, mines, and railroads) received indirect subsidies, and these subsidies would enable the new unions to finance the more comprehensive activities of their organizers. In some public sectors, the state actually paid trade union functionaries. In other sectors, by ignoring regulations (e.g., regulations limiting the number of days a worker could be absent from his or her post without loss of pay), the state indirectly financed some union activities.[30] Nevertheless, even after the recognition of the new union structure, there would still be major financial difficulties inherent in running the large national federations, *unions départmentales,* training schools, and international activities.

Although local employers, either indirectly as a result of French law or directly through subsidies, had been providing limited financial support to local trade unions in France for years, the AFL believed that it was neither feasible nor desirable to obtain funds from this source. To begin with, many employers were unwilling to finance the activities of the new leadership. Although a few local groups or individual employers were interested in reducing the CGT's power, the Patronat (the main organization of French employers) refused generally to engage in actions directly opposed to the CGT.

There is no supporting documentation in the AFL archives on this point, but Brown maintains that Patronat officials, like some noncommunist CGT officials, feared that if the Communists came to power, they would be compromised.

[28] Val R. Lorwin, op. cit., pp. 153–154.
[29] Ibid, pp. 258–259.
[30] Interview, Brown. These indirect subsidies accrued to all unions in the public sector.

Hence, they preferred to hedge their bets and refused to commit themselves.[31] Furthermore, the AFL was aware that if the new unions were successfully smeared with an employer or Patronat label, they would have a much more difficult time securing the support of militants and workers.

Socialist politicians were able to aid the new leadership indirectly by supporting it in local governments throughout the country, in parliamentary debates, and in the administration of the ministries they controlled.[32] This last source of support was extremely important, especially in the public sectors of the economy. But the AFL knew that the Socialists did not have the resources to finance trade union activities in the amount needed. Although Lovestone hoped that the Socialists would become involved with trade union organization,[33] he and other AFL leaders knew that the Socialists themselves needed financial assistance. Indeed, since the war's end, the Jewish Labor Committee and the ILGWU had sent money to the French Socialists for various purposes.[34] Furthermore, even if the Socialists had been in a position to aid the unions, the new organization's leadership could scarcely have relied on the financial support of a political party when one of its central tenets was removal of another political party's influence from the trade union movement. By closely allying itself with the Socialist party per se, the new leadership would have jeopardized the support of a large number of anarcho-syndicalists, Trotskyists, and other independent trade unionists.

The French government also was reluctant to finance the activities of the noncommunist leadership. Besides understanding the undesirable political repercussions of receiving government money, the AFL knew that the French government (which, of course, was still a coalition in which Communists participated) would not, with the aforementioned exception of 40 million francs (see footnote 32), finance the new organization.[35]

The remaining sources of potential financial support were foreign. The AFL believed that national and international groups within the labor family might be persuaded to provide the emerging organization with badly needed funds. Various sectors with a tradition of international solidarity (e.g., the transport

[31] Interview, Brown. Possibly, some employers also feared that new unions, to be competitive with their rivals, would escalate wage demands.

[32] Daniel Mayer was minister of labor and Jules Moch was minister of the interior in 1947 and 1948. The Ministry of Labor, in 1948, ruled that 40 million francs (about $114,000) owed to French labor as a result of Vichyite labor policies should be given to the new CGT-FO. See *FO Congrès Constitutif 1948 Compte Rendu*, pp. 16–17 and 126–127.

[33] Lovestone to Leon Denenberg, July 9, 1946 and Lovestone to Dubinsky, July 5, 1946.

[34] See for example Melech Epstein, *Jewish Labor in the U.S.A. 1914–1952* (New York: Trade Union Sponsoring Committee, 1953), pp. 348–353.

[35] Interview, Brown.

workers, miners, and metal workers) appeared to be potential donors.[36] Such sources, although suffering the disadvantage of being foreign, nevertheless would be far more desirable from the political point of view than French industry or government. The AFL soon realized, however, that other European unions were either unwilling or unable (because of their own domestic problems) to provide the large sums that were needed.[37]

In effect, this left only the American unions and the United States government as potential donors. The AFL foreign policy leaders had only limited funds at their disposal, given the number of countries in which their interests were involved and the prevailing apathy of the majority of their AFL colleagues. As was previously mentioned, it does not appear that a careful estimate of the AFL's foreign policy needs or resources was ever made. The AFL leaders simply perceived that they had been and would be able to obtain limited resources, but that even such finite resources could be of enormous strategic importance at a time when the new French organization was literally impoverished. As early as March 1946, Brown wrote to Woll about the potential of the new leadership in France. He concluded:

> We can be a great force for democracy. There are all sorts of people in France and in our embassy who look to us as a source of aid and comfort for the democratic forces. . . . We cannot let down hundreds of people all over the CGT and France who with a little aid at this time (and not later) can become prepared for the future showdown fight.[38]

AFL leaders, in other words, believed that they could make a major contribution to the future of the new organization. Just how much assistance would be required was never clearly ascertained. Nor did the AFL policy makers ascertain how much the AFL would be willing to donate.

Prior to the implementation of the Marshall Plan, as the AFL foreign policy leadership viewed the situation, the United States government demonstrated little understanding of the enormous importance of trade unionism in France. Although a few State and Defense Department officials shared some of the AFL's perceptions, Washington as a whole was not terribly interested.[39] With

[36] In January 1948, for example, the ITF sent a delegation to France which concluded that the chances of FO's success "would be considerably enhanced if it were possible to supply the new unions with some office equipment, more particularly typewriters and paper." ITF, "Report on Trade Union Situation in France," February 4, 1948.

[37] From 1947 to 1950, various trade secretariats and national federations or confederations in Europe made small contributions to the new organization. The AFL did not believe that these sums were anywhere near enough to ensure its viability. Interviews, Brown and Lovestone.

[38] Brown to Woll, March 14, 1946.

[39] Brown's reference to "people in our embassy" in his letters to Woll referred primarily to Ambassador Jefferson Caffrey and Labor Attaché Richard Eldridge.

the onset of the Russian offensive against the Marshall Plan in late 1947, however, the United States government became increasingly alert to the trade union situation in France and other countries. The Marshall Plan legislation envisaged the development of free trade unions, and United States officials realized that their plans could very well be derailed if the Russians were able to use organized labor to disrupt European recovery and Atlantic defense arrangements. Moreover, if it appeared that masses of European workers were opposed to the American initiatives, isolationist or simply opportunistic politicians in Washington would have a strong argument to buttress their underlying opposition to United States involvement in European affairs.

From the FO's political standpoint, of course, United States government financial support was not particularly desirable. However, alternative sources of supplementary funds were just not available. Moreover, the United States government was already aiding French business and other sectors through the Marshall Plan. Thus, the AFL believed that if Washington really understood the trade union situation and knew how it might channel aid to the new union structure, the United States government could become an important source of financial support.

From the preceding analysis, it is apparent that the AFL was far from certain that the militants opposed to working within the CGT would be able to prevent the Communists from dominating the French labor movement whether or not a new structure was created. What was certain, however, was that in the absence of increased unity and central coordination, additional moral support, and external sources of material assistance, the chances that the noncommunist leaders could succeed would be reduced virtually to zero.

Christian (Catholic) Trade Unions in France

The Catholic trade unions, organized in the CFTC, were another noncommunist group that refused to work within the CGT structure. Shortly after the Liberation, the Catholics rejected the CGT's blandishments and built up an independent organization of considerable size and strength in various economic sectors and geographic regions in France.[40]

But the Americans did not believe that the French Catholics in the long run could succeed in wresting control of the labor movement from the Communists. This was for two reasons. First, they were denominational. This meant that they could attract support in areas where the church was strong (e.g., in the northeast coal and steel communities) but would alienate non-Catholic workers and militants in other areas (e.g., the socialist Nord and Pas de Calais departments and the south of France). Indeed, Brown believed that many French workers

---

[40]For an analysis of CFTC policy during these years see Gérard Adam, *La C.F.T.C., 1940–1958* (Paris: Armand Colin, 1964), especially pp. 41–92.

and militants were anti-Catholic and that the CFTC as an independent organization would be unable to challenge the power of national secular unions.[41] Furthermore, to many AFL leaders, the CFTC appeared to be a dual union— which is to say, a divisive influence within the labor family. And locked as it was in the early postwar years in competition with the CIO, the AFL was hardly well-disposed toward dual unions.[42]

Second, the AFL believed that the CFTC leadership, by adopting a strategy of competing with the Communists in their radical economic demands, would sooner or later undermine noncommunist trade union forces. Some AFL leaders believed that this Catholic competition with the Communists was sheer opportunistic demagoguery. Others maintained that the CFTC's stress on economic demands was attributable to Catholic openness to the theory of stomach communism. Whatever its origin or motivation, the AFL leadership was united in its opposition to this CFTC tactic. The AFL believed that this approach would tend to undermine the economy and lead, in time, to united action and even united fronts with the Communists.[43]

In any case, the AFL believed that the Catholic unionists would find it easier than the new noncommunist leadership to remain in existence without external coordination, moral support, or material assistance. The CFTC already was recognized as a trade union organization, and this meant that it received various material subsidies as a matter of course. Then, too, the AFL leaders (and others) were convinced that the CFTC received financial and moral support from the Catholic church. Although most of this aid (assuming that there was aid) was limited to geographic areas where the church was strong, it would be extremely important in blighted postwar France.[44] Furthermore, the AFL believed that the influence of the church, church schools, worker-priests, and the Catholic faith provided CFTC leaders and militants with an important unifying force. Although there would continue to be major policy and personal conflicts within the organization, the CFTC did not generally suffer from the bitter conflicts that often

[41] Interview, Brown.

[42] Indeed, Abraham Bluestein, the first secretary of the Free Trade Union Committee, maintains that in late 1945 and early 1946, the AFL leaders were opposed to the CFTC primarily because they considered it a dual union. Given the struggle between the AFL and the CIO at the time, he points out, the AFL could hardly have been friendly to the CFTC. Interview, Bluestein.

There is an apparent contradiction between AFL support for a split in the CGT and AFL reluctance to support what they regarded as a dual union. However, AFL leaders would maintain that once the Communist party gained control of the CGT, it ceased to be basically a trade union. Therefore a split in the CGT was not the creation of two unions.

[43] Interviews, Brown, Lovestone, Meany, and Dubinsky.

[44] The AFL and French Communist and noncommunist trade unionists calculated that the CFTC could not possibly afford to pay the large number of organizers on its staff from dues alone. Interviews with AFL staff members and Communist and noncommunist trade unionists in Lens, Nantes, Marseilles, Metz, and Paris.

paralyzed the anarcho-syndicalists, Trotskyists, and Socialists. Catholicism, the AFL perceived, was an ideology that in some ways could function as a substitute for Marxism for large numbers of French workers.

Finally, Catholic unionists to some extent were organized internationally. Representatives from Catholic unions in six countries participated in the Christian International.[45] The AFL believed that the international would furnish its French brethren with moral support and political standing that the new noncommunist leadership would not readily acquire. The Americans were convinced, however, that the small, denominational international, acting alone, could never compete with the WFTU and the support it gave to the Communist cause in France.[46]

Instead the AFL hoped that the Catholics might be brought together with other noncommunist trade unionists in France and other countries. If the strength and solidarity of the former were fused with the secular militancy of the latter, the disadvantages of denominational trade unionism and the Christian International would be considerably reduced. In fact, as most European workers were either Catholics or Socialists, a unified organization, AFL leaders believed, would probably be appealing to workers throughout noncommunist Europe. A merger of Catholic and Socialist militants and material resources would add a dimension of strength to the noncommunist trade union forces. The major problem, as the AFL saw it, was how to bring about such a fusion.[47]

[45] See Adam, op. cit., pp. 117–119.
[46] Interviews, Brown and Lovestone.
[47] Ibid.

Chapter 7

AFL Foreign Policy

The major contention of this study is that a nongovernmental organization based in one country can influence developments in other countries. In this chapter, AFL policy affecting the international and European labor movements will be described. It will be shown that the AFL utilized a variety of channels to provide moral, material, and organizational support to European trade unionists who were resisting engulfment by and within Communist-dominated labor organizations. First, the AFL leaders attempted to demonstrate that resistance was both necessary and possible and that the Europeans were not alone in their efforts to avoid Communist domination. Second, the AFL leaders attempted to provide organizational leadership, particularly in France and in the international labor movement generally. Third, the AFL leaders gave material aid to the noncommunists who wanted to build independent unions. In the next chapter, the effectiveness of this policy will be assessed and the AFL's influence weighed.

AFL POLICY CHOICES

Early in the postwar period, the AFL rejected the strategy of attempting to gain control of Communist-dominated organizations or even of organizations in which Communists participated. The AFL leaders believed that the Communists cooperated with noncommunists only to increase their own strength and that they joined strategic noncommunist organizations primarily to use these organizations for Party purposes.

Communists, the American labor leaders believed, were able to gain control of noncommunist organizations by using a variety of covert and overt techniques. They used terror and intimidation whenever it suited their purposes. Recalcitrant workers in the mines and ports were physically intimidated, and employers were blackmailed. The AFL leaders also held the view that at the end of the war, the Communists financed their activities with Russian funds and with money stolen from banks and other institutions. In addition, they had the advantages of superior organization and central direction. The disunited democratic elements were almost helpless in the face of skilled, well-organized, and centrally directed Communist cadres. The AFL leaders were convinced that Communist elements sooner or later would gain control of key positions in almost every labor organization in which they participated and, once in these posts, would be almost impossible to unseat.

Finally and crucially, the AFL rejected the strategy of working with the Communists because doing this would tend to confuse and ultimately disarm noncommunist workers. At the end of the war, after all, many workers saw little reason to oppose the Communists. The Russians and European Communists, as participants in the World War II victory, enjoyed enormous prestige. British and French trade unionists were encouraging cooperation with the Communists in the WFTU and other international organizations. The AFL leaders reasoned that if European trade union leaders cooperated with the Communists, the rank and file would see little reason not to elect and appoint Communists to positions of power and accept them as brothers.

The British TUC and the reformist French CGT leaders believed that by working with the Russians and with French and other European Communists, the noncommunists would strengthen the labor movement and would be able to prevent the Russians from using organized labor for their political and military purposes. The AFL rejected this line of reasoning. The Americans believed also that the integration of the international trade secretariats into the WFTU's trade departments and the strengthening of the noncommunist militants in the CGT would not prevent the Communists from maintaining their control over these organizations. Quite the contrary, this strategy, they believed, would simply serve to confuse the noncommunists, strengthen Communist control, and ultimately lead to war or Russian domination.

The remaining AFL alternative was, as first order of business, to weaken the Communist-controlled organizations or at least prevent them from increasing and using their strength. The second element of this option was to strengthen national noncommunist organizations, encourage the creation of new noncommunist trade union centers, and integrate all these organizations into a viable noncommunist international.

The AFL leaders tended toward this strategy even before the end of the war. They were concerned about rebuilding democratic unions in the face of what they considered to be an implacable foe—the Russians and local Communist parties—and believed that they would have to remain heavily involved in European as well as Asian and Latin American politics. Even in 1944, at a time when most senior United States government officials thought that the United States would no longer have to be concerned with worldwide disruptive forces and that major conflicts would be resolved by the cooperation of the major powers in the United Nations, the AFL leaders deemed it necessary to create a million-dollar Free Trade Union Fund and Free Trade Union Committee to fight the Russians and rebuild democratic trade unions. Moreover, they believed that they would have to "educate" United States officials about what they, from their trade union perspective, believed were the realities of Russian imperialism and the inability of the United States to prevent war or preponderant Russian power if democratic trade union forces, particularly in Europe, were left to fend for themselves.

The specifics of AFL policy evolved slowly in the early postwar period. At first, the AFL leaders were unsure whether their assistance to noncommunist European, and particularly French, labor leaders could effectively impede or prevent organized labor from being used to support Russian objectives.

By the late spring of 1946, however, AFL policy in France began to take shape. The FTUC concluded that Brown was correct and that Jouhaux would not be able to regain control of the CGT. In March, Brown had implored the AFL leaders to make a decisive commitment to aid the noncommunists in their struggle to create free trade unions. In a letter to Woll he wrote:

> I do not claim there is any certainty about what can be done nor do I deny that the Communists have and will continue to control the CGT. But no one can deny that there is movement and restlessness that can be utilized in the ranks. There is a fundamental desire to re-establish trade unionism. There are coming events that will dramatize the great struggle that lies just beneath the surface. If and when the open fight comes or the split (which everyone mentions and looks forward to in the CGT) there will be more chance of success and victory if at the present the opposition forces are well constituted, organized and a cohesive force. There is little value in merely writing about this situation and not being able to help.[1]

Brown went on to say that he saw little value in his remaining in France if he could not provide material assistance to the noncommunists. In a scribbled note

[1] Brown to Woll, March 14, 1946.

on a carbon copy of his March 14 letter to Woll, he told Lovestone that he needed $100,000 but could make do with $10,000 to prepare for the April CGT convention. If he did not receive this support, he said he was "thinking seriously of resigning."[2]

By June, however, it appears that a decision had been made. The minutes of the FTUC meeting of June 5, 1946, included the following: "It was decided to cable Brother Brown that his budget is acceptable as sound in principle and that it will be supported provided definite arrangements are made that the American support be accompanied by broad material support from French labor itself."[3] After recording the committee's decision on policy with respect to Germany, Spain, and the United Nations Economic and Social Council, the minutes concluded with a report on "Brown's Status": "It was further decided to inform Brother Brown that we looked on his work with satisfaction and desire his resuming the same in Europe after his report (at the AFL Convention) here."[4]

Thus, by the summer of 1946, the policy first advocated by Brown in the early spring of 1946 apparently had been adopted by the FTUC.[5] It was not clear, however, just how much assistance the AFL was prepared to give the noncommunists attempting to create new trade union structures.

MORAL AND PSYCHOLOGICAL SUPPORT

Preserving the morale of European anticommunist trade unionists and, particularly, encouraging them not to accept the myth of unity with the Communists were major concerns for the AFL. During the "honeymoon period" immediately after World War II and later during 1947 and 1948, when it appeared for a while that the Communists would take power and that persons who opposed them would suffer drastic sanctions, these were difficult tasks.

To encourage resistance to the Communists, the AFL issued a continuous stream of policy resolutions and statements stressing the tyrannical nature of communism and the fate that befell workers when the Communists came to power.[6] For example, in the introduction to a pamphlet describing the fate of trade unions that fell under Communist domination in the Soviet Union and Eastern Europe, Woll pointed out,

It is no accident that reactionaries of every ilk, that despots of every hue and stripe, that totalitarian movements of every brand have singled out the basic

[2] Ibid.
[3] Minutes of the FTUC, June 5, 1946.
[4] Ibid.
[5] Brown in an interview also maintained that by mid-1946, the FTUC had decided to support this option.
[6] See especially *Proceedings*, 1946–1952.

organization of labor—the free trade unions—as their first target. To capture and control or to dissolve and destroy the trade unions is the first aim of all totalitarian tyranny.[7]

The AFL also pointed out that the Russians had established a system of forced labor in the Soviet Union and Eastern Europe. In 1949, the Federation published a book that included the affidavits of former inmates of Russian labor camps and descriptions of Russian attempts to extend the forced labor system to Eastern Europe. The volume documented the AFL's campaign against forced labor, a campaign that eventually resulted in a decision by the United Nations Economic and Social Council to adopt the AFL's proposal to conduct an international survey of forced labor and measures for its abolition.[8]

The AFL continued to explain its refusal to become associated with the WFTU and analyzed the dangers of Communist infiltration and control of trade unions in Western Europe and elsewhere. At the 1947 convention, the delegates approved the Executive Council report stating:

> It is only natural that the AFL, as the strongest body of free trade unions in the world should come into head-on collision with the WFTU. Everything that has happened since this caricature of a world federation of unions was set up has confirmed our evaluation of it as a camouflaged and delicately controlled instrument of Soviet imperialist interests and foreign policy. It has dismally failed to defend the interests of workers on the economic field. As an international body it has thrown its weight behind government coordinated unions in Czechoslovakia and has put the stamp of approval on the so-called trade unions in all the other Russian satellite countries. . . .
>
> A growing uneasy feeling now pervades the ranks of the WFTU affiliates west of the Iron Curtain. The rank and file is realizing more and more that there is something fundamentally wrong with an international trade union organization which dare not even discuss the problem of reconstruction, let alone try to help the rebuilding of war-wrecked economies and to foster the protection and promotion of the rights, liberties, and interests of the working people. In fact, many affiliates of the WFTU are now part of the Russian Fifth Column which is frantically seeking to sabotage post-war reconstruction and doom the toiling people to poverty, misery and chaos.[9]

On the affirmative side, the AFL vigorously supported the Marshall Plan. To prevent the Russians from using organized labor to obstruct the plan, the AFL

---

[7] ILRC, "What Happened to the Trade Unions behind the Iron Curtain," 1948, pp. 5–6.

[8] AFL, "Slave Labor in Russia, the Case Presented by the American Federation of Labor to the United Nations," 1949.

[9] *Proceedings*, 1947, pp. 470–471.

organized trade union support for the European Recovery Program (ERP). The 1947 convention endorsed the idea of the AFL "taking the initiative in calling a conference of the free trade union organizations in all the cooperating countries."[10] The AFL also proposed (prior to the United States government's decision to create NATO) the establishment of a military commitment in Europe:

> We believe that economic recovery within Europe must be buttressed by an increasing degree of cooperation covering Western European countries similar to the Inter-American Defense Treaty. Such agreements are provided for in the United Nations Charter and afford practical channels for organizing the necessary military protection.[11]

These statements and repeated declarations of support for the Marshall Plan and later for the NATO treaty and the Korean war effort were disseminated throughout the world.

In 1946, the FTUC began publishing the monthly *International Free Trade Union News* in English, French, German, and Italian. Soon almost every anticommunist trade union militant in Europe was receiving the publication.[12] In addition to featuring AFL resolutions and policy statements, the publication carried analyses and details of the suppression of free trade unionism in Communist countries and in such noncommunist dictatorships as Spain. The *International Free Trade Union News* also condemned the efforts of colonial powers to suppress noncommunist national liberation movements in Africa and Asia and, on occasion, supplied details of the AFL's actions to assist these movements. The FTUC also published, translated, and distributed anticommunist pamphlets. Also, Dubinsky, Woll, Green, Meany, and Brown were frequent contributors to journals and periodicals of general circulation.

Members of the Executive Council and AFL representatives and delegates repeatedly visited most of the European countries and gave numerous speeches.[13] The AFL also brought a number of European labor leaders to the United States in the late 1940s.[14] All these efforts were, of course, magnified by coverage in the mass media. The AFL issued press releases and fed information

[10] Ibid., p. 474.
[11] Ibid., p. 467.
[12] In June 1947, Brown reported that he was sending Lovestone a list of 12,000 French names and addresses. Brown to Lovestone, June 18, 1947. Total worldwide circulation was approximately 30,000. *Proceedings*, 1947, p. 187.
[13] In 1947, for example, the AFL's representatives in Europe, Brown and Rutz, made numerous appearances in France, Germany, Italy, Austria, Norway, Poland, Switzerland, England, and Denmark. *Proceedings*, 1947, pp. 186–189.
[14] The FO leader Pierre Ferri-Pisani, the chairman of the German Zonal Trade Union Council Marcus Schleicher, and the German Social Democratic leader Kurt Schumacher were invited to the United States to address AFL conventions. *Proceedings*, 1947, 1948, and 1950.

to selected journalists both in the United States and abroad.[15] Both the European and American press carried stories on the AFL's views and activities.[16]

Another type of assistance, rather more tangible, was that of providing noncommunist trade unions with food packages. In Germany, these packages amounted to a program of essential material assistance. In France, they were a further demonstration of the AFL's support for the democratic elements, especially in the mining regions where Communist militants received assistance from the Communist party.[17]

Thus, through a variety of means, the Federation attempted to provide moral and psychological support for the trade union forces that were resisting powerful Communist pressures. The AFL attempted to demonstrate that resistance was necessary and, of critical importance, that the Europeans were not alone in their efforts to prevent Communist domination.

ORGANIZATIONAL LEADERSHIP

Another major thrust of AFL policy was organizational leadership. The noncommunist trade unionists in most of Europe were too preoccupied with their internal and national problems to organize on a continental much less a worldwide scale. By contrast, during the early postwar years, the AFL was able to engage in interrelated organizational initiatives in a number of countries and in the international labor movement generally. Indeed, in a sense, the AFL became the organizational catalyst for Europeans who sought to weaken Communist-controlled labor organizations and to build and strengthen noncommunist alternatives.

The AFL's first international effort was to prevent the integration of the ITS into the WFTU trade departments. If American unions, which were not usually active in the ITS, could be persuaded to affiliate and participate in ITS politics, the AFL would have an opportunity to maneuver inside the secretariats. The American labor leaders then could use the "carrot" of American trade union strength, economic production, and financial resources and the "stick" of disaffiliation to ensure that the secretariats remained autonomous.

Toward this end, the AFL encouraged American unions already affiliated

[15]See for example Dubinsky's answers to questions by French and Dutch journalists cited in previous chapters. *Proceedings*, 1947, 1948, and 1950.

[16]Among numerous examples, see the London *Times*, November 26, 1947; *L'Humanité*, January 4, 1948; the London *Times*, August 2, 1948; *Le Figaro*, December 30, 1948; *L'Humanité*, September 22, 1950; *Le Figaro*, January 15, 1951; *Business Week*, March 17, 1951; *Time*, March 17, 1952.

[17]Approximately 500 CARE packages were sent monthly to Germany. Only a few packages were sent to France each month, except in late 1948, when over 1,000 packages were sent to the FO miners. FTUC archives, 1946–1949.

with a secretariat, the United Mine Workers of America (UMWA) for example, to increase their participation in the politics of its secretariat. The UMWA, which had not even been in the habit of sending representatives to the meetings of the miners' secretariat's leadership, was encouraged to attend and make the position of the Americans clear to the Europeans.

Then, too, the AFL attempted to secure increased American affiliation to the ITS. In the summer of 1946, for example, AFL policy makers approached the leaders of the American transport unions on the urgency of involvement. The FTUC also loaned the International Transport Workers Federation $3,000 for a delegation to be sent to the United States to secure American affiliation. In early February of 1947, the AFL Executive Council strongly urged the transport workers to affiliate with the ITF,[18] and on February 26 the *New York Times* announced the affiliation of the 700,000-member Railway Labor Executives' Association with the secretariat.[19] In 1948, the International Brotherhood of Teamsters, Chauffeurs, Warehousemen and Helpers of America also affiliated some 50,000 of its total membership with the ITF.

American affiliation to the ITF gave the AFL the opening to participate in the politics of the most important secretariat and greatly strengthened the hand of the Oldenbroek leadership. American representatives attended the ITF conference in April 1948 which was designed to bring transport unions together to discuss methods of trade union participation in the Marshall Plan. This was the first international trade union meeting to support the plan, and it was significant symbolically in both Europe and the United States. George Harrison and other American transport workers' leaders also attended the crucial ITF congress later in 1948. At this congress, Harrison argued decisively against ITF (and consequently ITS) affiliation to the WFTU and contributed to the vote that supported the Oldenbroek leadership.[20]

The AFL also attempted to secure the affiliation of other American unions to their respective secretariats. In the winter of 1946 and in January 1947, Brown encouraged the International Association of Machinists (IAM), which at that time was not even part of the AFL, to become affiliated with the IMF.[21] Brown's appeal was followed up by Woll on January 23.[22] Just days later, the IAM decided to affiliate with the IMF,[23] and a few months later the Machinists asked the IMF to hold its next Executive Committee meeting in the United

[18]Lovestone to Brown, February 10, 1947. FTUC archives, 1947.
[19]*New York Times*, February 26, 1947.
[20]"Report on Activities and Financial Report for the Years 1946–1947," *Proceedings of the International Transport Workers Federation Congress*, Oslo, July 19–24, 1948, pp. 172 and 200.
[21]Letter from Irving Brown to Harvey Brown, president of the IAM, January 13, 1947. FTUC archives, 1947.
[22]Woll to Harvey Brown, January 23, 1947. FTUC archives, 1947.
[23]Brown to Lovestone, January 31, 1947.

States.[24] Irving Brown, appointed an IAM representative, was elected to the IMF's Executive Committee.[25] The AFL leaders also attempted to secure more extensive American affiliation and closer working relationships with other secretariats, including the public service workers, white-collar workers, actors and artists, and clothing workers.[26]

Another AFL international initiative was the organization of a series of Marshall Plan trade union conferences that were catalytic in the processes that eventually split the WFTU. The AFL had immediately supported ERP. Meany agreed to become a member of the ERP Planning Commission, later known as the Harriman Committee, and several AFL staffers accepted positions in the ERP administration. Many WFTU affiliates, however, including the CIO and the TUC, kept their distance. After the Russian decision opposing the Marshall Plan, these organizations as a group also were reluctant to endorse the plan openly as they feared that doing this would precipitate a WFTU scission.[27]

The initiative for the ERP conferences appears to have come from Irving Brown.[28] In mid-October 1947, an AFL convention resolution endorsed the calling of a conference of trade union representatives from the 16 countries cooperating on a continental scale to rebuild the European economies.[29] To secure TUC support, Brown visited England at the end of November 1947. The AFL leaders believed that TUC support was essential. Without the British, the noncommunist Europeans, most of whom were affiliated with the WFTU, would be unlikely to participate in a conference that would probably exacerbate the conflict over the Marshall Plan in the WFTU. Also, the absence of the TUC, one of the most important trade union centers and the strongest noncommunist European labor organization, would emasculate a Marshall Plan conference.

Brown had concluded that the TUC would be reluctant to support the conference, and, even before he went to England, the AFL leadership had agreed that he should seek the assistance of Ernest Bevin, the British foreign secretary.[30] (Bevin, an ardent supporter of the Marshall Plan, was a former general secretary of the Transport and General Workers Union and still maintained close

[24]Mark Perlman, *The Machinists: A New Study in American Trade Unionism* (Cambridge: Harvard University Press, 1961), p. 127.

[25]*Proceedings*, 1948, p. 76.

[26]Minutes of the FTUC, January 22, 1947; Brown to Lovestone, January 27, 1947; Woll to Emil Rieve, president of the Textile Workers Union of America, May 31, 1947; *Proceedings*, 1948, p. 77.

[27]Among the best secondary sources on the TUC's relationship with the WFTU are Morton Schwartz, "Soviet Policies and the WFTU" (Ph.D. thesis, Columbia University, 1963) and John Windmuller, *American Labor and the International Labor Movement 1940–1953* (Ithaca, N.Y.: Cornell University, 1954).

[28]Brown to Woll, July 25, 1947.

[29]*Proceedings*, 1947, p. 474.

[30]Brown, confidential report to the ILRC, November 11, 1947. FTUC archives.

links with TUC leaders.) The AFL hoped that Bevin would bring pressure to bear on the TUC.

Although he did not see Bevin in November, Brown passed along the AFL's views to Christopher Mayhew, who had been asked by Bevin to see Brown.[31] In the latter half of December, Brown returned to England and conferred with Bevin himself. By January 3, 1948, he felt confident enough of the TUC's support to announce that the conference would probably be held in March.[32]

In the two months following, Brown conferred with representatives of at least 14 trade union federations, and, on March 9, a conference of 50 representatives from 15 countries convened in London. Léon Jouhaux represented the FO and Gaston Tessier, the CFTC. From the delegates' speeches, it was clear that they believed that the Marshall Plan served the interests of the working classes of Europe and North America and that the plan deserved the support of organized labor. Moreover, the delegates decided to elect a committee to maintain a continuing liaison with the ERP administration. The committee, to be known as the Trade Union Advisory Committee (TUAC), was to conduct the work of the conference between its meetings, convene future conferences, secure maximum unified action among constituent organizations, and seek contact with the Organization for European Economic Cooperation (OEEC) so as to assure maximum representation in its councils. The AFL supported these moves, believing that they were steps in the direction of creating a new noncommunist international labor body.[33]

At a TUAC meeting in June, an Emergency Committee was created to maintain contact and conduct negotiations with the OEEC. Jouhaux and Vincent Tewson, with the TUC's Donald Bowers acting as an economic assistant, were appointed to the committee.

In July, another major ERP trade union conference was held in London. Top labor leaders from 26 organizations in 16 countries attended. The French were represented by Jouhaux, Bothereau, R. Rous of the FO, and three CFTC leaders. The Italian noncommunist groups in the Communist-dominated CGIL sent a delegation headed by Giulio Pastore, who was soon to preside over the formation of a new noncommunist confederation in Italy. The AFL was represented by Brown and Dubinsky. The CIO, which after some initial hesitation had decided to support the Marshall Plan, was represented by James Carey, David MacDonald, Michael Ross, and Elmer Cope.

Administrator Averell Harriman and former AFL staff members occupying

---

[31] Brown to Lovestone, November 29, 1947.

[32] *New York Times*, January 4, 1948. See also Schwartz, op. cit., pp. 295–296.

[33] See especially Brown to Lovestone, July 5, 1948; *Proceedings*, 1948, pp. 75–76; Charles Ford, "The Role of Trade Unions in the Economic Development of Europe," ICFTU, Brussels, 1966, pp. 11–14.

important ERP staff positions addressed the conference. The Marshall Plan administrators told the delegates that they hoped labor would play a leading role in the ERP and pointed to specific ways in which American aid could be used to improve the lot of European workers, particularly with regard to health and housing programs and social security systems.

The conference decided that the TUAC should appoint a permanent representative in Paris to keep in close contact with OEEC. His duties would also include informing affiliated national centers of OEEC activities in the fields of manpower and trade union problems generally. It was agreed that Jouhaux should serve as the TUAC representative until a permanent appointment was made. The conference concluded by adopting a resolution reaffirming its pledge of support for the ERP, "upon whose success depended the continued efforts of millions of workers in the countries concerned" and which implied effective representation and participation of organized labor.[34]

As Professor John P. Windmuller has observed, the conference had important "symbolic" effects—and some effects that were a good deal more than symbolic. It gave the stamp of trade union approval to the Marshall Plan, it officially established a permanent administrative organization to ensure organized labor a role in the execution of the ERP, and it marked the first time that both the AFL and the CIO participated in an international meeting of trade union organizations.

This latter change in AFL policy, which eventually culminated in AFL-CIO joint participation in a new international trade union organization, came about as a result of two major factors. In the first place, AFL leaders believed that the survival of democracy in Europe required the coordinated efforts of both the AFL and the CIO as well as European unions to support a large-scale reconstruction program. As Windmuller noted, "A similar policy had prevailed throughout most of the war period when joint AFL and CIO participation in the defense effort and in such agencies as the War Labor Board had led to temporary retreat from the earlier attitude of intransigence toward the CIO."[35] Because the CIO was recognized both by the United States government and by many Europeans as the representative of some segments of organized labor in the United States, the AFL could not insist on excluding the CIO without damaging the cause of noncommunist unity in support of the Marshall Plan.

Then, too, by the late 1940s the CIO was in the process of expelling Communists from its ranks. The AFL wanted to encourage these activities and believed that it would be easier in the future to work with the CIO's noncommunist leadership.[36]

[34] Report by Jay Lovestone in behalf of the AFL delegation to the ERP trade union conference, July 29, 1948. FTUC archives. Ford, op. cit., pp. 14—15.

[35] Windmuller, op. cit., p. 133.

[36] Interview, Lovestone. For additional analysis see Windmuller, op. cit., pp. 131—132.

By the winter of 1948, as the WFTU was about to break up over the question of supporting the Marshall Plan, the AFL had begun lining up support for the creation of a new international labor organization. In early January, the FTUC and ILRC engaged in extensive planning for a new international.[37] The subject was also discussed privately at the fourth ERP-TUAC meeting on January 22, 1949.[38]

Shortly after the British withdrawal from the WFTU in early 1949, the ITS met in England. With the exception of the miners' international, all the major secretariats were represented. The delegates, representing 17 international organizations and more than 20 million workers, unanimously agreed to reject any and all relationships with the WFTU. The conference also took the first important international step, following the WFTU split, in turning toward the creation of a new international in which the trade secretariats would play a significant role. The conference agreed to create a coordinating committee that would represent the collective and common interests of the ITS. Brown participated in the conference as an IMF delegate and became an alternate on the Coordinating Committee.[39]

In the spring of 1949, the AFL and the CIO reached an agreement for joint participation in a new international labor body. An international planning conference took place in June, and, in November–December 1949, 261 delegates from unions in 59 countries attended the Free World Labor Conference that officially created the International Confederation of Free Trade Unions (ICFTU). The Americans attempted to bring the Catholic unions into the new organization, but this effort was blocked by the Europeans.[40] In the following months, cooperative arrangements between the ICFTU and the ITS were concluded by the new ICFTU general secretary, Oldenbroek.[41]

Activities in France

In addition to working with the international labor movement, the AFL also engaged in a number of activities in the major European countries. To trace such activities in one key country, France, it will be necessary to backtrack. As noted previously, the AFL leaders believed that France was the key to control of

---

[37]Minutes of the ILRC, January 31, 1949. FTUC archives, 1949.

[38]Brown, report on the ERP-TUAC meeting, Berne, Switzerland, January 22, 1949. FTUC archives, 1949.

[39]Brown, Report of AFL representative in Europe for the period December, 1948–October, 1949. FTUC archives, 1949.

[40]See Windmuller, op. cit., especially pp. 151–170.

[41]See Windmuller, op. cit., pp. 169–170 and "Report on Activities and Financial Report of the ITF, 1948–1950," pp. 84–90; for an account of the AFL's policy in the ICFTU from 1950 to 1952 see Windmuller, op. cit., pp. 171–190.

Western Europe. In the long run, Germany would be more important, but in the early postwar years Germany was prostrate. Italy was important, but Italy was also a defeated power. The AFL leaders believed that developments in France would be decisive for the rest of Europe. If the Communists gained control of France, in this view, they would split Western Europe and ultimately gain control of both Germany and Italy.

It is difficult to determine the extent of direct AFL organizational involvement in French and European politics. It is clear, nevertheless, that the AFL's organizational and financial resources were interrelated in a number of initiatives in France, Italy, and Germany as well as in a number of smaller European countries. Although Irving Brown, as the AFL's representative, traveled extensively throughout Europe and occasionally made trips to the United States and Asia, he concentrated his efforts in France. In addition to believing that France in the short run was the key to the future of democratic pluralism on the Continent, Brown liked the country, its people, and their life-style. Originally he had wanted to set up the AFL office in Paris. The AFL, however, was dissuaded from doing so by threats of Communist terror.[42]

Brown was a dynamic organizer. He had learned the rudiments of the trade working for the AFL in the 1930s. His life-style was well suited to his strategy of welding together small groups of militants. He enjoyed extensive and continuous traveling. Moreover, he was willing to work 18 hours a day, 6 days a week. His life was a constant round of traveling and meeting with noncommunist militants in every conceivable place at every conceivable time. And nothing less would do, as he saw it, to build, maintain, and coordinate the groups of dynamic militants.[43]

MATERIAL AID

The AFL also was able to weld these groups into an effective, continuing force with material support coming first from contributions channeled through the FTUC and, after the creation of Force Ouvrière, from the United States government. In the immediate postwar years, as was pointed out, noncommunists opposed to working with the Communists in the CGT were short of money and essential supplies and equipment. In some sectors, the nature of the industry facilitated organization and action. Railroad organizers, for example, were frequently able to travel free of charge around the country. PTT organizers found it relatively easy to communicate with one another. Also in these public sectors, once a union grouping was officially recognized, it received advantages that were unavailable to organizers in the private sector. Nevertheless, the leaders and

[42]Minutes of the ILRC, November 13, 1946. FTUC archives.
[43]See *Time* article describing his daily routine and style, March 17, 1952.

militants in both the private and the public sectors were, relatively speaking, impoverished.

Shortly after his arrival in France, in the winter of 1945, Brown discussed splitting the CGT with Jouhaux, Bothereau, and Albert Gazier (who soon left the trade unions after accepting a ministerial post). Even though Jouhaux was opposed to Saillant's equal status in the CGT, he did not, for the reasons cited in Chapter 6, want to split the organization.[44] As a result, after securing approval from the AFL leadership, Brown turned his attention to the noncommunist militants who opposed Jouhaux's strategy of accommodation.

The AFL's efforts focused on three strategic industries—coal mining, communications, and transportation, particularly the railroads (see Chapter 5). As far as can be determined from the FTUC archives, the AFL gave these groups from \$11,000 to \$20,000 between January 1946 and the CGT scission in December 1947.[45] The money was used specifically to finance the traveling expenses of organizers, the publication and distribution of anti-CGT newspapers and leaflets, and the campaigns of FO candidates in union and social security elections.[46]

After the general strike collapsed in December 1947, those Force Ouvrière militants who still remained in the CGT insisted that the noncommunists secede from the organization. Jouhaux and the other confédéré leaders, faced with the loss of their militants, agreed to leave the CGT formally and create a new organization[47] which they did in late 1947. In the following months, the PTT, the autonomous section of the railroad unions, and several other autonomous unions became affiliated with the new organization.[48] The AFL did not really play the leading role in the split. The Force Ouvrière militants had been determined for some time to create a new organization, and the AFL's moral and material assistance strengthened them and facilitated their actions—but the crucial determination was theirs.

Although the AFL leaders were delighted that a new national center had been formally created, they were opposed to the tactics of Jouhaux and his

[44] Interview, Brown.

[45] Analysis of FTUC correspondence reveals that the FTUC found it extremely difficult to raise even this amount and that Woll and Dubinsky had to engage in extensive fundraising activities. See for example ILRC, "Report to the Executive Council," January, 1948. It should be noted, however, that these were large sums in postwar Europe, and, moreover, Brown was able to exchange dollars for francs at extremely favorable rates of exchange. Brown to Lovestone, June 18, 1947.

[46] Interview, Brown, and letters from Brown to Lovestone, especially June 18, 1947 and August 7, 1947.

[47] See Val R. Lorwin, *The French Labor Movement* (Cambridge: Harvard University Press, 1954), pp. 123–126 and Georges Lefranc, *Les Expériences Syndicales en Europe de 1939 á 1950* (Paris: Montaigne, 1950), pp. 190–193. Lefranc also notes Carpentier's role in forcing the confédéré leaders to leave the CGT.

[48] See especially Lefranc, op. cit., pp. 194–197.

generation of FO leaders. These older hands wanted to remain involved in the WFTU and to retain the name "Force Ouvrière," which connoted wartime and Socialist resistance to totalitarian forces. The AFL favored the strategy of André Lafond and many of the younger provincial militants, who were against the FO's affiliation with the WFTU, against the name "FO" itself (which was not popular with many groups of noncommunists), and for a unified organization or at least united action with other noncommunist organizations such as the Catholic CFTC and anarchist Confédération National du Travail. The AFL believed also that the older leaders were too bureaucratic and too interested in preserving personal status. AFL leaders were convinced that the new union structure would never wholly replace the CGT as the trade union representative of the working class until younger, more dynamic elements moved into positions of leadership.

During the ensuing years, the AFL for the most part supported the vigorous organizational drives of the younger leaders and their attempts to unify all noncommunist trade unions. Not only did these groups occasionally receive financial assistance from the AFL, but the Americans also sent them vitally needed office equipment. In 1948, for example, the AFL sent 100 typewriters and 25 mimeograph machines to FO offices throughout France.[49] Moreover, in the summer of 1948, when the FO leaders ran out of the funds they had received from the French government (as noted above), the AFL "loaned" them $30,000.[50] Also, Brown helped coordinate and finance meetings that brought together militants from all over France to create FO federations in those sectors of private industry most difficult to organize, for example, the maritime trades.[51]

Also, the AFL helped secure the United States government's material assistance, in several ways. The AFL leaders encouraged the United States government to aid noncommunist unions generally. Marshall Plan funds were being used to aid in the recovery of French industry; management benefited directly from the plan, they argued, so why not labor? Moreover, they pointed out, the Marshall Plan would be endangered if the Communist-controlled unions maintained their hold over organized labor. The Communists were receiving funds from the Soviet Union to prevent the plan from achieving its objectives; so again, they argued, why not aid noncommunist labor groups to ensure the plan's success?

Moreover, the American labor leaders helped pinpoint reliable noncommunist militants who would put any United States assistance they received to most

[49]Thank you letters and receipts in the FTUC archives.
[50]Brown to Lovestone, May 5, 1948 and July 5, 1948. Harrison to Green, August 21, 1948. AFL archives.
[51]Pierre Ferri-Pisani, quoted in *Time*, March 17, 1952. Interview, Georges Picquemal. AFL participation in dockers' and seamen's unions will be elaborated on in the following pages.

effective use. The AFL and its staff were personally acquainted with most of the reliable and efficient noncommunist leadership, had been working with and exchanging visits with them for years, and had developed trusted contacts not only among trade unionists in the national centers but also among the less well known but dynamic groups of militants in the provinces.

The AFL also encouraged the unification of noncommunist labor organizations. At first, this was done through efforts to bring the autonomous unions into the FO. Brown's letters from 1948 to 1950 were studded with references to his efforts to encourage this tendency. As previously mentioned, the Federation also quietly attempted to bring together the predominantly Socialist FO and the Catholic CFTC. For a number of months, Brown worked closely with a segment of the CFTC under the leadership of Paul Vignaux, who had been a member of the wartime Committee of Exiles in New York guiding the Labor League's relief efforts. Brown's efforts were unsuccessful.[52]

Furthermore, the AFL did everything possible to arrange for the entry of the FO into the noncommunist international labor movement. This effort was designed, first, to increase the domestic and international prestige of the FO. Second, the AFL hoped that it would encourage the international movement to provide material assistance to a free French labor movement. A strong FO in turn, the AFL expected, would increase the strength of the international noncommunist labor movement. Third, cooperation between French and other European unions, the AFL believed, would increase the chances for European economic and political stability.

One of the clearest examples of the AFL's efforts in this area was the program of Franco-German cooperation that developed from an AFL initiative. As early as 1947, Brown had begun to bring together German militants with activists of the Amis de Force Ouvrière from the mining and metal trades. So soon after the war, this was considered a revolutionary initiative. In 1948, trade unionists from the Benelux countries were also brought into these meetings. Cooperation developed to the point that in March 1949, representatives from Benelux, France, Germany, and the United States met to create a permanent multinational secretariat to bring about trade union participation in the international control of the Ruhr and the entire northwest European coal, iron, and steel industries.[53]

Another AFL initiative was an institution known as the Mediterranean Committee. As has been pointed out, the AFL leaders, especially Brown, were concerned about Russian control of the maritime industry. In June 1949, the WFTU

---

[52] Interview, Brown. See also CGT-FO, *Second Confederal Congress*, October 25–28, 1950, pp. 181–217 and Gérard Adam, *La C.F.T.C., 1940–1958* (Paris: Armand Colin, 1964), pp. 158–168.

[53] Interview, Brown, and his "Report of the AFL Representative in Europe," 1949.

created a maritime trades department and a maritime bureau was set up in Marseilles. The AFL leaders believed that the new WFTU department and bureau were designed in part to disrupt Western European economic recovery and interrupt the transportation of American arms to Europe. Brown reported that Cominform agents were running the bureau in Marseilles and sent Lovestone a clipping from *Le Figaro* naming the responsible Cominform agents in France and Italy.[54]

In August 1949, Brown spoke with Oldenbroek and encouraged the ITF to impede these new Communist activities. At an ITF International Dockers and Seafarers Conference in Rotterdam, on August 26–30, Communist use of the maritime workers for political objectives was condemned and it was decided to create three regional "vigilance committees"[55] for the Baltic, North Atlantic and Mediterranean areas, the latter with Marseilles as the center.

The Mediterranean Committee had three major objectives. First, its aim was to ensure that American and Allied shipping in the Mediterranean (especially to France and Italy) carrying Marshall Plan goods and NATO-related equipment went on uninterrupted. Doing this required breaking Communist control of maritime labor organizations. Second, the committee attempted to create paramilitary cells on each ship to counter the Communist cells. As the French union leader and director of the Mediterranean Committee, Ferri-Pisani, spelled it out to the AFL convention, Communist propaganda activities on ships were a pretext for the creation of small Russian-controlled cells:

> What is attempted is to create an apparatus, a combination of small cells, whose members never present themselves on occasions of secondary importance. The visible part of the network is not essential. The secret part is operated by a political-trade union control but is actually directed from a political-military angle.[56]

Third, the committee attempted to mount an offensive of its own against communism.[57] The committee was designed to engage in positive anticommunist activities rather than merely to react to Communist initiatives.

To accomplish these objectives, Brown, together with Ferri-Pisani, organized groups of dockers and sailors in such major French ports as Marseilles, Bordeaux, Cherbourg, and Le Havre, as well as in Italian, Greek, and North African ports.

---

[54] Brown to Lovestone, August 19, 1949. *Le Figaro*, August 8, 1949. See Appendix C for examples of United States intelligence reports that tend to support the accuracy of the AFL assessment.

[55] ITF, "Report on activities and financial report, 1948–1950," pp. 52–53.

[56] *Proceedings*, 1950, p. 446.

[57] Irving Brown, quoted in *Le Monde*, January 16, 1951.

To strengthen the organization, the heads of the French railway, *Wagon-lits*, and road transport workers' unions also became members of the committee. A small professional staff was hired, supported at least initially with ITF funds,[58] to coordinate and sustain these organizational efforts.

The staff in Paris and the groups in each port engaged in a variety of tactics. The committee distributed enormous quantities of propaganda, designed to bolster the morale of its militants as well as to explain to the workers how the Communists were exploiting their economic grievances and the widespread fear of a new war. A particular attempt was made to explain that if the dockers in a given port withheld their labor, American ships would simply go elsewhere and eventually, as patterns of trade were interrupted, the port would become idle. In 1950, in addition to thousands of leaflets prepared locally, the committee began publishing a monthly magazine, *Air, Terre, Mer*, in French, English, and Italian, which was distributed throughout the Mediterranean area.

Another technique was to work with well-placed contacts in local Communist-controlled unions. In Cherbourg, for example, Jean Bocher, the head of the FO Officiers de Marine, was in contact with both Brown and Pisani. At the same time, he remained in contact with an old Socialist, one Lesvel, whom Bocher had encouraged to remain in the CGT dockers' union even after the split in 1947. Thus, in 1948 and 1949, when Benoît Frachon and other Communist leaders went to Cherbourg to encourage and to pay the dockers not to unload American ships, Bocher, in weekly contact with Lesvel, successfully sabotaged these efforts.[59]

The committee also engaged in activities to neutralize what it believed to be Communist terror and intimidation. This was accomplished in a variety of ways. One was to protect both professional and occasional dockers when the CGT called a dock strike, primarily by hiring strong-arm men to work alongside the dockers. Thus, the Communists would have to tangle with men experienced in the techniques of violence.[60] Because the dockers would be vulnerable to Communist terror when they left the piers, the committee also warned the Communist leaders in several ports that if dockers and sailors were physically assaulted, the noncommunist strong-arm men would retaliate not against the Communists' own goon squads but against the leaders themselves. Reportedly in Marseilles Pisani, who had many friends amongst the "milieu,"[61] marched to the Communist party's headquarters and delivered this warning personally.[62]

To enable members of the milieu to work on the docks, the committee

---

[58] ITF, "Report on activities, 1948–1950," op. cit., p. 119.

[59] Interviews, Brown and Bocher.

[60] Most of the strong-arm men were not professional thugs, but they were not, of necessity, *enfants des choeur* (choirboys) either. Interview, Picquemal.

[61] "*Le milieu*," slang for "underworld."

[62] *Time*, March 17, 1952.

cooperated with the Socialist Minister of the Interior Jules Moch and with local prefects. The prefects were also encouraged to use the police to crack down on the Communist strong-arm squads and to use the BMCO to deny work permits to persons who engaged in violent activity on the docks.[63]

From 1949 to 1952, the committee also encouraged the creation of small cells on French and other ships that sailed the Mediterranean. These cells maintained surveillance of Communist groups on the ships to prevent them from transporting propaganda and engaging in espionage and sabotage.[64]

In sum, it appears that the AFL leaders' policy choice was virtually dictated by their perspectives. The AFL leaders believed that if the Federation did not aid noncommunists who wanted to remain independent of Communist-controlled unions, it would be guilty of contributing to Europe's giving way to Russian domination. In adopting this policy, the AFL leaders attempted to affect the course of postwar politics by providing noncommunist labor leaders with moral and material assistance as well as organizational leadership. The Americans attempted to strengthen noncommunists in national and international labor organizations, encourage the creation of new international and national centers, and integrate all these groups and individuals into a strong noncommunist international labor movement. The AFL leaders believed that these activities would help prevent the Russians from using their control of international and French labor organizations to achieve hegemony on the European continent. An assessment of the effectiveness of this policy is the subject of the next chapter.

[63] Interviews, Brown and Jean Baylot.
[64] Interviews, Froideval, Bocher, and Philips. There are few references to these activities in the FTUC files.

Chapter 8

The Effects of the AFL's Foreign Policy

An assessment of postwar AFL foreign policy indicates that this nongovernmental organization played a significant role in European politics. While it is impossible to know what would have happened if the AFL had not assisted the noncommunists in Europe, principally those who wanted to maintain autonomous labor organizations, it appears that the AFL played a direct and multiple role in the international and French labor movements and, by doing so, an indirect role in postwar French and European politics.

The AFL played a direct role in weakening Russia's ability to use the international labor movement as an instrument of policy. The AFL first secured the affiliation of key American unions to their international secretariats. This helped prevent the secretariats from falling under WFTU control and from being used by the Russians to thwart European recovery and defense efforts. The AFL also exacerbated the tensions in the WFTU, contributed to the forces that led to the creation of the rival ICFTU, and thus weakened the WFTU's ability to support Russian objectives.

In France, among other countries, the AFL also impeded the Russians' ability to utilize the labor movement for political purposes. The moral, material, and organizational assistance provided by the AFL was one of several forces that bolstered labor elements resisting Communist domination. By helping to create FO and the Mediterranean Committee, the AFL reduced the CGT's ability to support Russian objectives in France and elsewhere.

The total effect of these activities, as well as similar activities in Italy and Germany, was significant in the world struggle for power. The Soviet Union's efforts to utilize organized labor to disrupt European recovery and stability was checked. The balance of domestic power within important European states, and particularly France, was maintained. Western Europe remained free from Russian hegemony and the global balance was not imperiled.

EFFECTS ON THE INTERNATIONAL LABOR MOVEMENT

As noted in the previous chapter, AFL policy in 1946 was in large part responsible for the American railway unions' affiliation to the ITF and the machinists' union to the IMF.[1] These American affiliations, coupled with the AFL's foreign policy posture generally, in turn bolstered the position of the dominant faction in the ITS, which was struggling to keep the secretariats from being integrated into the WFTU trade departments. George Harrison in the ITF and Irving Brown in the IMF lent the AFL's moral support to these forces. In crucial discussions and votes also, the Americans argued vehemently against joining the WFTU. Perhaps the most decisive example of this occurred at the July 1948 ITF convention, when George Harrison's speech appears to have prevented Arthur Deakin, the leader of the British Transport and General Workers Union, from securing a vote supporting the integration of the ITF and the WFTU's maritime trades department.[2]

If the ITF had in fact affiliated at this critical juncture, it is likely that the other secretariats would have followed suit. By helping to ensure that the ITS remained autonomous, the AFL helped maintain a nucleus for a new trade union international and kept the secretariats free to support the Marshall Plan, NATO,

---

[1] The AFL's role in securing the railway unions' affiliation was confirmed by Harrison. Dr. Mark Perlman's private notes on the IAM archives also tend to confirm Irving Brown's role in bringing the IAM into the IMF. (Dr. Perlman is one of the few scholars who has had access to the IAM archives.)

[2] "Report on Activities and Financial Report for the Years 1946–1947," *Proceedings of the International Transport Workers Federation Congress*, 1948, pp. 172, 200, and 243. In interviews, both Harrison and Becu confirmed Harrison's crucial role at the congress. If the policy of Oldenbroek and Becu had been reversed at the congress, this would have reopened the whole question of the relationship between the secretariats and the WFTU and might have given the forces that were trying to keep the WFTU together a shot in the arm. Windmuller, however, believes that the struggle was over by the time the ITF met in 1948. See his *American Labor and the International Labor Movement*, pp. 113–115.

and the Mediterranean Committee as well as European economic and political cooperation.

It would be misleading to claim flatly that the AFL "created" the ICFTU. It is more accurate to say that the AFL's willingness to create a new organization (and not withdraw into isolationism) and the AFL-organized Marshall Plan trade union conferences in 1948 were major forces that led to the creation of the ICFTU. Other forces were the WFTU scission, the TUC's and the Benelux unions' interest in creating a new international, and ITS support for a new organization. The WFTU split resulted, in large part, from the Russian decision to oppose the Marshall Plan and from subsequent attempts to use the trade unions to support this decision.[3] The AFL, of course, exacerbated the tensions in the WFTU by organizing the ERP trade union conferences and by constantly denouncing Communist attempts to use the WFTU in support of Russian political objectives.[4] By challenging the TUC's leadership in the noncommunist international labor movement and by supporting the independence of the ITS, moreover, the AFL contributed to the strengthening of forces that created the new international.[5]

The TUAC appears to have played only a minor role in ERP and early OEEC decision making.[6] OEEC administrators maintain that, for the most part, relations with the trade unions were conducted through the ERP labor advisers in the individual European countries. The OEEC was not anxious to have the TUAC take part in its decision making, and many European union leaders were less than eager to commit themselves to OEEC decisions on such sensitive questions as levels of productivity.[7]

The AFL's international activities diminished the political importance of the WFTU. The voice of the AFL, represented at the UN by the official AFL delegates Matthew Woll and David Dubinsky and in Europe, Latin America, and Asia by AFL and FTUC representatives, meant that the WFTU could not be considered as *the* voice of organized labor in the world. After the WFTU split and the creation of the ICFTU, the WFTU suffered an even greater loss in prestige, and its political role in international organizational affairs was further reduced.

---

[3]Morton Schwartz, "Soviet Policies and the WFTU" (Ph.D. thesis, Columbia University, 1963) and Windmuller, op. cit.

[4]See letter from Oldenbroek to Dubinsky quoted in Philip Taft, *The AFL from the Death of Gompers to the Merger* (New York: Harper, 1959), p. 380. For the AFL's attacks on the WFTU see for example *Proceedings*, 1946, pp. 433–434; *Proceedings*, 1947, p. 181; *Proceedings*, 1948, pp. 271–272.

[5]See Windmuller, op. cit.

[6]For a history of the TUAC and its relationship with the ERP and the OEEC, see Charles Ford, "The Role of Trade Unions in the Economic Development of Europe," ICFTU, Brussels, 1966.

[7]Interviews, Porter, Shishkin, and Saposs.

The AFL's continuous criticism of the WFTU's involvement in the politics of specific countries and the tensions within the organization itself made it extremely difficult for the WFTU to exert effective pressure on foreign governments.[8] Moreover, fears that the Communists were using their control of the international labor movement for political purposes resulted in close cooperation between Western governments and the noncommunist labor movement. A striking example of this can be found in the maritime industry. In the late 1940s, when the WFTU and its Communist affiliates attempted to disrupt Western military transportation, Western governments, the AFL, the ITF, and other segments of the noncommunist labor movement all coalesced in the Mediterranean Committee to prevent any disruption or sabotage of Western shipping.

EFFECTS ON THE FRENCH LABOR MOVEMENT

The AFL's moral and psychological support of the French forces resisting Communist domination appears to have been significant. Its views were well known throughout the country. The *International Free Trade Union News* and other FTUC publications had a wide circulation. Irving Brown made numerous public speeches, and the AFL's views were quoted and discussed in the French Communist and noncommunist press.[9] Indeed, it appears as if every anticommunist militant in France knew that he was not alone and that a large, powerful national trade union center was militantly anticommunist—and so, for that matter, did the Communists.

The AFL, of course, believed this assistance was extremely important. A major segment of the Federation's human and material resources was devoted to the effort. Many former Amis de Force Ouvrière leaders and United States government officials also believed that the AFL's efforts helped make resistance to the Communists a respectable and viable policy at a time when most national centers were cooperating with the Communists.[10]

Finally, the Communists believed that the AFL's encouragement of the anticommunist forces was significant. The Communists threatened Brown with violence if the AFL set up an office in Paris,[11] and this is a form of respect. Almost weekly the Communist press attacked the AFL. For example, Robert Bouvier, an editorial writer for the Communist daily, *L'Humanité*, and the weekly, *France Nouvelle*, stated:

[8]*Proceedings*, 1946, pp. 433–434 and *Proceedings*, 1948, pp. 271–272. The single best illustration of the AFL's effectiveness is the case of Germany, see Taft, especially pp. 345–360.
[9]See *Combat, Le Populaire, L'Humanité, La Vie Ouvrière*, and *France Nouvelle*, 1946–1952.
[10]Almost all the FO leaders and American officials interviewed maintained that the AFL's moral support was important in the early postwar period.
[11]Victor Riesel, "Inside Labor," *New York Post*, April 29, 1947.

One of the main objectives of the monopolists from across the Atlantic is to break the strength of a powerful and united CGT in France, just as, on the international scale, its objective is to cause a collapse of the unity achieved in the WFTU. . . .

As early as 1946, the AFL thereupon appointed a special agent in Europe, notably to operate in France. Irving Brown . . . was provided with a well-filled coffer of dollars and the job of causing, at any cost, a weakening and a schism in the CGT and later in the WFTU.[12]

The Communists also devoted a great deal of attention to the work of the Mediterranean Committee. Brown was accused of organizing and paying gangsters to break legitimate strikes. He was also accused of advocating provocative police practices so that the duly provoked Communist militants could be arrested.[13]

AFL leaders believed that their organizational and financial assistance to the Amis de Force Ouvrière militants and later to the incipient FO organization was "strategically" important. They were convinced that the noncommunists had created a de facto split in the CGT and eventually would have broken with the traditional organization anyway, quite apart from the AFL's actions. AFL activities in the 1940s, the American union leaders believed, strengthened the noncommunist forces to the point that when they did break away from the CGT, they were quickly able to create a national union structure that was rapidly assimilated into the international labor movement.

The AFL leaders also believed that they had played a role in educating United States government officials in the realities of postwar labor politics and the necessity for using Marshall Plan funds to aid provincial as well as national trade union centers.[14] In the early postwar period, the AFL leaders believed that the United States government as a whole was not sufficiently worried about Russian ambitions in Western Europe or the ways in which organized labor would be used to support Russian political and military objectives. The AFL leaders in their discussions with United States officials tried to convince them that the Soviet Union was intent on dominating the Continent and would use labor unions as a weapon. Moreover, after the creation of the Marshall Plan, the

[12]"The Trade Union Schism," *France Nouvelle*, December 27, 1947. The Communists were right in thinking that the AFL was trying to undermine the CGT and WFTU. This writer, of course, does not believe that they or the revisionists are correct, however, when they assert that the AFL was doing this at the behest of the "monopolists."

[13]*L'Humanité*, September 22, 1950. In January 1955, the monthly CGT newspaper published a long summary of Brown's activities in Marseilles. The AFL organizer was called a *"chef des nervis,"* a Marseilles expression for "gangster leader," and an accompanying cartoon depicted him as an Al Capone in an Uncle Sam uniform; *La Vie Ouvri*ère, January 1955. For additional Communist reaction to the AFL and Brown see *La Vie Ouvrière*, *L'Humanité,* and *France Nouvelle*, 1945–1952.

[14]Interviews, Dubinsky, Harrison, Meany, Lovestone, and Brown.

AFL leaders suggested not only that the United States government should use the ERP to support noncommunist national centers but also that support should be given to provincial leaders. The AFL feared that if aid were given only to the national centers, the national leaders would be tempted to use the money principally to bolster their own position inside their organizations. Able provincial leaders who were not necessarily close to the national leaders would not receive the support they needed to do an effective job.

Other authors and commentators have maintained that the AFL's role was more decisive. The controversial Tom Braden has stated that the AFL "organized Force Ouvrière."[15] In an interview, James Carey, former secretary-treasurer of the CIO and a partisan of the "reformist" CGT tendency, maintained that the AFL "split" the CGT.[16] The Communist CGT leader Benoît Frachon, in an interview, also maintained that Brown and the AFL, acting as agents of the United States government, split the CGT and created Force Ouvrière.[17]

Needless to say, the AFL, the CIO, the CGT, FO, and the United States government all have vested interests and their views on the AFL's role in French politics appear to coincide with their institutional perspectives. The AFL did not want to appear to be too involved in the CGT scission. The CIO opposed the scission. The CGT preferred to blame everything on the imperialist forces. The United States government did not want to be openly implicated in the trade union politics of other states. Nevertheless, from the available evidence, it does not appear as if the AFL alone, or in cooperation with the United States government, split the CGT and created or organized Force Ouvrière. It is more difficult, however, to determine the effects of the relationship between the AFL, the United States government, and FO after FO came into existence in late 1947 and early 1948. On the basis of the information available, it is impossible to come to any clear-cut conclusion about who affected whom and on what issues during this later period.

While it is possible that the AFL and the United States government made secret arrangements to split the CGT and create a new union structure, the evidence (leaving aside Frachon's assertions) does not support this contention. First, American and AFL officials deny that they worked together to create FO in 1946 and 1947. Braden, moreover, claims that the AFL "organized Force Ouvrière on its own," and that only later did the United States government

---

[15]Tom Braden, "I'm Glad the CIA Is 'Immoral'," *Saturday Evening Post*, May 20, 1967, p. 11.

[16]Carey maintained that in his lifetime, he had organized a number of trade union scissions and that the AFL's actions were decisive in splitting the CGT. For a discussion of CIO policy during this period see Windmuller, op. cit. and Joseph Carwell, "The International Role of American Labor" (Ph.D. thesis, Columbia University, 1956).

[17]Frachon maintained that he had received information from sources in the United States and French governments confirming his opinion.

support noncommunist unions in France and Italy. Second, as has been discussed, in the very early postwar period, the AFL leadership and most senior United States officials differed sharply in their assessment of Russia's ambitions in Western Europe and the potential use of unions in the Russian scheme. And United States officials did not at that time have the means to engage in political operations even if they had wanted to. In interviews, United States officials and AFL leaders maintain that, prior to 1948, United States officials (with some exceptions) did not really understand the significance of Communist control of the labor movement. Moreover, after the OSS was dismantled in the fall of 1945, the United States government did not begin to set up another significant political operations unit until the fall of 1947, when the CIA and the Office of Policy Coordination were established. Finally, examination of the AFL and FTUC archives reveals that the AFL was desperately short of money, but there was no discussion of or, at that time, hope of obtaining money from the United States government. AFL correspondence and FTUC minutes reveal that the AFL, acting almost alone, provided limited financial and organizational assistance to militants, primarily in the mines, railroads, and PTT, who wanted to create a new union structure.[18]

Although the AFL's assistance in the early postwar period was doubtless significant, Carey and Braden appear to be overstating the AFL's role in the creation of FO. To begin with, the AFL did not engineer the CGT scission. Brown's early letters to the FTUC, especially the previously cited request of March 14, 1946, for funds to aid the Amis de Force Ouvrière militants and his report on the April 1946 CGT congress, clearly indicate that he believed that there was already a de facto split in the CGT and that a formal break was inevitable. Undoubtedly, the AFL strengthened the forces that split the CGT and created FO, thus nudging the "inevitable" along. The AFL's financial assistance was used to support the activities of anti-CGT militants. Financing FO organizers was, of course, exceedingly important. Although there may be a number of reasons why workers join a given union, all the FO leaders interviewed pointed out that where Amis de Force Ouvrière militants were supplied with funds for traveling and other organizational expenses, the FO flourished. Where FO could not sustain field organizers, workers either remained in the CGT or became apathetic. (There is also some statistical evidence to indicate that where French union organizers were active, workers joined unions in great numbers.[19])

Nevertheless, almost every FO leader interviewed maintains that the AFL's assistance merely facilitated the decision of the Amis de Force Ouvrière to leave

[18]There are indications in the FTUC files that the ITS and other fraternal labor groups also were sending small, not very significant, sums to Amis de FO militants at this time.

[19]Richard F. Hamilton, *Affluence and the French Workers in the Fourth Republic* (Princeton: Princeton University Press, 1967), pp. 234–235.

the CGT and create a new organization. The AFL, they pointed out, was helpful but not decisive. The FO militants had fought the Communists before and during the war, and many of them, in Résistance Ouvrière, had just fought the Nazis. In interviews, they insisted that they were not about to let the Communists keep control of a major organization for which they had just risked their lives in a six-year war.[20] Brown, they pointed out, was a dynamic organizer, but he was only one person. The AFL's financial contributions were significant, but the Amis de Force Ouvrière were already creating an autonomous structure when the AFL assistance began in mid-1946.

It is more difficult to measure the direct effects the AFL's policy had after FO came into existence. Again, FO and AFL leaders believe the Federation's financial and organizational support was significant. FO, however, received much more aid than the $30,000 the AFL gave to the FO national office and the 100 typewriters and 25 mimeograph machines that were distributed throughout the country.

In general, the AFL encouraged the United States government to subsidize FO and particularly local FO leaders. It is difficult to determine, however, if the AFL was ultimately influential. United States officials, including Ambassadors Averell Harriman and Jefferson Caffery, maintain that the AFL did, on occasion, provide them with useful suggestions and information. They insist, however, that the government's own staff was well acquainted with the various tendencies in French labor and that the United States government did not rely on the AFL's information and suggestions. A recently declassified 1949 U.S. Embassy review of the labor situation in France tends to support this view. The United States government was well informed about various labor groupings, and the embassy maintained that "encouragement and assistance" should be given to provincial militants from FO and the autonomous unions rather than to the FO leadership in Paris. Whether the embassy reached this conclusion on its own or whether information supplied by the AFL was decisive in the embassy's deliberations cannot be determined until all the relevant United States government files become available.[21]

[20] It should be noted that Auguste Lecoeur, who was a leading member of the Communist party and the head of the CGT miners' union in the early postwar period, also maintained in an interview that the AFL's assistance was not decisive. Lecoeur, who has since broken with the Communist party, believes that AFL aid to FO militants can be likened to giving a car to a man on a long journey who has only a bicycle. The man is determined to reach his goal, and the car is of considerable help but not decisive in reaching the objective. Interview, Lecoeur.

[21] See "Review of the Labor Situation in France since the Schism within the CGT of December, 1947," U.S. Embassy, Paris, no. 327, April 4, 1949. It should perhaps be noted that there is no indication that the AFL used its leverage in Washington to pressure Truman into financially supporting European labor groups. AFL leaders maintain that in 1948, they would have supported Truman's reelection regardless of the United States government's aid to free trade unionism in Europe. Interviews, Lovestone and Dubinsky.

It is clear that the AFL played a considerable role in the creation of the Mediterranean Committee. Every significant participant in the committee's activities, including the ITF, FO, and French and United States government officials, credits the AFL with the major role in the committee's creation and subsequent actions. Brown together with Ferri-Pisani mobilized the most important participants and secured the financial assistance for the committee's activities.[22]

EFFECTS ON FRENCH AND WORLD AFFAIRS

The existence of FO and the Mediterranean Committee appears to have had mixed effects on French trade unionism and the economic and social conditions of French workers. Until the creation of FO, non-Catholic workers on the whole were represented by a union structure dominated by a political party. Although the interests of trade unionism and the Communist party sometimes overlapped, the CGT was clearly guided primarily by party interests. In other words, the CGT's no-strike policy between 1945 and 1947 and the general-strike policy in 1947 and 1948 resulted primarily from CP directives rather than from trade union interests.

FO leaders were free from this determining constraint. Although many FO leaders and militants were Socialists, the FO's lack of financial and organizational indebtedness to the Socialist party enabled it to remain aloof from Socialist party politics when it decided that the party was not pursuing the workers' best interests. This does not mean, of course, that FO always pursued the best interests of French workers. It seems reasonable to conclude, however, that FO was freer than the CGT to pursue what it conceived to be these interests.[23]

The existence of two rival non-Catholic union structures also led to competition between the two confederations. On the one hand, this was useful in that competition and rivalry encouraged militant trade unionism. Each confederation, to secure the greatest possible support from the workers, wanted to appear to be the more militant. Hence, each had to outbid the other in attempting to secure better economic and social conditions for the workers. On the other hand, the then Socialist minister of labor, Daniel Mayer, insists that competition

[22] Interviews, Oldenbroek, Becu, Brown, Lovestone, Picquemal, Baylot, and Caffery.

[23] As was discussed in Chapter 2, especially footnote 4, almost all noncommunist scholars believe that the CGT was controlled by a Communist party loyal to Moscow. Edward Shorter and Charles Tilly, however, insist that the Communists should not be blamed for diverting the CGT into political concerns and away from bread-and-butter matters and effective organization. They maintain that these political activities prevailed in the mass production industries since the beginning of the century and that the postwar innovations in strike activity had little to do with changes in local union structures. Shorter and Tilly, *Strikes in France 1830–1968* (New York: Cambridge University Press, 1974), p. 184.

with the Communists led FO to make irresponsible, inflationary wage demands.[24]

A number of critics of the AFL and the FO have maintained also that the CGT split in 1947 led to the weakening of the French labor movement. Indeed, there is some evidence that the split, like previous trade union scissions in France, was in fact damaging to the labor movement. Apparently, when a French labor or political grouping splits into two factions, not all the militants take sides. Rather, one group remains in *la vieille maison*, a second part follows the scissionists, and a third, finding itself unable to choose between the first two, becomes apathetic and leaves the movement altogether. The overall result is a weakening of the movement.[25] Critics of the AFL and FO maintain that this happened in the late 1940s and that French labor still has not recovered.

The partisans of FO, however, point out that prior to the split, the CGT, because it was being used so blatantly to serve the Communist party, was already losing large numbers of militants. They point to the declining strength of the CGT in social security elections, the increasing number of wildcat strikes, and the increasing strength of independent and Amis de Force Ouvrière labor groupings as evidence of the CGT's decline prior to the official scission.[26] Far from weakening the labor movement, they maintain, the creation of FO strengthened organized labor by providing disillusioned noncommunist and non-Catholic trade unionists with a viable alternative to the CGT.

Another criticism of the AFL centers on the organization of the Mediterranean Committee. A number of noncommunist critics maintain that the committee's concern with political-military affairs was detrimental to the building of trade unions. Specifically, these critics maintain that the committee frequently adopted expedient methods to unload ships (e.g., hiring strong-arm men) instead of engaging in organizational drives and militant trade unionism. Ferri-Pisani, the committee's director, they argue, was a dynamic and intelligent man, but he was not a good union organizer. He spent little of his time on the mundane but necessary tasks of organization and administration. Furthermore, it is argued, the committee's organizers relied on ITF and American financing. When these funds were no longer available in the mid-1950s, the strength of the FO maritime unions, which had been built up through the Mediterranean Committee, declined drastically.

This criticism has also been applied to other sectors that received American aid. It is maintained that American aid did not encourage dynamic organization

[24] Interview, Mayer.
[25] "Les Effectifs de la C.F.D.T.," *Les Études Sociales et Syndicales*, December 1965, p. 14. This article goes on to point out that this hypothesis is applicable to the CFTC split in 1965 which produced the CFTD.
[26] Val R. Lorwin, *The French Labor Movement* (Cambridge: Harvard University Press, 1954), pp. 115–116 and Georges LeFranc, *Les Expériences Syndicales en France de 1939–1950* (Paris: Montaigne, 1950), pp. 172–181 and 212–213.

and that the organizers were led to believe that they could continue to rely on external assistance. Moreover, these critics allege that the recipients of the aid were politically disadvantaged by the general knowledge that they were in fact relying on external sources of financial support.[27]

The committee's supporters, however, maintain that without external sources of support, it would have been impossible to engage in organizational drives, especially in the private sectors of the maritime industry. While they admit that the committee engaged in a number of non-trade union activities, they point out that vast amounts of human and material resources were deployed to trade union activities. These activities did not lead to sustained organizational efforts because external financial aid was cut off. Without external financial assistance, they point out, it is impossible to sustain strong unions in key sectors of the maritime and other private industries. The workers alone will not finance union organizers. The private as opposed to the public sector will not sustain union organizers. Hence, unless external assistance is forthcoming, the unions cannot employ the sizable numbers of organizers that they need if they are to remain effective.

Although several observers have maintained that the French (and Italian) labor movements were "impotent,"[28] there are indications that the trade unions played a significant role in postwar French politics. It appears that organized labor was influential in the political socialization and indoctrination of trade unionists and probably other workers in contact with union militants.

A number of scholars have maintained that the unions provided French workers with their political perspectives or "frames of reference." These scholars have pointed out that where Communist unions are strong (e.g., in France and Italy), the Communist party tends to have a large electoral following. Where Communist-controlled unions are weak (e.g., in Belgium), the Communist party is electorally weak.[29] The contentions of these scholars were confirmed by numerous interviews with French Communist and noncommunist union leaders and militants.

[27]Interviews, Lapeyre, Hebert, Froideval, and Becu. Joseph La Palombara in *The Italian Labor Movement: Problems and Prospects* (Ithaca, N.Y.: Cornell University Press, 1957), pp. 57–58 maintains that external financial support was "dysfunctional" in Italy. There is no evidence, however, that French unions "lost their autonomy" or that AFL funds were used to support "oligarchical patronage." Indeed, the AFL consistently disseminated its funds and equipment in the provinces rather than relying on the FO leaders, whom the AFL regarded as bureaucratic.

[28]See for example Walter Galenson, *Trade Union Democracy in Western Europe* (Berkeley: University of California Press, 1961), p. 1.

[29]See Hamilton, op. cit. passim; Charles Micaud, *Communism and the French Left* (New York: Praeger, 1963), pp. x, 86–88, and 107–108; Hadley Cantril, *The Politics of Despair* (New York: Basic Books, 1958), pp. 83 and 100–102. These writers stress the flow from the unions to the Communist party. They do not analyze the flow from the Communist party to the unions. Another indication that unions can be a major socializing force can be found in John H. Magill, *Labor Unions and Political Socialization: A Case Study of Bolivian Workers* (New York: Praeger Special Studies, 1974).

If these scholars and union leaders are correct, the creation of FO and the support of anticommunist militants would appear to have reduced the Communists' electoral strength and counteracted, in part, the CGT's indoctrination of French workers. By bolstering morale and supporting anticommunist militants, the AFL also appears to have contributed to the French public's support for the Marshall Plan, the Atlantic Alliance, the European Coal and Steel Community (ECSC), and the Korean war, all of which were bitterly opposed by French Communists and their trade union forces.

The existence of FO may also have impeded the CP's ability to sabotage the government's policies. Two of the clearest examples of this are the Marshall Plan and the ECSC. In both cases, the Communists and the CGT refused to participate in government planning and administrative committees. FO, however, gave the government its complete cooperation, thus helping to ensure that the interests of the French workers were taken into consideration in developing programs and that the workers did not oppose the government's policies. Indeed, Georges Levard, a former CFTC leader, has suggested that if FO and the Catholics had not supported the ECSC in 1950, other pressure groups (e.g., agricultural groups), following the trade unions' example, would have proved far more reluctant to support the Treaty of Rome when it came up for ratification in the late 1950s.[30]

FO's connection with the AFL also increased FO's bargaining power in French and United States government circles. As Paul Porter, a former Marshall Plan administrator, has pointed out, French and American officials knew of the close relationship between the AFL and FO and knew that if they opposed FO, they might very well have to face the AFL's pressure in France and in the United States.[31]

There is also considerable evidence indicating that FO and the Mediterranean Committee may have been instrumental in preventing the Communists from successfully organizing political strikes. The tactics of the Mediterranean Committee have already been described. The Amis de Force Ouvrière and, later, FO militants also urged workers not to engage in what they considered to be political strikes. If there already was a walkout, they distributed propaganda explaining how the strike was being used to support Communist and Russian political objectives.[32] When they felt it was tactically wise and physically possible (e.g., when they believed they would not be assaulted by Communist strong-arm squads), they led the return to work.

[30] Interview, Levard.
[31] Interview, Porter. Jean Bocher, the FO and Mediterranean Committee leader in Cherbourg, also has given me copies of letters he exchanged with United States government officials. In these letters, Bocher, referring to his close association with the AFL's representative Irving Brown, requested that American ships be diverted to Cherbourg to ensure that the dockers did not remain idle.
[32] In their propaganda, the FO militants frequently referred to the CGT as the "CGT-K," the "K" standing for "Kominform."

Many workers either were unsympathetic to the CGT's political aims or believed a given strike was not tactically wise. Fearing psychological, economic, or physical intimidation, however, they did not dare break trade union solidarity and return to work. When the FO militants led the return to work, many of these workers followed suit, thus forcing the CGT to call off the strike.

For example, the United States consul general in Marseilles, reporting the closing of the FO Dockers' Union and Mediterranean Committee office in October 1953, noted:

It is true of course that during 1949–1950, a successful fight was waged on the docks against the communist CGT union which was trying to paralyze the Marseilles docks by getting workers to refuse to load cargoes for Indo China (See Congen's despatch No. 59 December 7, 1950). This struggle was carried out by the newly organized F.O. Dockers Union. . . . This victory of the anti-communist forces at this time effectively broke the hold of the CGT on the dock workers and the communists have never since been able to rally them behind any political agitation.[33]

Even before FO was established, small groups of Amis de Force Ouvrière militants in some sectors of the railroad and communications industries or independently in the mines were instrumental in breaking Communist strikes. Not only did these small groups on occasion keep an entire sector functioning, but also the anticommunists first encouraged and then led the return to work in the general strikes of 1947 and 1948.[34] Although these efforts did not prevent the CGT from seriously crippling the economy and impeding French economic recovery in 1947 and 1948, by 1950 most observers—including AFL, FO, Catholic, and Communist trade union leaders—believed that the Communists needed the support of the FO, with its relatively small number of adherents, to organize a successful strike. As Irving Brown reported in 1951,

The CGT remains the dominant trade union in France and still commands a 60 to 70% vote in trade union elections, especially in the basic industries. . . . Yet, the curious thing about this CGT vote is that although they could get 75% in the Renault Works Council elections, the CGT in a strike ballot in April could get only 25% of the vote. It has become almost an absolute rule that the CGT can get the workers' vote in elections by an

[33] "Recent Developments in Union Activity among the Dockers of Marseilles," American Consulate General, Marseilles, no. 44, December 1, 1953. It should be pointed out that the French government's decision to "get tough" with the strikers in 1947 and 1948 and later on the docks in 1949 and 1950 was also partially responsible for the failure of the strikes. The French government acting without some trade union support, however, would probably have had a much more difficult time breaking the strikes. Interviews, Brown, Moch, Baylot, Carpentier, and Philips.

[34] In the middle of the strike, Maurice Thorez traveled from Russia to France on trains run by members of Lafond's autonome.

overwhelming majority, yet they cannot get workers to march either in a political or economic strike unless F.O. and the Christians are participating.[35]

Brown went on to point out that the Communists were aware of this, and that is why they placed heavy emphasis on their united-action policy. Indeed, a few years later, Frachon to some extent openly confirmed Brown's contentions. The CGT leader pointed out that securing the support of the Catholic trade unions, while easy, was insufficient. To carry the masses, especially in a strike, he said, it was necessary to bring about unity of action with FO, and he encouraged the Communist militants to do everything possible to bring this about.[36] All the FO leaders, CFTC leaders, and former officials of the French government familiar with postwar labor politics also confirmed these contentions.[37]

It is more difficult to evaluate the role of FO and the Mediterranean Committee in impeding Communist attempts to use the CGT for espionage, paramilitary activities, and coups d'état. Val Lorwin has written that "Force Ouvrière could say with much justice that its action had saved France in 1947 from the fate of Czechoslovakia."[38] Jules Moch, however, maintains that the Communists did not attempt to organize a coup de Prague until 1948. In an interview, Moch maintained that as minister of the interior in 1947–1948, he received information that convinced him that the French Communists in 1948 had adopted the strategy that brought the CP to power in Czechoslovakia. The CGT strikes, he believed, were used to blackmail the government into accepting Communist ministers or to prevent anticommunists from occupying key ministerial posts.[39] After this was accomplished, the Communists planned to use their cadres and their control of strategic industrial sectors (e.g., electricity) to bring about a coup.

In the absence of additional information, it is, of course, impossible to confirm these contentions. It should be noted, however, that even if the Communists did not consciously adopt in France the strategy they had employed in Czechoslovakia, the general strikes they organized created an insurrectional

[35] Report by Irving Brown, September 19, 1951. FTUC archives.

[36] Benoît Frachon, "Interventions," *Cahiers du Communisme* XXX (June–July 1954), pp. 797–799.

[37] See Appendix B for list of those interviewed.

[38] Vai R. Lorwin, "French Trade Unions since the Liberation, 1944–1951," *Industrial and Labor Relations Review* V (July 1952), p. 531.

[39] Moch maintains that the French government in 1947 and 1948 had excellent sources of information in high Communist circles in France. Usually, Moch received detailed information on the French Communist party's Central Committee meetings within 24 hours of the meeting's conclusion. See also Jules Moch, *Rencontres avec Leon Blum* (Paris: Plon, 1970), pp. 319–332.

atmosphere and gave rise to what historically might be called "revolutionary conditions." As Barrington Moore, Jr., has suggested, "The main factors that create a revolutionary mass are a sudden increase in hardship coming on top of quite serious deprivations, together with the breakdown of the routines of daily life—getting food, going to work, etc.—that tie people to the prevailing order."[40]

Certainly FO and the Mediterranean Committee alone did not prevent these conditions from arising, nor did they prevent the Communists from following the strategy they had used in Czechoslovakia. But as Lorwin, Moch, and FO and AFL leaders have pointed out, FO's cooperation with what was then "the prevailing order" substantially reduced the chances of a revolutionary change in the French political system.

It seems reasonable to assume that the Communists may have used their control of the CGT for espionage and paramilitary activities. Reference has already been made to previous Communist efforts to use the trade unions for this purpose, and examples of the tactic's occasional use in the postwar period have come to light. In 1952, for example, French transport workers in and around the naval base at Toulon admitted that their CGT union superiors had ordered them to collect information on the numbers, armaments, and morale of French troops.[41] Again, FO and the Mediterranean Committee alone were unable to prevent these activities, but the existence of these organizations may have facilitated efforts to impede them. The Mediterranean Committee's activities have already been described. FO's cooperation with the French and United States governments resulted in the hiring of politically reliable skilled and unskilled workers at military bases and in classified projects of one kind or another.[42]

Thus, it appears that American trade unions, by influencing developments in the international labor movement as well as in key European countries such as France, were able to play a role in postwar world politics. The AFL's actions furthered European economic recovery and stability by helping ensure that European unions kept their economies running smoothly and cooperated with the Marshall Plan. Similarly, the AFL helped restore the internal balance of political power and prevented a shift to the extreme Left. By assisting those union organizers who wanted to avoid political involvement, the AFL helped prevent organized labor from being used to bring Communists closer to power.

In turn, by preventing the Russians and their Western European allies from using organized labor, the AFL helped maintain a global balance of power. By

[40] Barrington Moore, Jr., "Revolution in America?" *New York Review of Books*, January 30, 1969, p. 8.

[41] *New York Times*, June 11, 1952.

[42] Interviews, Brown and FO leaders. In 1950, the French minister of the Merchant Marine denounced the CGT maritime unions as Cominform agencies and prohibited them from dealing with the loading of military related ships. ITF, *Journal*, February 12, 1951.

preventing the Russians from exploiting Europe's economic weakness and political instability, the AFL helped prevent the Soviet Union from acquiring control of the European continent. It is, of course, difficult to know what would have happened if the Russians had managed anyway to impose their hegemony on Western Europe. The United States had just fought a second war in the twentieth century to prevent a totalitarian German elite from acquiring control both of Europe and Western Russia, and it is quite likely that the United States would have fought to prevent a totalitarian Russian elite from doing the same thing. If not, the United States ultimately might have been faced with the combined might of a revived Europe and Russia under Russian leadership. Thus it does not seem excessive to conclude that the AFL played a role in world politics—a substantial role, indeed—and helped save the United States from again intervening militarily in Europe or ultimately facing the preponderant power of the Soviet empire.

Chapter 9

The AFL in Postwar
Europe and the
AFL-CIO Today

The general purpose of this study has been to demonstrate that states and government leaders are not the only important actors in world affairs. More specifically, it has sought to show that one kind of nongovernmental organization in particular, the trade union, also can be significant. As the case of postwar Europe reveals, trade unions can be significant in their own right as well as when they are under the control of governments. And they need not be concerned solely with economic issues. They can play a crucial role in national security affairs. Indeed, as the preceding analysis has sought to show, they can affect the entire global balance of power.

If these conclusions are correct, those who seek to understand or to shape world affairs can ignore nongovernmental organizations and particularly trade unions only at the risk of imperfectly understanding the course of international relations. Major nongovernmental forces must be analyzed and their aims, methods, resources, and opportunities for action assessed. Similarly, practitioners will have to take these organizations into account as they plan their strategies. Trade unions and other nongovernmental forces can be important allies and can assist in the attainment of objectives. Or they can be impediments to action, as both the United States and Russian governments discovered in the early postwar years.

This study, however, does not show that trade unions are always significant actors. What it does suggest is that some conditions or circumstances apparently enable nongovernmental organizations to play a significant role; absence of these circumstances may preclude such role playing.

At the end of World War II, a number of circumstances existed together which apparently enabled the AFL to play a role in European and world politics. It is difficult to say even now what the relative importance of each condition was, but among the most important were these.

1 An independent Europe was crucial to the global balance of power. The AFL was able to play a significant role insofar as it helped maintain that independence.

2 The Soviet Union, seeking to dominate Europe, sought to use European trade unions for this purpose. The AFL was in a position to help prevent the successful implementation of this strategy.

3 Postwar Europe was weak economically and politically and susceptible to external influence. Because of this susceptibility, the AFL was able to provide material and human resources that influenced developments on the continent.

4 European nongovernmental forces welcomed AFL involvement. If they had not, it is difficult to see how the Americans could have affected European politics to the extent they did.

5 The United States and Western governments at first tolerated and later encouraged the transatlantic nongovernmental coalition. If they had not at least tolerated it, it probably never could have developed. That they later encouraged and participated in the coalition probably made it more effective.

6 The American nongovernmental actor was able to affect European and world affairs because it was a special type of private organization. If its leadership had not been highly motivated and had not possessed material and human resources and unique expertise, the AFL would have been unable to influence world politics.

Whether these conditions were necessary or sufficient to cause the nongovernmental organization's influence is uncertain. Clearly, though, if many of these conditions reappear, it should be no surprise if American labor continues to play a significant role in world politics. Indeed, it would seem that a number, though not all, of the characteristics of the early postwar period are now present or reappearing.

THE GLOBAL BALANCE OF POWER

The first important characteristic is that Europe's fate still is a crucial variable in world politics. If Western Europe's industrial base and military potential were to fall into the hands of the Soviet Union and its allies, the global balance of power would be radically changed. It should be noted, for example, that North America produces approximately 30 percent, the Warsaw Pact nations, approximately 20 percent, and Western Europe (NATO and other European states), about 25 percent of the world's goods and services. Of the remaining 25 percent, Japan accounts for approximately 7 percent and China 4 percent.[1]

Needless to say, it is not always possible simply to extrapolate military and industrial power from GNP statistics.[2] In this case, however, the relationship among them is clear. There is little doubt that if Europe's resources were aggregated under the control of the Soviet Union, that is to say, if the Soviet Union were able to more than double its resources and deploy over half the world's GNP, global power relationships would be drastically altered. Even aside from the likely disruption of the North American economy, which is tied in with the Western European economy in what some call a "trade-dependent geostrategic region,"[3] there would be the emergence of the Soviet Union and its European allies as the predominant global power bloc.

An occasional commentator has suggested that United States security could still be assured in such a world,[4] but this is decidedly the minority view. Moreover, the United States has shown no disposition to alter its traditional position that it will not allow a single power to dominate militarily both Russia and Europe. This was a *causus belli* during World War I and World War II and potentially was one in the post-World War II period as well. It appears to remain so today.

RUSSIAN GOALS AND CAPABILITIES

A second circumstance that affected the AFL's influence during the postwar period was the Russian strategy for attaining European hegemony. Are there contemporary parallels? Although the leadership of the Soviet Union is now engaged in a "relaxation of tension" policy (*razriadka* in Russian), the Russians themselves see little change in their goals or methods.[5] They insist that the destruction of capitalism and its social system and the triumph of communism and classless society is still their long-term goal.

[1] These statistics are derived from U.S. Arms Control and Disarmament Agency, *World Military Expenditures and Arms Trade 1963—1973*, Publication 74 (Washington, D.C.: U.S. Government Printing Office, 1975).
[2] See for example Klaus Knorr, *Military Power and Potential* (Lexington, Mass.: D.C. Heath, 1970).
[3] Saul B. Cohen, *Geography and Politics in a World Divided*, 2d. ed. (New York: Oxford University Press, 1973).
[4] See for example Robert Tucker, *A New Isolationism: Threat or Promise* (New York: Universe Books for Potomac Associates, 1972), especially pp. 47 and 77—86.
[5] For short but comprehensive descriptions of Russian views of their own policy, see Foy Kohler, Mose Harvey, Leon Goure, and Richard Soll, *Soviet Strategy for the Seventies: From Cold War to Peaceful Coexistence* (Miami, Fla.: Center for Advanced International

Détente

Changing the global balance of power in favor of the Soviet Union is their current overall objective. "Peaceful coexistence" remains, as it has been since the time of Lenin, a strategy or stage that can be used along the way. As both Lenin and Stalin pointed out, states with different social systems can coexist for limited periods of time, and peaceful coexistence should be used to strengthen the Communist camp. *Razriadka* is merely a type of peaceful coexistence (*mirnoya sosuchchestvovaniye*), and the Russians, until recently anyway, have used the latter term when referring to "détente."

The major difference in peaceful coexistence now as compared with earlier periods, Russian analysts maintain, is that there has been a shift in Western thinking and policy. They feel that although the Soviet Union has always followed the policy of peaceful coexistence, the West has only recently developed a more "sober" and "realistic" attitude. This shift in Western policy has been caused, so these analysts go on to say, by the increasingly serious crisis in the imperialist camp and the shifting power balance in favor of the Soviet Union. These factors have caused the West to be more cautious in its dealings with the Soviet Union and also have forced the United States to establish closer economic relations with the Soviet Union so that the United States can compete more effectively with rival capitalist states.

Although some Russian analysts are less enthusiastic about or see different benefits in *razriadka* than others do, they all generally maintain that *razriadka* will further the interests of the Soviet Union and only temporarily help capitalism. In the long run, they argue, "contradictions in the imperialist camp" will be heightened. For example, because the Soviet Union will no longer appear to be threatening, it will become increasingly difficult for the Western military-industrial complex to justify its rule and maintain the cohesion of its military alliances. In the meantime, the power of the Communist camp will grow and there will be a gradual change in the global balance of power in favor of the Soviet Union.

For the Russians, peaceful coexistence does not mean the abandonment of all forms of class struggle. Even the use of force against capitalist countries or even within the Socialist camp is not completely ruled out. Although Stalin's successors have allowed for the possibility that thermonuclear war between the two systems may not be fatalistically "inevitable" and that states representing different social systems can coexist without resorting to general violence, Com-

---

Studies, 1973) and Walter Laqueur, "Détente: Western and Soviet Interpretations," Strategic Studies Center, Stanford Research Institute, January 30, 1975. The following account is drawn largely from these sources.

On possible Russian responses in the event of a failure of détente see William Carpenter, Stephen P. Gilbert, and William Lackman, "U.S. Strategy in the Event of a Failure of Détente," Strategic Studies Center, Stanford Research Institute, April 1975.

munists in the West have been warned to be prepared to use violence in support of or to protect "the revolution."

Apart from using peaceful coexistence to strengthen the Socialist camp economically—by obtaining credits, investments, and the like—the Russians also will "intensify" the ideological struggle. This is not something that will be left to the philosophers. Political and economic struggle will be increased. There will be peaceful coexistence between states but not between social classes. The Soviet Union is to guard itself against Western efforts in this regard and also is to wage offensive ideological war.

The Russian leadership today maintains that it harbors no territorial aspirations in Western Europe.[6] Indeed, during the past few years, the Russians have pushed hard for formal European acceptance of the territorial status quo on the Continent. However, the Russians still indicate that they want to influence events in Europe— in at least two ways. First, they would like to see the Warsaw Pact and NATO dismantled and the United States military presence withdrawn. They propose instead the establishment of a pan-European collective security system and a permanent European secretariat to help regulate affairs on the Continent. Second, they believe it is their duty to assist the "working class" in Europe (and elsewhere) in its increasing struggle against "monopoly capital."[7]

For the Russians, the developed capitalist world, particularly Europe, has entered a new period. They maintain that especially since the downturn in the United States economy in the early 1970s, the "crisis in capitalism" has continued "to deepen." During the past few years, the so-called contradictions in capitalism have intensified and the working class has reacted massively. According to one Russian analyst, "In five years, from 1969–1974, the total number of those taking part in strikes and other mass demonstrations of workers in Europe, North America, and Japan has risen to 225 million as against 164 million during the five preceding years. . . ." The most massive and intense struggles for demands carried out during recent years have taken place in such "citadels of capitalism" as the USA, Italy, France, Great Britain, the Federal Republic of Germany, and Japan.[8]

As the Russians see it, working-class forces must unite across state boundaries to take advantage of this situation and must be prepared to use a variety of means to promote the destruction of the imperialist camp. As one Russian analyst put it,

[6]See for example the authoritative and seminal speech of Leonid Brezhnev, "From the Report to 24th CPSU Congress," in *On the Policy of the Soviet Union and the International Situation* (Garden City, N.Y.: Doubleday, 1973), pp. 67–79.

[7]Ibid.

[8]C. Chernikov, "The Economic Struggle and the Deepening Class Struggle in the Capitalist Countries," *World Trade Union Movement*, January 1975, pp. 7–9. In recent issues, this journal, the official organ of the WFTU, has carried articles on "the deepening capitalist crisis." Another article in the same issue, for example, is entitled "France: A Crisis or the Crisis" as if the final crisis in capitalism may be upon us. This point is repeatedly made in Russian and Moscow-oriented Communist publications.

The consolidation of the international working class and the democratic movement undermines the social and political foundations of state monopoly capitalism. It creates favorable opportunities for fruitful struggle against monopoly capital, for peace, democracy and socialism. At the same time reality shows that the most reactionary bourgeois circles are always ready to use violence to export counter revolution to stop political and economic progress. All progressive forces of the world must set themselves the new task of effectively rejecting the policy of the bourgeoisie. . . .[9]

Although there are some differences in emphasis among Russian specialists,[10] they are in general agreement about goals and the methods best calculated to achieve them. The same cannot be said, however, of Western analysts of Russian policy. In both Europe and the United States, there are two major schools of thought.[11] One argues that there has been a basic change in the direction of Russian policy. As Adam Ulam might characterize members of this school, they believe that the Russians' need for coexistence has finally prevailed over the impetus for expansion. They argue that although the Soviet Union has not given up its professed historical mission, it will do little, if anything, to further world revolution or acquire hegemony over Europe or other strategic areas. A variety of factors, they maintain, have led to the search for genuine coexistence and a stable world order—among them the fear of nuclear war, the fear of China and the desire to avoid a Sino-American alliance, the economic problems of the Soviet Union, and the bureaucratization of the Communist elite.

Russian policy in Europe, according to this view, is leading or has led to the termination of the cold war. The major cause of tension from shortly after World War II through the early 1960s, Western fears that the Soviet Union and its allies were seeking to dominate Western Europe, has been alleviated. The Russians have agreed to the territorial status quo, and they have solemnly pledged to abstain from harassing Western rights pertaining to West Berlin or

---

[9]Chernikov, op. cit.

[10]From time to time, some Kremlinologists refer to these differences in emphasis as an indication of a debate in the Politburo; for example, Victor Zorza has suggested, based on various Soviet publications, that a debate is under way between the hard-liners, who favor taking immediate advantage of the crisis of capitalism and pushing Western European Communists into more militant action, and those who favor a more "dovish" approach. However, it could be argued that the differences in emphasis reflect different functional responsibilities. For elaboration and a brief listing of those with different responsibilities and their orientations, see Dimitri Simes, "Monthly Report on Foreign Policy, Arms Control, and Strategic Issues in the Soviet Media," no. 10, Georgetown University Center for Strategic and International Studies, Washington, D.C., October 15, 1975.

[11]For brief descriptions of the two schools see Adam Ulam, *Expansion and Coexistence*, 2d ed. (New York: Praeger, 1974), pp. 726–776; see also U.S., Congress, House, Committee on Foreign Affairs, "Détente, Hearings Before the Subcommittee on Europe," 93rd Cong., 2nd sess, 1974 and Richard Pipes, ed., *Soviet Strategy in Europe* (New York: Crane Russak, 1976).

unilaterally altering the status of the city. Moreover, they are negotiating for new security arrangements and mutual force reductions. Finally, they are not seeking to bring Communist governments to power in Western Europe through force or paramilitary activities. In fact, they seem quite happy to deal with European governments led by conservatives such as DeGaulle or Pompidou, even if the interests of local Communist parties are not served thereby. Viewed from this perspective, future scholars will recognize this period as one of major transformation in Russian policy.

Future scholars instead may agree with the views of a second school of analysts. This group concludes that the Russians have merely changed their tactics, not their fundamental goals and methods of operation—and this is precisely what the Russians have done in almost every decade since the Bolsheviks came to power. The reasons cited for the change in tactics are much the same as those cited by the analysts who argue that there has been a fundamental change in Russian policy: the fear that Khrushchev-like adventurism is too dangerous in a nuclear world (at least until the Soviet Union obtains clear-cut nuclear superiority), the desire to avoid driving the United States and China together, the hope of obtaining Western economic assistance in the face of internal economic difficulties, and, finally, the cautious nature of the aging bureaucratic leadership in the Soviet Union.

The Russians, the second group of analysts points out, not only continue to stress their fundamental goals but also are pressing for hegemony in Europe and elsewhere. The Russian military buildup is spectacular, particularly when compared with declining American strength. Russian nuclear as well as conventional forces and bases in Third World countries continue to increase while the United States is in a process of retrenchment.

In Europe, members of this second school argue, although the Russians merely promised to do what they were obligated to do anyway in Berlin, it was the Western powers that made concessions by formally accepting the Russian-imposed territorial status quo. Although the Russians are willing to discuss future European security arrangements and force reductions, they are asking for an arrangement that will dissolve NATO, erode the United States commitment, and, through a pan-European approach, give the Soviet Union a preponderant role in future European security affairs. Moreover, while the Russians are willing to talk about mutual force reductions, they are actually strengthening their forces in Central Europe so that they may be in a better position to threaten military intervention at a later time.

Finally, this line of analysis goes on, while the Russians have not encouraged European Communist parties to seek power by revolution, they have not abandoned this instrument and, through the détente policy itself, have increased its potential. By appearing to be less threatening and by making the Soviet Union appear to be uninterested in changing the balance of power in Europe, the

Russian leaders have helped improve the political appeal of European Communist parties. Now these parties are becoming respectable political partners who
once again can be accepted into the mainstream of European life. Moreover, by
cooperating with conservative governments, the Russians not only have improved their own respectability; by putting some distance between themselves
and their local allies, they also have further increased the political respectability
of the local Communist parties. The Russians have never renounced their willingness to assist their allies in Western Europe and continue to work with "progressive forces" in an effort to weaken Europe and American monopoly capitalism.
When the Russian leaders judge that the "objective conditions" are suitable, they
will encourage and assist Communist, pro-Russian, or other malleable forces to
come to power.

From this perspective, détente is only a transitional phase in Soviet strategy:
it is not immutable. If the Soviet Union should become much stronger relative to
the United States or China, or if future younger Russian leaders are less cautious,
there may be a return to tougher and much more aggressive tactics.

Russia's Tactics with Organized Labor

While it is impossible to be certain about the direction of Russian policy, and
without accepting either school's analysis wholesale, some conclusions are plain
enough. The Kremlin clearly is still attempting to use organized labor to achieve
its purposes. There is no question, for example, that the Russian "trade unions"
remain instruments of the Party leadership at home and abroad. The Politburo
and the "unions" do not hide their relationship. In fact, they are proud of it. As
a recent plenum of the Soviet All-Union Central Council of Trade Unions
(AUCCTU) emphasized, "The Soviet trade unions ... wholly and completely
support the Communist Party's foreign policy and devote all their strength to
the implementation of its historic plans ... the entire work of the Soviet trade
unions is aimed at the practical implementation of the decisions of the 24th
CPSU Congress in the foreign policy sphere ..."[12]

Moreover, the Russians take the international labor movement and organized
labor in Europe very seriously. For example, the International Affairs Department of the AUCCTU has a staff of about 100, with at least 6 or 7 specialists
working on Europe alone (apart from the Ministry of Foreign Affairs, the KGB,
and the Central Committee Secretariat and various research institutes that also
employ a number of international labor specialists), and the daily trade union
newspaper, *Trud*, devotes nearly half its coverage to foreign affairs.

[12]Edwin Morrell, "Communist Unionism: Organized Labor and the Soviet State"
(Ph.D. thesis, Harvard University, 1965). For more recent restatements of the relationship
between the Party and the unions, see Petr Pimenov, "Toward Unity on a Class Basis,"
World Trade Union Movement, March 1973, p. 7 and "An AUCCTU Plenum," *Trud*, May
29, 1975.

Russian labor organizations continue to support the Party's objectives in Europe in at least three ways. First, organized labor is used as a propaganda and pressure vehicle in an attempt to influence voters and political parties. A major part of the peaceful coexistence effort in the trade union area is spent on the exchanges of delegations and the issuance of declarations. Russian unions report that whereas they exchanged several hundred delegations with 50 to 60 countries annually in the 1950s, they are now exchanging over 1,500 delegations annually, and they are issuing joint declarations with or "actively cooperating" with trade unions in 128 countries.[13] Glowing accounts of these exchanges then are printed in the Western and Third World presses. In addition, the Russians and the WFTU organize propaganda conferences and seminars almost monthly. These multitudinous activities have helped make détente and peaceful coexistence respectable in the West and have reduced European interest in an anti-communist posture and in defense expenditures.

Second, the Russians are trying to use organized labor to take advantage of what they see as the inherent weaknesses of the Western World. They are attempting to reduce Western strength and cohesion by increasing the strains and tensions in Western society, or what is sometimes referred to as "the contradictions in capitalism." In Europe, this has meant promoting economic difficulties as well as strengthening "working-class forces," that is, unions and Communist parties that can take advantage of the crisis of capitalism.

The Russians see the increasing economic crisis in the West, which has been expected to appear sooner or later, as a favorable trend.[14] Moreover, while they did not, of course, engineer the Arab oil embargo and price rise, they have, within the limits of détente, encouraged the Arabs to continue them.[15] At the same time, the increasing militance of the workers in England, France, Italy, and elsewhere—who have been hard hit by these developments—is seen as a natural defense of their interests in a capitalist economy and is applauded and encouraged.[16] The Russians, in other words, are helping to increase the strains in the West not only by encouraging the oil producers but also by promoting trade union militance that in some cases is designed to hinder the "capitalist" economies yet more. Although the Kremlin today is not promoting the immediate use of strikes to altogether wreck Western economies and systems of government, it is not unreasonable to conclude that it tries to subtly push in this direction whenever this direction promises a momentary payoff. In Britain, the Russians are helping in a small way to aggravate the country's economic difficulties by encouraging both Communist and noncommunist trade union leaders to take

13Morrell, op. cit., pp. 562–567 and "An AUCCTU Plenum."

14See for example the monthly *World Trade Union Movement* and especially the previously cited article by Chernikov.

15See for example Robert O. Freedman, *Soviet Policy toward the Middle East* (New York: Praeger Special Studies, 1975), p. 140.

16Chernikov, op. cit.

advantage of the unsettled industrial relations and hyperinflation. For example, a major tactic employed by the British Communists, encouraged by the Russians, is to join with noncommunists, try to discredit the moderates, and demand very high wage increases, frequently way above the increase in cost of living. If these very high wage claims are granted, this further increases inflation and undermines confidence in the British economy; if they are not, the Communists blame the moderate union officials and push for strikes, which are also damaging to the economy. In France, the Russians encourage the Communist party and the CGT to engage in similar, though not identical, tactics. On occasion, the Communists and the CGT have gone even further; in the fall of 1974, for example, they tried to organize a general strike. In Italy, the Russians and the Communists for a while encouraged militant strike action to defend the workers' interests, but with the Italian Communist party seeking sufficient respectability to enter into a coalition government, recently there has been much less emphasis on high wage claims and strikes— although the WFTU did congratulate the CGIL for waging a successful one-day general strike in April 1975.[17]

The Russians also are materially supporting trade union strike activities as well as organizations that they favor. It is impossible, of course, to ascertain the full extent of this support. Nevertheless, it is clear that they have assisted strike activities. On occasion, communist-bloc financial support for a labor movement has been acknowledged.[18]

---

[17]Ibid. and the WFTU publication, *Flashes*, May 7, 1975.

[18]Although, as noted, it is impossible to determine the precise extent of Russian financial support for European trade unions, the tip of what very well may be an iceberg can be seen. For example, according to Radio Moscow, August 11, 1972, Jimmy Reid, then secretary of the Scottish engineering workers, thanked the Russian authorities for giving his union approximately $50,000 for strike actions. Cited in Brian Crozier, "Soviet Union's New Takeover Bid," *Forum World Features*, August 1973. In another Radio Moscow program, in January 1974, Leslie Dixon, a member of the Amalgamated Union of Engineering Workers Council, was quoted as saying that Russian unions had made a substantial financial contribution to his union's "dispute fund." See Brian Crozier, "Soviet Interest in Industrial Unrest," *Soviet Analyst*, February 14, 1974. In another article, Crozier, a British political analyst, also listed several of the main KGB, AUCCTU, and CPUSSR secretariat officials who he maintains are helping to coordinate strikes in Great Britain. "New Light on Soviet Subversion (1)," *Soviet Analyst*, March 28, 1974.

Secretary of State Kissinger has estimated that in a 12-month period, the Soviet Union sent $50 million to the Portuguese Communist party. *New York Times*, April 18, 1975. Undoubtedly, some of these funds were used to help establish Communist control of the Portuguese national trade union center, Intersyndical. Indeed, Fletcher School of Law and Diplomacy professor and columnist John Roche has a xeroxed copy of a telegram from the Soviet Bank for Foreign Trade to a Lisbon bank transferring $28,570 to the Intersyndical. "The Portuguese Labyrinth II," King Features, August 26, 1975. Moreover, in a rare acknowledgment of organizational assistance, an East German labor leader stated that his organization has given the Portuguese unions 1 million escudos and has promised additional aid for union buildings, duplicating machinery, etc. "Voice of the GDR," August 2, 1974 (BBC, SWB, EE/4669/AI/I).

Although there is some statistical evidence to indicate that Communist parties and Communist-controlled unions appear able to affect the prevalence of strike activity,[19] this should not be taken to mean that industrial strife and economic difficulties in Europe have been caused in the main by the Russians. Almost certainly they have not. Rather, it would be closer to the truth to suggest that the Russians have been encouraging European Communists to take advantage of whatever forces are at work to increase Western economic and political difficulties.

The third approach the Russians employ in the trade union area is the promotion of "working-class unity" under their influence. For decades, the Kremlin has attached great importance to bringing Russian labor organizations and Communist-controlled unions in the West into the mainstream of the international labor movement. This, they continue to feel, will give them much greater access to labor and political forces in the West. They expect Communists in the labor movement to become more influential as a result of this entreé. Ultimately they should be able to outmaneuver the noncommunists, gain complete control of the entire trade union movement, and be in a position to use labor, and political parties in which trade unions are influential, as an instrument of Party policy.

Although they made a number of attempts to recover from the splits of the late 1940s and to recapture the unity that was achieved in the early postwar period, the Russians did not meet with much success until the early 1970s.[20] Specifically, in addition to the bilateral contacts they have now established with almost every European national center, they have successfully brought together the ICFTU's and WFTU's European affiliates under the umbrella of the ILO, and they are encouraging more meetings of this kind. They also have encouraged and have been the beneficiaries of efforts to unify the European labor movement on a pan-European basis. The Communist-dominated Italian central body, CGIL, has been accepted into the recently formed European Confederation of Trade Unions. The French Communist CGT also has recently applied, and, if it is admitted in the future, a move to bring in Eastern European labor organizations can be expected.

At the same time, the Russians and the Communist unions in Western Europe have encouraged unity in the industrial internationals. Communist unions have been admitted into one or two European trade secretariats (e.g., the European Metal Workers Federation). In Italy, the three main national centers—

[19]Douglas Hibbs, *Industrial Conflict in Advanced Industrial Societies* (Cambridge: Center for International Studies, Massachusetts Institute of Technology, April 1974).

[20]The best sources of information on trade union unification are polemical. The WFTU's monthly, *World Trade Union Movement*, carries at least one article on this subject almost every month. For a brief historical but critical analysis of Soviet policy see Claude Harmel, in the French bimonthly, *Est et Ouest*, March 1–15, 1975, pp. 12–24.

the Communist CGIL, the predominantly Catholic CISL, and the Socialist Unione Italiana del Lavoro (UIL), which broke away from the CGIL in the late 1940s—are close to merger.

The extent to which the Russians have prepared to or intend to use unions for such purposes as paramilitary and espionage activities cannot be ascertained. Presumably, Western security services have some idea of their capabilities and intentions, but only occasionally do tidbits of information on this subject come to light.[21]

It should be noted, however, that there may be a significant difference between the early postwar Russian ability to manipulate European Communist parties and trade unions and the current situation. Certainly the relationship is more complex now. Although it may never have been very easy, a number of factors, such as the change of leadership and rapid turnover of membership, currently make it much more difficult for the Russians to manipulate the European Communist parties. Moreover, some students of European communism and labor also suggest that the Italian and French parties no longer have complete control of the CGIL or CGT.[22] If this is indeed the case, then it also may be much more difficult for American labor today to form the kinds of coalitions with noncommunist trade union leaders that were formed when it was possible to point to a fixed foreign enemy, manipulating European unions for its own purposes.

In sum, while there is no doubt that the first precondition for American labor's effectiveness still prevails—namely, Europe's crucial role in the power

[21] For example, the British expulsion in 1971 of 105 Russian "diplomats," several of whom were accused of working with British unions and preparing for sabotage activities.

[22] As was noted in Chapter 2, almost all observers believe that shortly after the liberation, the major trade union centers in France and Italy fell under the control of Communist parties subservient to Moscow. For discussion of the more complex current relationships between the Russians and the major European Communist parties, see Donald M. Blackmer and Annie Kriegel, *The International Role of the Communist Parties of Italy and France* (Cambridge: Center for International Studies, Harvard University, 1975); Donald M. Blackmer and Sydney Tarrow, eds., *Communism in Italy and France* (Princeton: Princeton University Press, 1975); Neil McInnes, *The Communist Parties of Western Europe* (London: Oxford University Press, 1975). Some writers differ on the extent of present Russian and Communist party control of the CGT. See André Barjonet, *La CGT* (Paris: Seuil, 1968); the debate between Gérard Adam and Jean Ranger in *Revue Française de Science Politique*, June 1968, pp. 524—539 and December 1968, pp. 182—187; Jean-Daniel Reynaud, "Trade Unions and Political Parties in France: Some Recent Trends," *Industrial and Labor Relations Review*, January 1975, pp. 208—226. However, Walter Kendall in *The Labor Movement in Europe* (London: Allen Lane, 1975) argues that the CGT and CGIL are still controlled by the French and Italian Communist parties, and the French journals *Les Études Sociales et Syndicales* and *Est et Ouest* provide detailed information to indicate that the CGT and CGIL are still controlled by Communist parties that remain basically loyal to Moscow. For an example of a commentator who believes that the CGIL is no longer an instrument of the Italian Communist party, see Peter R. Weitz, "Labor and Politics in a Divided Movement," *Industrial and Labor Relations Review*, January 1975, pp. 226—243.

balance—the same cannot be said for the second. Although the Russians themselves maintain that they have not altered their goals or overall policy, a number of Western analysts maintain that there has been a fundamental policy shift, that détente is for real. Others believe that the Russian leaders, for a variety of domestic and international reasons, remain expansionist and are trying to weaken the West and increase their own power. Whatever the Russians' goals, however, there is little doubt that they continue to regard organized labor as an instrument of policy. Although almost certainly they cannot manipulate even European Communist-oriented unions as effectively as they did immediately after World War II, they are trying to use labor to promote their overall policy of peaceful coexistence as a vehicle for weakening the West economically and politically and, by unifying the labor movement, as a method of securing greater control of important political forces in the West.

These interpretations and Russian activities in the labor field are similar in many respects to those that prevailed from 1945 to 1947. Then, too, there were two schools of thought about Russian intentions, and the Russians were promoting peaceful coexistence and seeking to unify the labor movement. After 1947, when they switched to tougher tactics and clear-cut use of labor to impede European recovery and defense efforts, those Western political and trade union leaders who had been relatively sanguine about Russian intentions changed their position.

The AFL, however, had accepted the more pessimistic view of Russian policy well before 1947 and had decided to work with those Europeans who shared its view to prevent the European labor movement from falling completely under Russian influence. The Federation's role became more pronounced and visible when Russian tactics became more aggressive in late 1947—and apparently confirmed the pessimists' estimate of reality.

Today a number of pessimists on both sides of the Atlantic, while recognizing a more complex relationship between the Russians and the European labor movement, again are sounding the alarm. If the optimists are wrong once more, if the Russians become tougher and are able to manipulate their Communist labor allies, American labor may be able to replay postwar history by helping to prevent the Russians from controlling the European labor movement. But this assumes that a number of other preconditions also are present.

ECONOMIC AND POLITICAL STATUS OF EUROPE

A third factor in the AFL's postwar activities was early postwar conditions in Europe. A number of these conditions obviously no longer exist. Others do, and several present-day variants of early postwar conditions may again enable American labor to become effective.

Although there are some regional exceptions, Europe's major powers—West

Germany, France, Italy, and Britain—are no longer in ruins. Moreover, they are no longer completely dependent on the United States for their economic recovery. They also are not compelled by immediate practical necessity to seek American labor's assistance in dealing with the United States government. These changes in the economic status of the Continent and the nations' dependence on the United States have tended to reduce the capability as well as the entreé of all but the most powerful external actors to influence events—a marked contrast to the early postwar period, when external actors, especially American actors with limited resources, could be quite significant.

Europe's economic and political security is, however, still in large part dependent on external forces, particularly the United States. Europe's house still is not in order, and the Europeans have not developed sufficient political unity to stand on their own. The 1973 Middle East war and the ensuing oil crisis demonstrated once again the myth of a united Western Europe, if such a demonstration were needed.

Obviously, American labor by itself can do little to overcome the divisions in Europe. As part of a transnational coalition, however, American labor again may be able to play a significant role in transatlantic affairs. Most importantly, in 1947–1948, government, labor, and business on both sides of the Atlantic recognized the need to combine economic aid and recovery with a political approach to Western European unity and Atlantic security. American labor played a role in the process both in the United States and in Europe. Without this linkage between economics, European unity, and Atlantic security and without the support it received from public and private groups on both sides of the Atlantic, early postwar history might have turned out very differently. Although a great deal of progress was made in linking the economic with the political in the Marshall Plan days, a great deal remains to be done today if the disarray among the Western democracies is to be overcome.

For example, several of the economic conditions the Europeans are facing now have major political ramifications and significant implications for transatlantic labor's involvement. First, several key countries are suffering from serious "stagflation" and balance-of-payments difficulties that may become much worse and may even degenerate into major political crises. Italy and Britain are in the worst shape, and France also is in trouble. They are suffering, in one degree or another, from low rates of production, high inflation, and chronic surpluses of imports over exports which, without outside assistance, would make it almost impossible for them to keep paying for the oil and other materials they need to keep their economies functioning.[23] Within these states, the democratic

---

[23]For quarterly economic analyses, see the reports of the Commission of the European Communities, for example, "The Economic Situation in the Community," Directorate General for Economic and Financial Affairs, Brussels, March 1975.

centrist parties have been unable to solve these problems. Their failure has tended to discredit the center and in some instances open the way to extremists who maintain that they have the solutions.

The extent to which American labor can become involved in solving international or foreign economic problems is not at all clear. Except in their support for and role in the Marshall Plan, American labor leaders only rarely have been involved in this type of endeavor. As part of a transatlantic coalition of moderate trade union forces that can coalesce with employers and elements in government, however, they may have new opportunities for nongovernmental influence. Indeed, Irving Brown, reappointed AFL-CIO European representative in 1973, has already spoken of the need for a second (if somewhat different) Marshall Plan and of revitalization of the trade union role in the Organization for European Cooperation and Development (OECD). These actions, he has suggested, may enable labor organizations on both sides of the Atlantic to influence governments and contribute to solving pressing economic problems.[24]

In this regard, a second economic condition is also relevant. Although, as was noted, Europe is no longer completely dependent on the United States, the Western economies in general have grown more interdependent. The American economy is affected by developments in Europe, and vice versa. This interdependence further increases the opportunities for labor, management, and governments on both sides of the Atlantic to influence one another. For example, as a result of the growth of predominantly American-owned multinational companies and banks, Americans are in a position to affect the European economy, particularly developments in the major European states.[25] Although its influence may be limited, to the extent that American labor can affect multinational companies and banks either directly or through the American government, it will be a position to influence European developments. Similarly, to the extent that the AFL-CIO can work with European labor to affect European and American business and Western governments, it will, to some degree, be in a position to affect European affairs. One such approach might involve the passage of an American law that would require American-owned companies to afford similar benefits and collective bargaining rights to all employees of the company irrespective of the nation in which the company is located. This approach would open the door to all sorts of cooperation between European and American unions and could have far-reaching effects on the corporations as well as on the international labor movement.

[24] See the interview with Brown in the French publication, *Intersocial*, no. 2, February 1975.

[25] The full extent of American ownership of control of European industry is unknown. Most estimates place it at around 15 percent, but it is much higher in some countries than others and it is much more extensive in some strategic sectors of the economy. See for example the UN study, *Multinational Corporations in World Development*, ST/ECA 10, New York, 1973.

Although northern European states have largely reestablished a stable political equilibrium since World War II, the balance still remains precarious in the southern half of the Continent. Italy and France still have not created a stable balance because the ruling Christian Democrats in Italy and the succession of centrist and moderate-to-Right governments in France have not solved many of the major economic, social, and civic problems they face. There remains a constant search for a governmental ingredient, or even an alternative to the ruling parties, particularly in periods of economic distress. To obtain this ingredient or alternative, many voters now look to the Communist parties, particularly the large parties in France and Italy, which have not been included in governmental arrangements since 1947. Only the Communist parties seem able to provide an added element of order, stability, and perhaps even industrial productivity. However, bringing the Communists into government would vastly increase Communist strength. Mainly for this reason, it appears, the voters and key governmental and nongovernmental institutions, such as the military and industrial groups, have resisted this step.[26]

But if economic and social problems build up to the point where the moderates appear unable to find solutions, the Communist alternative will become more desirable. This will become increasingly likely if the Communist party appears to be efficient, modern, moderate, and either independent of the Soviet Union or capable of securing Russian friendship and cooperation in the solution of Europe's problems. Although the Communist parties are nowhere nearly as strong in Greece, Portugal, and post-Franco Spain as they are in France and Italy, these countries also are far from stable, and the Communists remain a key force that many observers feel will have to be included in government.

Britain and Germany are much more stable. In Germany, the extremist parties are insignificant electorally and the centrist parties have done reasonably well in solving the major economic and social problems facing the Federal Republic. In Britain, however, although the Communist party is not at all important in electoral politics, it remains an influential, although far from the dominant, force in the labor movement.[27] Moreover, because the major parties have

---

[26]*The Economist* of London frequently reports on local pressures for and against bringing Communists into government in southern Europe. For a detailed discussion of Italy, see the special section in the issue of March 29, 1975. See also Bernard Nossiter, "Italy's Fate Turns on Role of Unions," *Washington Post*, June 23, 1974.

On the "systemic" economic and political crisis that Europe may be facing see Edward Friedland, Paul Seabury, and Aaron Wildavsky, *The Great Détente Disaster* (New York: Basic Books, 1975).

[27]In the last general election (1974), roughly 0.1 percent of union members voted Communist, yet out of 350 executive members in Britain's 13 largest unions, 50 are actually members of the Communist party. *The Economist*, May 24, 1975. On the extent and significance of Communist influence in British unions see the House of Lords debate. *Hansard*, vol. 357, no. 52, February 25, 1975. However, Communist strength has declined considerably in recent elections in one of the most important British unions. See *The Economist*, November 22, 1975.

been unable to solve Britain's most pressing economic problems, the Communists and assorted extreme leftists have been given increased room to maneuver in trade union and Labor party circles.

In these situations, organized labor can either help maintain or undermine stability. In Italy, France, and Britain, for example, organized labor can make life extremely difficult for the democratic parties by exacerbating economic problems. Conversely, by helping to solve political and economic problems, trade unions can help maintain the political balance. Again, to the extent that American labor can work with moderate European unions, develop joint approaches, and build an influential transatlantic coalition that helps to solve current problems, the AFL-CIO will be in a position to affect the political balance in a number of states.

The European labor movement, however, also has changed since the 1940s. In many respects, it is not open to the same kind of influence the AFL exerted in the 1940s; in other respects it is. Unlike during the postwar period, for example, at the present time Europeans in general are not particularly well disposed toward American involvement in their affairs. Not only has the glow of wartime cooperation worn off, but also American involvement is no longer considered as essential, and, in many parts of the Continent, there is obviously a mild form of nationalistic reaction toward things American. Europeans still seem to be interested in the nonpartisan and nonpolitical style of collective bargaining that characterizes the American labor movement, but they still are tied in one degree or another to political parties. This sometimes makes it more difficult for American labor to interact with them. The AFL-CIO, for example, is not constrained by the interests of a political party such as the German SPD, which may want to use the labor movement to promote its foreign policy aims. Furthermore, noncommunist unions in Germany, France, and Italy now are more or less self-sustaining national organizations. In contrast to the way they were during the early postwar period, they are not dependent on external sources of financial or moral support. They are also much more self-confident, and some of them play a greater role in their national life than they did 30 years ago.[28] These factors have also tended to reduce the ability of an external actor to influence them.

Although there have been changes, in many ways industrial relations, particularly in the Mediterranean countries, have not made much progress. Although the use of collective bargaining, shop stewards, and, to some extent, dues paying has increased in Southern Europe, the Southern European labor movement remains underdeveloped when compared with the strength and services of trade

[28]See for example Solomon Barkin, ed., *Worker Militancy and Its Consequences, 1965–1975* (New York: Praeger Special Studies, 1975); Kendall, op. cit.; the symposium on unions and political parties which discusses the strength and self confidence in the European labor movement in two issues of *Industrial and Labor Relations Review*, October 1974 and January 1975.

unions in Germany and in the United States. In this situation, external labor centers still have an opportunity to influence the still emerging movements in Southern Europe.[29]

In France, for example, within the structure of the existing broad industrial unions, it might be possible to create special sections based on skill differentiation, if not American-style craft unions. The current building trade organizations in France or Italy provide very little by way of employment services and technical training for their members. If American unions were to establish union-to-union programs with their French and perhaps Italian counterparts and assist in setting up these services and training programs, they might very well be able to influence the future organization of segments of the labor movement in these countries.

For example, approximately 1.5 million, or about 20 percent, of French industrial workers are employed in the construction industry. About 10 percent of the construction workers are unionized. FO officials maintain that the CGT has attracted 50 percent of this membership and has at least eight full-time officials in Paris and four regional organizers. FO has over 25 percent of the unionized construction workers, but because of this limited membership and because dues paying is still rare, it has a small staff—four full-time officials in Paris and four in the provinces.

If FO were to secure American labor's financial and technical support for five years and used these resources to train and provide technical services for skilled building trades workers, it might very well produce a breakthrough in the trade union organization of the French construction industry—as well as increase productivity in France. For example, although there are about 10,000 cranes and other pieces of heavy equipment in France, only about 2,000 people have the skills necessary to utilize these machines effectively. An FO vocational training program (perhaps run in cooperation with the employers), a journal to keep qualified workers up to date on new techniques, construction codes, and various other services would probably attract thousands of additional workers to FO. Once they were organized and trained, they would be expected to pay dues, and if they continued to receive services and increases in pay as a result of their training and increases in productivity, a strong section of the construction industry, roughly equivalent to the Operating Engineers in the United States, could be built up. This section, by virtue of its strategic role in the industry and strength as a union, would become the master of the work place. As a result, it would be in a position to organize less skilled segments of the industry as well as other industries where skills involving heavy equipment are in demand, for example, the docks.

[29]Ibid. For a discussion of French efforts to find new forms of trade unionism see also Lucien Rioux, *Clefs pour le Syndicalisme* (Paris: Seghers, 1972) and Jean Daniel Reynaud, *Les Syndicats en France* (Paris: Seuil, 1975), vol. I.

Finally, the state of European morale may not be as important as it was in the reconstruction period after World War II, but it still may be significant. European trade unionists, like many European and United States officials, must be wondering about the future. If they perceive that the United States and American labor are abandoning them, they may decide that although Europe is reasonably strong economically, it will not be able to transfer its economic strength into political and military might. Instead, they may decide to make their accommodations with what they perceive to be the dominant forces in their region—the Soviet Union and its Western European political and trade union allies. American labor not only may be able to help prevent this by encouraging the United States government to remain involved, but also may itself be able to affect European affairs by providing moral support to those in need of it.

OPENNESS TO AMERICAN INVOLVEMENT

The active encouragement of American involvement by European trade unionists was another factor—the fourth precondition—that enabled American labor to play a role after World War II. Thirty years later, the Europeans are still encouraging American labor to remain involved, although once again several of the major labor centers in Europe and the AFL-CIO differ over preferred types of cooperation. Among the most fervent advocates of American involvement are the revived and powerful German DGB, the British TUC, the French FO, and major elements in the Italian UIL and sections of the CISL. Specifically, they want communication and contact with the AFL-CIO. With the exception of FO, however, they do not want a repetition of the anticommunist campaign of the early postwar period. Rather they want American labor to work with them in a number of ways—dealing with problems posed by the emergence of multinational businesses and the interdependent global economy; helping to maintain the United States commitment to Europe; serving as a counterweight, in international and national forums, to Russian and European Communist labor organizations; and, in general, acting as an anchor in the unsettled economic, political, and military relationships that characterize the Atlantic world.

The AFL-CIO, however, looks with dismay on what it views as European labor's tolerance of Russian repression, its admission of Communists into its ranks, and the role it is playing in the erosion of Western defense efforts.[30] In this respect the cycle has turned 360 degrees. American labor is again warning its European counterparts about the dangers posed by the Soviet Union and

---

[30] For a brief overview of contemporary AFL-CIO policy see this writer's "American Labor's Continuing Involvement in World Affairs," *Orbis*, Spring 1975. For more detailed accounts of AFL-CIO perceptions and policy resolutions see the monthly AFL-CIO *Free Trade Unions News*.

Western European Communists. The major trade union centers, much as they were after World War II, are not impressed by the warnings. The Europeans also want the AFL-CIO to participate in various international labor bodies, and some of them want American unions involved in organizational activities in a number of states. The AFL-CIO, however, has withdrawn from the ICFTU mainly but not exclusively on the grounds that the Europeans, while paying lip service to the principles of free trade unionism, are fraternizing more and more with Communist unions and thus negating the purpose of the organization. AFL-CIO unions have stepped up their activities in the ITS. In contrast to the early postwar period, when only a few AFL-CIO unions were affiliated with their respective secretariats, today over half of the AFL-CIO's 110 unions are affiliated. However, if the ITS accept Communist membership to any significant degree, as some Europeans are proposing, American withdrawal can be anticipated. Similarly, if Communist labor organizations and their allies in the Third World continue to use the ILO for overtly political purposes, the AFL-CIO and the United States government may very well follow through on their threat to withdraw.[31]

Thus, although the Europeans may want contacts with the AFL-CIO and its participation in various international bodies, the major concerns of the two groups are not identical at the moment. In these circumstances, it would be difficult for the AFL-CIO to be effective in pursuit of its policy objectives.

AFL-CIO presence and diplomacy may, however, over a period of time, be influential in altering the perspectives or constraining the choices of the European labor leadership. If the Europeans have little or no contact with the AFL-CIO, they are not likely to find their own views challenged. Communication and debate with the AFL-CIO conceivably may begin to alter their perspectives of Russian policy and in the long run may lead them to be more cautious in their dealings with Russian labor and Western European Communists. In this way, the AFL-CIO may be effective in the future. Moreover, the Europeans seem quite anxious to meet with AFL-CIO leaders to discuss interdependence and mutual economic and social problems. These conferences could very well open the door to new kinds of American labor involvement in Europe, although cooperation on economic matters will not necessarily lead to a joint policy toward the Russians.

The extent to which the Europeans want American labor involved in various organizational initiatives is uncertain. Certainly few, if any, elements in the German DGB and the British TUC see any great need for the AFL-CIO to be involved in their countries. However, some Germans and some elements in the TUC privately may value AFL-CIO efforts to help prevent the unification of Communist and noncommunist organizations in Italy and Communist domina-

[31] On AFL-CIO support for official notification of United States withdrawal from the ILO see the statement by the AFL-CIO Executive Council on the International Labor Organization, July 30, 1975.

tion of organized labor in other Southern European countries. They also might wish to see further AFL-CIO support or assistance to FO. Although some elements in FO, the CISL, and the UIL probably would object to AFL-CIO efforts to bolster their organizations or build new ones if the noncommunist and Communist organizations were merged, significant labor leaders in France, Italy, and elsewhere in Southern Europe would probably welcome this assistance, depending upon how it was given.

Although a number of FO leaders probably would not wish to see any basic change in the size or structure of their organization and others would not want American labor's assistance, many of the younger FO leaders favor greater American involvement. In Italy, a group in the CISL already is opposed to the merger with the CGIL, and the UIL also is opposed. If the merger does take place and there is a split in the CISL, it would not be unreasonable for many, if not all of those opposed to the Communists to work closely with the AFL-CIO. Similarly, it would not be unreasonable to expect a number of Portuguese, Greeks, and Spaniards who are trying to build democratic labor organizations in the face of both hostile governments and Communists to turn to the AFL-CIO for support.

In sum, while there are major differences between the dominant group of Europeans and the Americans on the degree of hostility that should be shown to the Soviet Union and Communist elements in Europe, the Europeans continue to welcome American involvement in other matters. Unless there is a fundamental shift in the thinking of Europeans, particularly in Germany and Britain, there is little likelihood that the AFL-CIO can be effective in mounting any kind of sustained and effective anticommunist drive in the international labor movement or in Northern Europe. Over a period of time, however, through dialogue the AFL-CIO may be able to affect the views of the Europeans, and joint actions may enable American labor to affect the development of joint policies to deal with the pressing problems of interdependence and economic growth and, beyond that, the evolution of the labor movement in Southern Europe.

GOVERNMENTAL ENCOURAGEMENT

A fifth factor that enabled the American nongovernmental actor to play a role in postwar European affairs was the toleration and, later, the encouragement of the European and United States governments. In Northern Europe, France, and Italy, there are today no governmental obstacles to AFL-CIO involvement. Although AFL-CIO's views on Russian policy and the proper Western response differ considerably from those of the United States and most European governments, there is little to prevent the AFL-CIO from propagating its views and trying to build support for its position in most European countries. In Portugal, Spain, and perhaps Greece, however, this may be another matter. The governments of these countries are sensitive about efforts to organize trade unionists.

Nevertheless, even if it could not operate directly within these countries, the

AFL-CIO could seek to affect developments there by supporting trade union educational programs and activities among the millions of migratory workers from these countries who temporarily reside in Northern Europe. With AFL-CIO assistance, hundreds of organizers could be trained so that when they returned to their native lands, they would be in a position to bolster the democratic labor movement. In addition, after they returned to their homes, they could also receive Western assistance either directly or through trade secretariats. For years the American and European labor movements have been supporting even the clandestine activities conducted by underground labor groups in Spain for example.[32]

Although the European and United States governments, because of their policy of détente with the Soviet Union, are unlikely to encourage anticommunist AFL-CIO and European activities in Northern Europe, they appear willing to help trade union leaders on both sides of the Atlantic get together to discuss matters of mutual interest.[33] If a transatlantic labor coalition develops, it would not be surprising if the Atlantic governments facilitated and even cooperated in its work.

The German and United States governments reportedly are also concerned about the increasing influence of Moscow-oriented Communists in Southern Europe at least, and they might be expected to assist efforts to organize noncommunist trade unionists there. To the extent that they are willing to help finance trade union activities, they are likely to increase the effectiveness of the nongovernmental transatlantic labor coalition, although much will depend upon how this assistance is handled.

THE AFL-CIO TODAY

Finally, the AFL was able to affect postwar world politics because its leadership was highly motivated and the Federation was able to mobilize significant human and material resources. Today the broad strands of AFL-CIO policy and the general perspectives of the leadership are unchanged.[34] However, there are several differences between the postwar AFL and the present AFL-CIO. For one thing, AFL-CIO President Meany, who has become principal policy maker, is skeptical about what can be achieved on the political front in Europe. As Meany sees it, the Europeans have forgotten the lessons of the early postwar period and are too preoccupied with accommodating themselves to the Russians and Euro-

---

[32]On AFL-CIO and European views and activities pertaining to Spain see this writer's "The International Confederation of Free Trade Unions and Spanish Politics" (M.A. thesis, Columbia University, 1967).

[33]Both the German and United States governments are directly and indirectly financing travel and meetings between union leaders on both sides of the Atlantic.

[34]Godson, "American Labor's Continuing Involvement in World Affairs."

pean Communists.[35] Presumably with this in mind, the AFL-CIO has been reluctant to invest large amounts of material resources in propagating its views and trying to win the support of key European centers for a policy the Europeans adhered to in the late 1940s and 1950s. The AFL-CIO itself has also been reluctant to involve itself in a major way in Southern Europe. This is not for lack of human resources. Indeed, Irving Brown still is a dynamic organizer, working six days a week, writing, traveling, speaking throughout the Continent. Undoubtedly the AFL-CIO could find other younger, if not as experienced, organizers. Nevertheless, for the moment at least, the present AFL-CIO, unlike the AFL in the early postwar period, is unwilling to mobilize a large number of skilled organizers and provide them with the moral and material resources that might make a difference in Europe.

The only area in which the AFL-CIO has shown some willingness to become more involved is that of economic problems and interdependence. Although relatively little has been achieved so far, more American involvement is likely in the future. Irving Brown's appeal for a second Marshall Plan has already been noted. AFL-CIO leaders and staffers have been attending more international conferences and meetings. It remains to be seen, however, whether the AFL-CIO will become seriously involved in a grand coalition of labor and political groups that can affect developments in Europe and perhaps also European-American relations.

In sum, there are important similarities and there are equally important differences between the conditions that existed at the end of World War II and the current situation. These similarities and differences make it difficult to judge whether the AFL-CIO can be an effective actor today. Certainly some factors—such as the significance of Europe, Russian interest in using organized labor to increase its power, new opportunities arising from the interdependence of the Atlantic world, and several other economic, political, and trade union conditions—suggest that it can. Other indications that the American nongovernmental organization can be influential include the interest of many European labor leaders in AFL-CIO involvement, the toleration and possibly the encouragement of several Atlantic governments, as well as the unchanged AFL-CIO policy and ability to mobilize significant resources. However, the greater complexity of relationships in the international Communist movement and the reduced aggressiveness of Russian tactics, the increased stability in Western Europe, and the reconstructed noncommunist labor movement make it much more difficult for the

---

[35]Meany has said that the Europeans, after fraternizing with the Communists for several years, will relearn the lessons of the early postwar period. "Address to the American Labor and International Affairs Course," AFL-CIO Labor Studies Center, Washington, D.C., April 22, 1974. Similarly, asked whether the AFL-CIO intended to rejoin the ICFTU, Meany answered in the negative. "Those fellows [the West's labor leaders] will soon get a bellyful of the communists anyway," as quoted in Lester Velie, "The Soviet Design for Free World Labor," *Reader's Digest*, June 1975, p. 111.

AFL-CIO to be effective. When these conditions are coupled with the anti-anti-communist impulses in the European labor movement, the negative reaction to things American, and the AFL-CIO president's views that little can be achieved unless there is a change in the thinking of the Europeans, it is far from clear that the AFL-CIO will significantly affect European politics in the foreseeable future. If, however, there should be a change in these negative factors—if, for example, the Russians become overtly more aggressive and there is a change in European attitudes, or if the AFL-CIO steps up its efforts at coalition building around other issues—American labor again may very well be able to play a significant role.

Thus, while this case study has demonstrated that an American nongovernmental organization was able to affect world affairs and that the subject of nongovernmental, particularly labor, organizations merits our attention, it has also sought to show that there are limits to this type of influence. Much more attention must be given to the subject and many more empirical studies must be undertaken, however, if we are to determine under what precise conditions and in what precise ways labor and other nongovernmental organizations can affect public affairs.

Archival Documentation

Although there are gaps in the AFL's archival materials, most, if not all, relevant records are available for scholarly perusal.

The archives that pertain to this study can be divided into two parts. The first part consists of the official papers of William Green, the early postwar AFL president, and other files relating to the work of the ILRC. These materials are available at the main AFL-CIO office in Washington, D.C. (A microfilm version is housed at the University of Wisconsin, Madison.) It should be noted that these records appeared incomplete. Sometimes there were no written materials in the files even when other archival material suggested that there should be written exchanges with Green and his immediate staff.

This writer was denied access to the AFL Executive Council minutes, but this does not seem to have been a serious limitation. The noted labor historian, Philip Taft, who extensively examined these minutes, informed this writer that they were in such summary form as to reveal little that could not be ascertained from the public record.

The second part of the AFL archives consists of the files of the FTUC. This writer was the first systematically to examine the records of this crucial foreign policy-making body. During the time that this examination took place, the FTUC files were housed in a warehouse in New York City. These records appeared to be almost complete, particularly for the period after 1946, when Jay Lovestone became executive secretary of the committee.

It should be noted, however, that the private papers of key AFL policy makers were unavailable. Among the most significant were those of Matthew Woll and David Dubinsky. Woll's papers appear to have been destroyed, and Dubinsky was utilizing his materials to complete an autobiography. However, although there were some limitations, there were no serious impediments to the study of American labor's policy.

The opposite was the case in Europe. Most European labor organizations will not permit independent scholars to examine their contemporary archives. This, of course, made it impossible to document with precision internal developments in the CGT and FO during the period of this study, although as mentioned in the Introduction, a number of French trade unionists who were interviewed supplied the writer with letters and documents from their personal papers to substantiate their accounts of postwar events. Wherever possible, these materials are cited in footnotes.

Unfortunately, in spite of the Freedom of Information Act and the assistance of archival officials, it was impossible to obtain access to substantial bodies of relevant official United States materials. Although a number of heretofore classified State Department, War Department, and Central Intelligence Agency materials have been studied and in some cases used in the text and footnotes, other significant materials on United States perceptions and activities are unavailable. Precisely why this is so is not completely clear.

Purportedly, almost all classified materials 30 years old or older and State Department material at least through 1947 are supposed to be available to the public. Indeed, a number of scholars, particularly revisionists such as Gabriel Kolko and Gar Alperowitz, refer to recently released government records in such a way that one might be led to believe that almost all relevant material about United States government perceptions and activities concerning Europe and the Soviet Union is available. This, however, is not the case.

The files relating to activities of the major United States intelligence services at the end of the war and in the early postwar period simply are not available for public scrutiny. The relevant files of the OSS; its operational successor, the War Department's Strategic Services Unit; and the Central Intelligence Group in the Executive Office of the President, all of which had major responsibilities for providing the Executive Branch with information on Russian policy and political conditions in Europe from 1945 until the establishment of the CIA in late 1947, now are supposed to be in the hands of the CIA. For 18 months this writer sought access to these materials. At his request, the CIA undertook a search of these files to ascertain if there were any materials pertaining to the subject of this study which could be declassified partially or completely. After an exchange of numerous letters and several conversations with those responsible for the search, the CIA did provide the author with a small number of declassified or sanitized documents, but it has been unable to find and/or declassify additional materials.

In a letter to this writer, the Agency has maintained that, for cost reasons, materials from the 1940s were not included in what it called "more advanced systems of information storage and retrieval," and thus the Agency was forced to search the old records "with limited archival indices and searching aids, and without the institutional memory that smoothed the workings of the organization of an earlier day." This problem was compounded, it maintained, by "the rather haphazard pattern of records disposition at the end of the war. The dissolution of the OSS was part of a much broader demobilization of our armed forces with all too little thought given to the desires and needs of the Professor Godsons of a later day. In fact we know now that some OSS personnel must have felt that OSS papers were part of their personal papers and took them with them into civilian life for reasons known only to themselves."

The Agency also implied that at the end of the war, little attention may have been paid to Russian intentions and interests in European labor. "The OSS was very much a part of the armed forces sharing the common goal of winning the war—the enemy being the Axis powers. The problem and potential threat represented by the Russians were not overlooked, but the overriding concern was intelligence on the immediate enemy so that the war could be shortened and the new postwar patterns of international relations effectuated."

Also under the Freedom of Information Act, the Agency found and either declassified or sanitized a small number of CIA and State Department documents that pertained to developments in the European labor movement for 1947 to 1952, the remaining years of the study. Clearly, however, the major part of the record was not made available.

The early postwar records of the State Department, which are supposed to be open to the public, also are neither complete nor completely accessible. This became apparent when an effort was made to examine the records of various sections of the Department of State. For example, an effort was made to examine the files of EUR-X, a small but significant section that was concerned with postwar labor activities in Europe and also was in contact with American unions. Inquiries at the National Archives in Washington revealed almost nothing about the existence of EUR-X or the location of its records. Based on interviews conducted during the course of the study, the writer ascertained that EUR-X was created in the 1930s to study the international Communist movement. It was a small section headed by Raymond Murphy, who kept voluminous files, prepared reports for senior State Department officials, and may have engaged in some operational activities in Europe. Just what happened to the files and reports of EUR-X no one seems to know.

Moreover, scholars are not permitted to peruse the State Department records held in the National Archives. They must inform the archivist what precisely they are looking for, and then they are given the materials the archivist believes pertains to the request. If the scholar cannot identify with precision the materials he is searching for or if the archivist decides that there are few relevant records, that is, so to speak, the end of the line.

In sum, while the records in the National Archives and the available declassified and sanitized documents were useful, they were far from sufficient to permit the systematic and comprehensive study of United States perceptions, let alone Unites States policy, in the closing months of World War II and the early postwar period. This, of course, limits the conclusions drawn in this study. It also affects other studies dealing with United States policy during this period.

It should also be pointed out that it was impossible to obtain access to *any* of the relevant files of the Russian or key European governments—perhaps an even more serious limitation for those interested in nongovernmental organizations and world politics.

Interviewees and Date and Place of Interviews

Marcel Babeau
Former Secrétaire, Union Départmentale, Bouches-du-Rhône, FO

Marseilles, France
9 July 1968

Michel Barbat
Secrétaire, Union Départmentale, Puy-de-Dôme, FO

Clermont-Ferrand, France
11 July 1968

Jean Baylot
Former Préfet Bouches-du-Rhône and Préfet de Police, Paris

Paris, France
24 December 1968

Omer Becu
Former President, ITF

Paris, France
17 July 1968

Roger Blanckaert
Secrétaire du Cartel Artisanal de la Batellerie

Lille, France
29 June 1968

Abraham Bluestein
Former Executive Director, Labor League for Human
Rights and first secretary of the FTUC

New York, N.Y.
24 February 1968

Jean Bocher
Former Secrétaire, Fédération de la Marine Marchande,
FO

Cherbourg, France
1 July 1968

Gondecourt Bradfer
Former Secrétaire (adjoint), Fédération des Mineurs,
FO

Paris, France
17 July 1968

Irving Brown
Former FTUC representative in Europe

25 December 1967
23 February 1968
24 June 1968
18 July 1968
31 August 1968
2 November 1968
26 December 1968
29 December 1970

Jefferson Caffery
Former United States Ambassador to France

Rome, Italy
23 December 1968

James Carey
Former Secretary-Treasurer, CIO

Washington, D.C.
13 September 1968

Jules Carpentier
Former Secrétaire Union Départmentale, Pas-de-
Calais, FO

Lens, France
28 June 1968

Oscar Catenne
Former militant, Fédération des Mineurs, FO

Lens, France
29 June 1968

Georges Delamarre
Former Secrétaire, Fédération des Métaux, FO

Beaumont sur-
Oise, France
17 December 1968

David Dubinsky
Former President, ILGWU

New York, N.Y.
14, 15 June 1968

Jean Duniau   Paris, France
Former official, Fédération des Ports et Docks,   21 June 1968
Bordeaux FO

Leon Faburé   Lens, France
Former Secrétaire, Syndicat des Mineurs, Dourgls, FO   29 June 1968

Pierre Felce   Paris, France
Secrétaire, Fédération des Transports, FO   25 June 1968

Benoît Frachon   Paris, France
Former Secrétaire Général, CGT   27 December 1968

Raymond Froideval   Paris, France
Former Editor, *Air Terre, Mer* (publication of the   16 July 1968
Mediterranean Committee)

Claude Harmel   Paris, France
Editor, *Les Études Sociales et Syndicales*   26 June 1968
                                                         16 December 1968

Averell Harriman   Washington, D.C.
Former Administrator, ERP   10 May 1969

George Harrison   Cincinnati, Ohio
Former Vice-President, AFL   2 November 1967

Alexandre Hebert   Nantes, France
Former member, Résistance Ouvrière   2 July 1968

Daniel Horowitz   Washington, D.C.
Former Labor Adviser, European Affairs, U.S. De-   28 November 1968
partment of State

Louis Johnson   New York, N.Y.
Former Publicity Director, Labor League for Human   14 June 1968
Rights

Madame (Léon) Jouhaux   Paris, France
Wife of former Secrétaire Générale of CGT and   17 July 1968
CGT-FO

Jean H. Laffont
Former Secrétaire, Fédération des Métaux, Gironde, FO

Bordeaux, France
4 July 1968

Harry Lang
Former Editor, *Jewish Daily Forward*

New York, N.Y.
15 June 1968

Roger Lapeyre
Secrétaire, Fédération des Travaux Publics et Transports, FO

Paris, France
16, 21 June 1968

Antoine Laval
Former Secrétaire, Union Locale, FO

La Cordiere, France
8 July 1968

Auguste Lecoeur
Former Secrétaire, Fédération des Mineurs, CGT

Paris, France
20 June 1968

Roger Lerda
Former Secrétaire, Union Départmentale, Bouches-du-Rhône, FO

Marseilles, France
6 July 1968

Georges Levard
Former Secrétaire Général, Confédération Française des Travailleurs Chrétiens

Paris, France
16 December 1968

Lucien L'Honorey
Former Secrétaire, Fédération des Marins, FO

Le Havre, France
30 June 1968

Jay Lovestone
Former Secretary, FTUC

New York, N.Y.
11 November 1967
31 March 1968
29 April 1969

Roger Magail
Former official, Mediterranean Committee

Paris, France
25 June 1968

Pierre Magnier
Former Secrétaire, Fédération des Livres, FO

Paris, France
21 June 1968

Daniel Mayer
Former Minister of Labor, France

Paris, France
19 December 1968

George Meany
Former Secretary-Treasurer, AFL

Washington, D.C.
28 November 1968

Maurice Mercier
Secrétaire, Fédération des Textiles, FO

Paris, France
18 December 1968

Jules Moch
Former Minister of the Interior, France

Paris, France
26 December 1968

Camille Mourgès
Former Secrétaire, Fédération des PTT, FO

Paris, France
19 June 1968

J. H. Oldenbroek
Former President, ITF and former Secretary-General
of the ICFTU

Dover, England
31 December 1968

Jean Philips
Former Secrétaire, Fédération des Officers des Marins,
FO

Paris, France
18 December 1968

Georges Piquemal
Former Secrétaire, Fédération des Ports et Docks, FO

Bordeaux, France
4 July 1968

Paul Porter
Former Assistant and later Chief Administrator,
ERP

Washington, D.C.
16 April 1968

Frank Rosenblum
Former Vice-President, Amalgamated Clothing Workers of American and Vice-President, CIO

New York, N.Y.
3 September 1968

René Schwob
Secrétaire, Union Départmentale, Moselle, FO

Metz, France
14 July 1968

Boris Shishkin
Former Labor Adviser to ERP Administrator Harriman

Washington, D.C.
15 April 1968

Arnold Steinbach
Formerly Manpower Division, U.S. Army, Europe

Washington, D.C.
9 September 1968

René Tainon
Secrétaire, Fédération des Spectacles, FO

Paris, France
26 June 1968

Vincent Tewson
Former General Secretary, TUC

Barnet, England
2 January 1969

Urbain Thevenon
Former Editor, *Révolution Prolétarrienne*

Vagnas, France
10 July 1968

David Saposs
Former Section Chief, Manpower Division, U.S. Army, Germany

Washington, D.C.
4 May 1968

Roger Vaillant
Former Secrétaire, Union Départmentale, Loire-Atlantique, FO

Nantes, France
2 July 1968

Paul Vignaux
Former wartime liaison between the French resistance movement and the Labor League for Human Rights

Paris, France
25 June 1968

Michel Urbaniak
Former militant, Fédération des Mineurs, FO

Lens, France
29 June 1968

Charles Zimmerman
Vice-President, ILGWU

New York, N.Y.
30 September 1968

U.S. Intelligence Reports

(Note: in chronological order not numbered)

QUARTERS DETACHMENT
th REGT. OSS (Prov)
APO 512, U.S. ARMY
Italian S.I.

Subject: DOCUMENT: COPY OF INSTRUCTIONS TO RUSSIAN AGENTS ON
           COMMUNIST PROPAGANDA AND ACTIVITY.

November 6, 1944

(This document covers instructions to the Russian
Labor Delegation on propaganda for Italy a ttached
to the memorandum given the Delegation by the Soviet Government. See reports #JR-1156, summary of
master memorandum, #JR-1177 and #JR-1178 relative
to this memorandum.)

DIRECTIVES FOR COMMUNIST PROPAGANDA IN ITALY

Contacts of Soviet Delegates charged with communist propaganda in Italy.

Constant contact must be kept. The meetings will take place in
the headquarters of the Communist party and in the residence of Delegates Beliuk and Sirmiov.

Beliuk may receive a Communist party delegate also in the Russian
Embassy, now occupied by the Russian military mission.

Decisions to be taken with the Executive Committee of the Communist
party will always be referred by the Soviet Delegates to a Delegate which the Soviet government will assign to Rome permanently.

For the time being, the Soviet delegates Beliuk and Sirmiov will
only have simple contacts with Velio Spano, editor of the communist
organ L'Unita'.

Direct contacts with Italian communist groups.

These contacts of the Soviet government, through its delegates, will
only take place with those groups located in provinces where positive communist activity is in progress, viz., at the present, t
the groups of

Viterbo	Bagnoli
Isola Liri	Civitavecchia
Terni	Livorno

Declassified by 006687
date 7 MAR 1975

The Soviet Delegates, in accord with a representative of the Communist party, will direct propaganda mainly toward the youth
sections. In newly formed feminine sections no propaganda is to
be carried out. Only activities of these sections will be reported
on. In this connection it must be remembered that the Communist
movement in liberated Italy finds a serious obstacle in the Christian
Democratic party, especially in the rural districts, where
communist propaganda is still weak among the male population, and finds a fundamental opposition among women. In
cities, the feminine movement will find good ground only
in the outskirts, where workers' sections are mainly located.

COMMUNIST HEADQUARTERS

In liberated Italy there are 5 communist headquarters
controlled by Soviet delegates:

1. <u>CATANIA</u>: Catania is entrusted to the Sicilian section
           of the Communist party and it has a program
of agricultural propaganda. In this city the Chamber of Labor is completely communist. It is organizing a Communist U-
nion of the citrus fruit industry.

2. <u>NAPLES</u>: Naples is entrusted to the Naples Communist section.
           It is active exclusively in the workers' field
especially in the ports and in the industrial section of Ba-
gnoli.

3. <u>TARANTO</u>: Taranto is entrusted to the local Communist
           section and it has a strictly workers' program
(Sections of the Navy Yard and of the port).

4. CIVITAVECCHIA AND 5., These two sections are combined into
   <u>TERRANOVA PAUSANIA</u>: one, but carry on separate activities.
                      Civitavecchia for the newly formed
section of port workers, Terranova Pausania for the mass of
workers in the coal mines of Monteponi and for the organization,
which is rather difficult, of Sardinian shepherds. About to
be formed are two headquarters at Pisa and Florence.

PRESS OFFICE.

Delegate Sirmiov has as a co-worker for propaganda Mr. Battistoni,
who, however, is not officially assigned to this service. He is
waiting to work for Tass as soon as this news Agency begins operations. In addition Sirmiov has with him two Italian agents.
They are:

   <u>Ferrari</u> - the son of former communist deputy Ferrari,
   exiled to Russia in 1919.

   In 1920, when he was 14, he was hired as an usher
   at the Russian Embassy in via Gaeta. Ambassador
   Kamereff brought him to Russia, from whence he has
   now returned as Sirmiov's collaborator. He knows
   Russian well and is also an interpreter for the Russian military Mission. Lives at the Embassy in Via
   Gaeta.

   <u>Alessandra</u> Montagna. - (Sister of Battistoni's mistress).
   Writes for L'Unita', which publishes in its second
   page articles of Russian propaganda under the alias
   "Rita Montagnana" (1)

----

(1) She may be Rita Togliatti, consort of the Italian
communist leader. She has been writing under the
name Rita Montagnana. The name Alessandra Montagna
is not known to us.

****

HEADQUARTERS DETACHMENT
2677th REGT. OSS(Prov)
APO 512   U.S. ARMY
ITALIAN DIVISION, SI, MEDTO

Subject: SOVIET EMBASSY ENLARGED BY ADDITIONAL 60 PARTY
WORKERS, ORGANIZERS AND TECHNICIANS.

---

24 November 1944

1. Sixty new members of the Soviet Embassy to Italy have
    arrived in Rome. They are not effective diplomats but
    almost exclusively Communist party workers, men and wo-
    men propagandists, organizers, reporters and technicians.
    In addition women with officer rank are also reported to
    have arrived in Rome. They are charged with carrying on
    Communist activity and with organizing new Communist sec-
    tions in Italy.

2. A group of Soviet propagandists (men and women) left
    Rome for Taranto on 7 November. Their Chief was a Russian
    woman with the rank of Captain. This woman is described
    as extraordinarily clever and possessing a perfect know-
    ledge of Italian.

There's another on Taranto

P&0 091 *Italy* T.S.

Director of Plans and Operations,
Department of the Army

FW # 3/5

TOP SECRET

NSC 1/2

COPY NO. 10

Revised 17 March

A REPORT

TO THE

NATIONAL SECURITY COUNCIL

by

THE EXECUTIVE SECRETARY

on

THE POSITION OF THE UNITED STATES WITH RESPECT TO ITALY

February 10, 1948

WASHINGTON

TOP SECRET

NSC 1/2   ~~TOP SECRET~~

February 10, 1948

NOTE BY THE EXECUTIVE SECRETARY

to the

NATIONAL SECURITY COUNCIL

on

<u>THE POSITION OF THE UNITED STATES WITH RESPECT TO ITALY</u>
Reference: NSC 1/1

   In approving NSC 1/1, the National Security Council
agreed that this report should be revised no less than 45 days
before the elections in Italy in the light of the political
situation existing at that time.

   Accordingly, the enclosed revision of NSC 1/1 has
been prepared by the National Security Council Staff with the
advice and assistance of representatives of the Departments
of State, the Army, the Navy, and the Air Force, and of the
Central Intelligence Agency.

   The enclosed report is submitted for consideration
by the National Security Council at its next meeting. It is
proposed that this report as adopted by the Council be submitted to the President with the recommendation that he approve
the conclusions contained therein and direct that they be implemented by all appropriate Executive Departments and Agencies
of the U. S. Government under the coordination of the Secretary
of State.

                 SIDNEY W. SOUERS
                 Executive Secretary

Distribution:
   The Secretary of State
   The Secretary of Defense
   The Secretary of the Army
   The Secretary of the Navy
   The Secretary of the Air Force
   The Chairman, National Security
    Resources Board

NSC 1/2   ~~TOP SECRET~~

D R A F T

February 10, 1948

REPORT BY THE NATIONAL SECURITY COUNCIL

on

THE POSITION OF THE UNITED STATES WITH RESPECT TO ITALY

THE PROBLEM

1.   To assess and appraise the position of the United
States with respect to Italy, taking into consideration the
security interests of the United States in the Mediterranean
and Near East Areas.

ANALYSIS

2.   The basic objective of the United States in Italy
is to establish and maintain in that key country conditions
favorable to our national security. Current US policies toward Italy include measures intended to preserve Italy as an
independent, democratic state, friendly to the United States,
and capable of effective participation in the resistance to
Communist expansion.

3.   The National Security Council has concurred in the
following:

> "...The security of the Eastern Mediterranean and
> of the Middle East is vital to the security of the
> United States. ...The security of the whole East-
> ern Mediterranean and Middle East would be jeopard-
> ized if the Soviet Union should succeed in its ef-
> forts to obtain control of any one of the following

countries: Italy, Greece, Turkey, or Iran. In view
of the foregoing, it should be the policy of the
United States, in accordance with the principles and
in the spirit of the Charter of the United Nations,
to support the security of the Eastern Mediterranean
and the Middle East. As a corollary of this policy
the United States should assist in maintaining the
territorial integrity and political independence of
Italy, Greece, Turkey, and Iran. In carrying out
this policy the United States should be prepared to
make full use of its political, economic, and if
necessary, military power in such manner as may be
found most effective. ...It would be unrealistic
for the United States to undertake to carry out such
a policy unless the British maintain their strong
strategic political and economic position in the
Middle East and Eastern Mediterranean, and unless
they and ourselves follow parallel policies in that
area...."

4.   The majority of the Italian people and the present
Government of Italy are ideologically inclined toward the
Western democracies, friendly to the United States and conscious
of the fact that US aid is vital to Italian recovery. The
Government is now under strong and persistent Communist attack
aimed ultimately at the creation of a Communist dictatorship
subservient to Moscow. The political position of the Communist

party is stronger in Italy than in any other country outside
the Soviet orbit. This strength stems primarily from the
prevailing economic distress which is conducive to agitation
and unrest, and secondarily from Communist success in obtaining election support from other left-wing parties through
formation of a "People's Bloc."

     5.   The current Communist campaign of strikes and politi-
cal agitation appears to be the preliminary phase of a major
effort to take over the Government either by winning the national elections now scheduled for April, by use of the general
strike to create chaos, or by armed insurrection. However, the
Communists will probably not resort to the general strike or
armed insurrection until the elections are over, possibly not
until the US Congress has acted on the European Recovery Program. If ERP is not implemented before expiration of US interim aid on March 31, or if rations are further reduced, the
"People's Bloc" will be stronger in the April elections and
may win participation in the government. If the Communists
fail to gain admission to the government and if ERP is implemented, the Kremlin may then order armed insurrection in a
final effort to prevent Italian recovery under a Western-orient-
ed regime.

     At present a Rightist threat to democratic govern-
ment in Italy is too remote to require consideration.

     6.   The Italian armed forces, although numerically ade-
quate, require additional modern equipment in order to enhance

NSC 1/2   - 3 -

August 12, 1949

POSSIBLE COMINFORM STRIKE ACTION AMONG
DOCK WORKERS OF THE WORLD

1. The Embassy recently transmitted to the Department a
despatch (No. 954 of July 19, 1949) on the Second World Congress of the
WFTU. This despatch stated in part –

"Undoubtedly one of the most important, if not the
most important, accomplishment of the Congress was the
work done on the development of International Trade
Departments. Previous to the opening of the Congress
itself three different founding congresses of Trade
Departments: Textile Workers, Metal Workers and Leather
Workers were held in Lyons, France, Turin, Italy, and
Gottwaldorf, Czechoslovakia, respectively. It was pointed
out in this congress how in the future world strikes of
categories could be carried on to accomplish the ends
sought in any one country. Organized on a horizontal world
basis, the significance of such a strike and the potential-
ities on a world basis might well be worthy of some reflec-
tion. By the end of the year, according to official estimates,
12 Professional Departments will be functioning and others
will be in the process of formation. The Constitution of the
WFTU has been modified to allow the inclusion of Trade
Department delegates in the Executive Committee to the number
of 1 to every four. Thus there will be one representing the
three Departments already founded, and at the next congress,
in 1951, it is contemplated that the number will be raised
in proportion to the number of Trade Departments functioning."

This report also stated that on July 14 a founding conference
of maritime and port workers had been held at Marseilles on or about
July 14.

2. LAVORO, Italian weekly publication of the WFTU, stated on
August 8 that a constituent congress of maritime and port trade unions
was held some days ago at Marseilles which elected as its directors the
following delegates:

President, Harry Bridges; Vice Presidents, Gudanov (USSR),
Elliot (Australia), Di Stefano (Italy) and a representative of the Chinese
Popular Government who had not been named.

- 2 -

3. Simonini, an astute and well-informed Italian labor leader
(PSLI), advised the Embassy some days ago that he had reason to believe
that widespread strikes and disturbances would be unleashed by the
Communists in all Italian communicating facilities (ports, railroads,
etc.) some time this Fall. The Embassy had previously learned that
the Communists were also planning strike action this Fall in the
agricultural field, especially during the olive harvest, a basic and
extremely important harvest from the Italian economic point of view.
Simonini advocated the organization of counter measures before the
Communists showed their hands. He specifically proposed a counter-
propaganda campaign exposing the Communist move as a political measure
and a special organizational campaign among the Italian railroad and
port workers. A great part of these workers are not Communists but
many of their union leaders are either party members or members of the
Communist-controlled CGIL. Specifically, Italian dock and maritime
workers (most of whom are not Communists) belong to cooperative unions
which collect a set percentage fee on the value of each cargo for
payment to members of the cooperatives. Leaders of these cooperatives
(Di Stefano in Naples, a non-Communist but a follower of the Communist
line, and Giulietti, an Independent Republican who also is a member of
the CGIL and follows the Communist line) are, generally speaking,
fellow-travellers.

4. Irving Brown, European Representative of American Federation
of Labor, who has just arrived in Rome, states that from information
he has acquired in France, he feels convinced that the Communists are
preparing plans for widespread strike action throughout the Continent
of Europe this Fall which may be described as a Cominform offensive
against the Marshall Plan, the Atlantic Pact and the Military Aid
Program. He attributes the British dock strike, the recent Italian
maritime strike, and similar disorders in Australia and the West Coast
of the United States as a mere preview, a trial run, of what the
Communists have in mind. In this connection the Embassy has learned
from a reliable source that the Communist Party of Italy contributed
Fifty Million Lire (approximately $90,000) to support the Italian
maritime strike. He notes that although the British strike was finally
settled, a Communist-controlled strike committee continues to exist.
He states a maritime committee of the International Maritime Trade
Department, mentioned in paragraph 1, has been set up in Marseilles
with two Cominform members, one of whom is presumably Gudanov. The
head of this Committee is a certain Friessonet (General Secretary).
A sub-Committee has been established in Genoa. Mr. Brown maintains
that this is a straight Cominform operation reminiscent of Comintern
operations in German and Dutch ports in the early 20's and 30's so
well described by Jam Valtin ("Out of the Night"). Efforts will be

- 3 -

made to extend the strike action to worldwide proportions. If
this operation is successful, it will be a body blow to the
Marshall Plan and an alarming proof of strength of Communism and
the WFTU over the working forces of the world. Mr. Brown states
that he believes that the two focal points of the action will
probably be in France and Italy, especially among the dock workers
and he maintains that the Communist wheels have already begun to
roll in France with meetings of the Marseilles Committee and
manifestos demanding improved working conditions for the dock workers.
In his dramatic way he has stated "The Cominform is on the March!"

    6. Mr. Brown is of the opinion that the Italian and French
non-Communist labor authorities, as well as governmental people
should immediately take steps to nullify to as great an extent as possible
this Communist offensive. Even should such an offensive not materialize,
the proposed steps, and the financial means necessary to insure their
efficacy involve a mere pittance of effort and money in comparison
to the tremendous losses which European and American economy would
undergo should Cominform plans take form and substance. Specifically
he recommends:

    (a) An immediate propaganda and publicity offensive on the
part of the Italian Free Trade Union Committee and its counterpart in
France, which, through press, handbills, posters, agitators, etc.
would expose the real political aims of the Cominform (defeat of the
Marshall Plan, undermining of the economy of Europe, retarding MAP,
etc. because of Soviet foreign policy). Such a campaign must anticipate
and precede the Cominform action, place it on the defensive and thus
take much of the wind out of its sails.

    (b) An immediate organizational campaign among the port,
railroad and other communications workers for the primary purpose of
bringing the true picture to these workers, of setting up anti-Communist
cells and nuclei, of prevailing upon non-Communist leaders not to abide
by orders issued by the Communist-dominated CGIL or CGT, etc.

    (c) Close coordination between the French and Italian
non-Communist labor union forces for the purpose of forestalling,
defeating or weakening Cominform action in the communications field.

CENTRAL INTELLIGENCE AGENCY

INFORMATION REPORT

REPORT NO. SO SC764

CD NO. 6749

COUNTRY France

SUBJECT French Labor

PLACE ACQUIRED France, Paris

DATE OF INFO. 30 September 1949

DATE DISTR. 18 NOV 49

NO. OF PAGES

NO. OF ENCLS. (LISTED BELOW)

SUPPLEMENT TO REPORT NO.

SANITIZED COPY

	GRADING OF SOURCE						COLLECTOR'S PRELIMINARY GRADING OF CONTENT					
COMPLETELY RELIABLE	USUALLY RELIABLE	FAIRLY RELIABLE	NOT USUALLY RELIABLE	NOT RELIABLE	CANNOT BE JUDGED		CONFIRMED BY OTHER SOURCES	PROBABLY TRUE	POSSIBLY TRUE	DOUBTFUL	PROBABLY FALSE	CANNOT BE JUDGED
A.	B.	C.	D.	E.	F.		1.	2.	3. X	4.	5.	6.

THIS IS UNEVALUATED INFORMATION

SOURCE

185

1. The Confederation Generale du Travail (CGT) is not planning at present to start a general strike in any one particular industry or for the whole of French industry. Its chief aim is to achieve unity of action as the basis necessary for any such over-all movement. In the meantime, the CGT advises trial strikes and strength-testing strikes, such as those at the Provence yards and shops of Port de Bouc, Bouches-du-Rhone.

2. A general strike will be called by the CGT only if all elements of success are present. However, if the CGT-Force Ouvriere (CGT-FO) or the Confederation Francaise des Travailleurs Chretiens (CFTC) should begin a strike, the CGT will undoubtedly, according to its usual tactics, join immediately, try to assume the leadership and claim all the credit. The manpower of the two smaller federations is too small and limited in influence in each industrial plant to enable them to call strikes of any scope.

3. In source's opinion, although not always the instigators of CGT strikes, the Communist Party of the Soviet Union or the Cominform do support them financially. These groups also aid such strikes with sabotage teams which work without direct contact with the CGT. The possibility does exist that a CGT-called strike would have repercussions abroad, particularly among seamen and dockers, metal workers, and miners.

4. Most of the departmental unions of the CGT show a deficit. Neither the main offices of the CGT nor those of its component unions seem to be in possession of important sums of money, but they do usually control the centralization and distribution of funds, which are derived partly from dues and partly from subsidies provided by unions, foreign political organizations or the WFTU. It is probable that in the case of an important strike the CGT will be furnished funds from abroad. Funds of this type are used first of all to pay the cadres and militant unions and to underwrite propaganda. They provide only the most paltry amount of help to individual strikers.

186

5. The CGT-FO and the CFTC have great difficulty in keeping their treasuries

STATE	X	NAVY	X	NSRB	X
ARMY		AIR	X	FBI	

DISTRIBUTION

- 2 -

full. They could not be able to spend large sums and by financial means alone maintain a strike of long duration. The only foreign subsidization these federations would receive would come from any foreign, non-communist, union organizations (CIO, AFL, etc.) which decided to support international unionism.

CLASSIFICATION SECRET/CONTROL - U.S. OFFICIALS ONLY

CENTRAL INTELLIGENCE AGENCY

INFORMATION REPORT

COUNTRY	Italy
SUBJECT	Partito Comunista Italiano (PCI) Plans for Port Strikes in Italy
PLACE ACQUIRED	Italy, Milan
DATE OF INFO.	4 January 1950

REPORT NO.	SO 35510
CD NO.	
DATE DISTR.	10 Feb 1950
NO. OF PAGES	1
NO. OF ENCLS. (LISTED BELOW)	
SUPPLEMENT TO REPORT NO.	SO-34832*

Return to CIA Library

GRADING OF SOURCE

COMPLETELY RELIABLE	USUALLY RELIABLE	FAIRLY RELIABLE	NOT USUALLY RELIABLE	NOT RELIABLE	CANNOT BE JUDGED
A.	B.	C.	D.	E.	F.
	b	c			

COLLECTOR'S PRELIMINARY GRADING OF CONTENT

CONFIRMED BY OTHER SOURCES	PROBABLY TRUE	POSSIBLY TRUE	DOUBTFUL	PROBABLY FALSE	CANNOT BE JUDGED
1.	2.	3.	4.	5.	6.
		3. X			

THIS DOCUMENT CONTAINS INFORMATION AFFECTING THE NATIONAL DEFENSE OF THE UNITED STATES WITHIN THE MEANING OF THE ESPIONAGE ACT 50 U.S.C., 31 AND 32, AS AMENDED. ITS TRANSMISSION OR THE REVELATION OF ITS CONTENTS IN ANY MANNER TO AN UNAUTHORIZED PERSON IS PROHIBITED BY LAW. REPRODUCTION OF THIS FORM IS PROHIBITED.

THIS IS UNEVALUATED INFORMATION

SOURCE   An individual with good contacts in Italian police circles.

1. During the past two months, the Directorate of the Partito Comunista Italiano (PCI), "on orders of Moscow and Cominform leaders," in union with the French Communist Party, has allegedly prepared a vast plan of sabotage in Italian and French ports when United States vessels with war materials are to arrive.

2. Officers of the Soviet service are stated to have recently visited port zones and, through the payment of large sums of money, succeeded in identifying points of landing and unloading cargo of the American ships.

3. It is stated that Russian officers were in Taranto on 12 December 1949 where an Italian Lieutenant Colonel, with the cover name of "Leone," received the sum of 300,000 lire to carry out intelligence activity and possibly sabotage.

Declassified by CO6687
date 6 March 1975

STATE		NAVY	X	NSRB		DISTRIBUTION:
ARMY	X	AIR	X	FBI		

189

CENTRAL INTELLIGENCE AGENCY

INFORMATION REPORT

REPORT NO.

CD NO. SO-58664

COUNTRY Belgium

DATE DISTR. 12 APR 51

SUBJECT Summary Report on the Belgian Communist Party

NO. OF PAGES 4

PLACE
ACQUIRED Belgium, Brussels

NO. OF ENCLS.
(LISTED BELOW)

DATE OF
INFO. 1947 – January 1951

SUPPLEMENT TO
REPORT NO.

	GRADING OF SOURCE *					COLLECTOR'S PRELIMINARY GRADING OF CONTENT					
COMPLETELY RELIABLE	USUALLY RELIABLE	FAIRLY RELIABLE	NOT USUALLY RELIABLE	NOT RELIABLE	CANNOT BE JUDGED	CONFIRMED BY OTHER SOURCES	PROBABLY TRUE	POSSIBLY TRUE	DOUBTFUL	PROBABLY FALSE	CANNOT BE JUDGED
A.	B.	C.	D.	E.	F.	1.	2.	3.	4.	5.	6.

THIS IS UNEVALUATED INFORMATION

*SOURCE   Usually reliable with good contacts in Communist circles.

The following summary was prepared by source in answer to a specific inquiry on certain activities and capabilities of the Belgian Communist Party.

BCP Liaison with Foreign CPs

1. There is no definite information concerning the various ways by which instructions are received by the Belgian Communist Party (BCP). It would appear, however, that the directives from the Cominform come to the BCP via the French Communist Party (FCP), and particularly through such liaison agents as Jacques Duclos, acting head of the French CP, Benoît Frachon, head of the French General Confederation of Labor (Confederation Generale du Travail - CGT), and Marcel Cachin, prominent old time leader of the French CP. It is also believed that the directors of the BCP receive instructions whenever they travel abroad.

2. It has not been possible to establish whether or not members of the Soviet and Satellite missions maintain contact with the foreign Communists, e.g., the French CP, the Dutch CP. It is during the course of various congresses, such as the Partisans of Peace Congress, that these diplomats are able to contact other foreign Communists.

3. Although numerous individuals suspected of espionage belong to the BCP and may even be Communist propagandists, it has not yet been established that any of them report to the USSR through the intermediary of the Party. It is evident, however, that the USSR is interested in the BCP. The Soviet directors utilize, by preference, the services of individual Belgian Communists. According to information received, the USSR reportedly possesses an "homme de confiance" in every large Belgian center who is classified clandestine by the other members of the Party.

191

4. The higher echelons of the Party are partially aware of this activity, because of the aid which they are sometimes obliged to lend to foreigners. In these cases, it is only individually, however, that the members of the Party intervene in such activity. Normally, foreigners engaged in suspect activity avoid contacting members of the Party for fear that such individuals are too closely surveilled.

Declassified by 058375
date ‾‾‾ 5 MAR 1976

CLASSIFICATION

| STATE | | NAVY | X | USBB | X |
| ARMY | | AIR | X | FBI | |

DISTRIBUTION

80100 (D)

SECURITY INFORMATION — U.S. OFFICIALS ONLY

CENTRAL INTELLIGENCE AGENCY

67-5305

-2-

5. The Communist elements are always strongly interested in foreign groups within the country. The USSR and the Satellite countries have organized their loyal subjects residing in Belgium into groups such as the UPS, Union des Democrates Hongrois (Union of Hungarian Democrats), Union des Patriotes Polonais (Union of Polish Patriots). Such individuals are active propagandists among their

countrymen opposed to the Communist ideology. This propaganda is directed particularly toward the DP's who are encouraged by all means to repatriate themselves.

BCP Plans to Go Underground

6. Before the crisis over the Royal Question was settled, the BCP envisaged the Party going underground, and in order to prepare for this eventuality, they decided to destroy the files concerning members of the BCP and the Union Belge pour la Defense de la Paix (Belgian Union for the Defense of Peace - BDP). It is probable that copies of these files have been given to trusted Party members who are, however, little known for any political activity.

7. A work plan has been set up similar to that in France and in Luxemburg. Each member of the Politburo reportedly has been asked to find a safehouse and a courier, a member of the Party or sympathizer whose Communist connections are unknown to the authorities. Raymond Dispy, National Political Secretary, is reportedly responsible for seeing that this plan is carried out, but the plan has been so conceived that even Dispy will be unaware of all the liaison personnel and the safehouses. The movement underground will be set off automatically by war with Russia and the outlawing of the Party. The question of establishing a false list of Party members has already been discussed but it is not known whether or not it has been completed.

8. Until 1947, a Hungarian subject living in Brussels under the real or assumed name of Denis Clavel was the Comintern instructor assigned to the BCP. He fulfilled the functions of national "responsable" for cadres, and in this capacity held the reins of the Party. Clavel presently holds an important position in the Hungarian Government. The identity of Clavel's replacement is not known.

BCP Reorganization

9. No noteworthy progress has been made by the BCP in its reorganization program. Party activity remains stationary and rivalries in the heart of the Party still exist.

10. There is no indication at present that a purge of "Titoist" elements is under way in the Party. This, however, does not prevent the directors of the Party from accusing such members as have been indiscreet enough to criticize the Party line, or members who have been excluded, of being "Titoist". This was the case with Formaid Demeny.*

11. If Titoist or Trotskyist elements exist within the Party, they have been successful in not being discovered. They are too weak, if they do exist, to reorient the general line of the Party.

Front Organizations

12. The president of the American Bulgarian Committee (Union of Bulgaro-Soviet Friendship Association - ABS), Bernard Jaffe, upon his return from the USSR and the Soviet cultural society with a revived intent to support the efforts of the ABS and to materially aid it by scarce specialists from foreigners or theatrical groups. The greater part of the brochures and leaflets distributed by the ABS are supplied to it gratis or for only a nominal fee.

13. Neither the ABS nor the Union has maintained contacts between these organizations — USS is actually a part of the BCP, but contacts exist between these organizations and the Party. Members of the UBS attend meetings of the BCP and even furnish funds, notably on the occasion of an electoral campaign. The UBS has been

194

sub-licensed by the Soviet Embassy on such rare occasions as that when the funds for publishing its organ Sovietsky Patriot were exhausted, but the contribution was so slight as to be almost unnoticeable. The Soviet Commercial Mission lends, or rents for a nominal sum, films to the UPS by which the latter organization obtains funds. The mission also delivers pamphlets, brochures and newspapers free of charge.

14. There are only approximate figures available concerning the number of effectives in the UBDP, but they seem, however, to give a relatively true estimate. At the end of December 1949, this group comprised between 3000-4000 members, not including various associations which have requested to be affiliated with the UBDP. At present, the effectives still number approximately 3,500. The Rassemblement des Femmes pour la Paix - RFP (Women's Rally for Peace) numbers several hundred members. The BCP lays down the political line to be followed by the above two groups.

BCP Relations with Industry

15. It is not known that any industrialists financially support the BCP. It is possible, of course, that at the time the Party controlled certain ministries

(notably Supply), various merchants and industrialists supplied funds to the Party in order to put an end to investigations opened against them.

16. At the Fabrique Nationale the influence of the Party is not great even though a Communist cell does exist there. This is also true of the Fonderie des Canons. There is no evidence of the existence of a Communist cell at the Fonderies Reunies.

BCP Membership

17. In 1945, the BCP had increased its membership to around 100,000. Since then the number has continually decreased until now there are 85,000 registered and 25,000 dues paying members. The number of sympathizers, judging by the last electoral results, can be set at about 234,000. There is no information concerning the number of members on whom the Party could depend for acts of sabotage, revolutionary action or aid to Soviet troops in the event of an invasion.

Para-Military Activity

18. Weapons, ammunition and explosives have been discovered at the homes of certain militants, especially former members of the Communist resistance organizations, Front de l'Independance (Independence Front - FI) and Partisans Armes (Armed Partisans - PA) known for their activity during the German occupation, but these are isolated cases. There is not evidence of arms traffic or the construction of depots on orders of the Party. It is certain that Party leaders seldom go out unarmed, especially since the assassination of Julien Lahaut, former president of the BCP, but there is no evidence of armed units within the Party. The activity of the Communist propaganda groups known as Brigades

...developments is practically non-existent. The Brussels section of this group was dissolved on 11 January 1959 because of embezzlement and the incompetence of one of its directors. Members of the group have not as yet been incorporated into other such sections, and rather into special groups designated by the PA.

19. In the army, there is no Communist activity worthy of being mentioned. The recent hunger strike organized by a Communist among the troops in Germany in the guise of protesting against prolonged military service is one of the best examples of this. The army, however, is not free from propaganda organized by the Party and addressed to the young people of military age and to the young soldiers. To combat the ban on Communist publications in the barracks, it is reported that small sealed editions of such papers are sent to Communist army cargo. It has been reported that a plan has been designed to demoralize the army; the realization of this plan is reportedly entrusted to a Spanish and a French captain.

Communist Labor Unions

20. At the present time in spite of the interventions of the World Federation of Trade Unions (WFTU), the situation of the Communist independent trade unions is not very strong. Latest reports indicate that the CGU will be almost abandoned by the Party (its activity has never, it is true, been very great), while the setting up of Communist cells within the Federation Generale des Travailleurs Belge will reportedly be carried on on a large scale.

21. The Communist influence in the Confederation Generale des Services Publics (General Confederation of Public Service ~~Unions~~) had always had rather strong necessity, however, it has been greatly reduced. For example, two Communist elements, Roger Abel Lefebre and Martial ~~Dul,~~ have been removed from the national cadre. Charles Crevecœur is ~~still,~~ however, one of the national secretaries. The results of the election which caused the removal of Lefevre give an idea of the Communist strength in the CGSP. Lefevre obtained 24,367 votes against 79,435 for his opponent.

22. A group known as "ministeres" exists and was reportedly comprised of approximately 500 government employees, most of whom are found in the ministries which were affected by the Communists after the liberation. Following the government decision to remove Communists from government positions, the number dropped to about 425.

** See SO 41881

INFORMATION REPORT

CD NO.

COUNTRY France

SUBJECT Recent developments in the French Communist Party

PLACE
ACQUIRED Paris

DATE
ACQUIRED BY SOURCE 15 May 51

DATE OF INFORMATION

DATE DISTR. 20 June 1951

NO. OF PAGES 3

NO. OF ENCLS.
(LISTED BELOW)

SUPPLEMENT TO
REPORT NO.

1007260

	COMPLETELY RELIABLE	USUALLY RELIABLE	FAIRLY RELIABLE	NOT USUALLY RELIABLE	NOT RELIABLE	CANNOT BE JUDGED
GRADING OF SOURCE BY OFFICE OF ORIGIN	A.	B. X	C.	D. /	E.	F.

SOURCE'S OPINION OF CONTENT	TRUE	PROBABLY TRUE	POSSIBLY TRUE	DOUBTFUL	PROBABLY FALSE	CANNOT BE JUDGED
	1.	2.	3. X	4.	5.	6.

THIS IS UNEVALUATED INFORMATION

199

1. Labor Unity: The French Communist Party considers CGT-sponsored labor unity as responsible for the victory of the striking employees of the nationalized enterprises, and the resultant wage revision in private industries. This victory of CGT is undeniable. Now no agreement which excludes CGT can be made, something which has been attempted often in the past. The Party is now in a position to play off the other two great worker groups against each other. This statement was confirmed by the 25 April incident of the hotel, cafe and restaurant employees, when leaders of CGT and CFTC denounced the agreement with management signed by FO (Force Ouvriere) and CGC (Counter Intelligence Corps). At the first session of the "Commission Superieure des Conventions Collectives" on 22 March, the CGT encountered difficulty when it stood alone in demanding a minimum wage of 20,125 francs. However, the situation changed in its favor when, because of the rise in living costs, the Commission was obliged to convene again and meet the figure demanded by CGT. The Communist Party is now more convinced than ever that coordinated action committees controlled by CGT should be set up and given the power of decision. This foreshadows new achievements: a sliding wage scale, general wage increases, cuts in taxes required for rearmament, and, above all, coordinated action, not only by unions, but by the entire working class.

2. To create the proper atmosphere, simplified slogans appealing to the workers are being put out, as an example: "There is no difference been an FO dish and a CFTC or CGT dish—all are alike, and none very full." These slogans are always interesting to study, because they reflect the party line laid down by Moscow. The most recent one (25 April) sheds a good deal of light: "Bread, Peace, Liberty", precisely the slogan of the popular front of 1936.

3. Coordinated action on a broad base is vital to the Communist Party, which always fears isolation. On 25 April a meeting of all committees for coordinated action was held at the Annexe de la Bourse du Travail, Rue du Chateau d'Eau. Jean Cassot

was appointed by the Communist Party as the responsible officer of the Service of Order, demonstrating that the Communists are trying to set up a new "popular front." Moreover, only one item that could be called Stalinist was on the agenda, and it appeared in fourth place: "Defense of Peace by a treaty of the Five." This is the current key-formula, and also the slogan most easily acceptable to fellow-travelers, since it was accepted by the General Council of Marne on 20 March (3 Communists out of 33 members), the Municipal Council of Pantin on 24 April (13 Republican and Resistant Union, 2 Independants, 10 RPF, 3 Socialists, 1 Radical), and the Congress of Agricultural Workers of Allier (400 delegates representing 13,000 labor unionists).

CLASSIFICATION

STATE		NAVY	X	NSRB	X
ARMY	X	AIR	X	FSI	X

DISTRIBUTION

SANITIZED COPY

- 2 -

4. Communist successes through this plan should not be underestimated. There was a meeting on 6 April at the "Cite de la Fraternite", a Catholic group of Romainville. Among those attending were:

Drs. Rosenfeld, Dupas, and Boenich of the Conseil Communal de la Paix

Giry of the French Communist Party

Gilbert Desouche, a director of CFTC

Robert Calmejane, a local leader of RPF who, in spite of appearances, has a good deal of contact with Stalinites.

Robert Mailson, a director of "Cite de la Fraternite"

Robert Lucchini, a member of "Cite de la Fraternite"

Roger Kremer, Roger Decressat, Gerard Croene and Jean Malbet, directors of "Cite de la Fraternite"

Jean Roberti Zane, an officer of the MRP and a director of the ACJF, who presided.

5. Pacifist and Anti-American Activity: August Lecoeur reported on 25 April to the Central Committee of the Communist Party on the following subjects: "The constant growth of the danger of war; tasks of Communists in the struggle for peace; our country's contribution to the world movement and to the National Committee for Peace." It is increasingly clear that the Communists have been ordered by Moscow to push ahead fast. Within the Party, one hears constantly that "the next months, even the coming weeks, may be decisive." Doubtless the reason that the effort against German rearmament has been relaxed in recent weeks is to devote practically all efforts to the fight for a "Five Power Treaty". Such action would furnish a base for wider support. Lecoeur siad that during the "just and in-

202

dispensable campaign against German rearmament", the struggle against the "rearmament of France and her occupation by American troops" had sometimes been neglected. Andre Soupquiere added that the two tasks were not contradictory, but complementary, "the struggle for a Five Power Treaty being today the most important, and itself helping to prevent German rearmament." The campaign for a Five Power Treaty has received the utmost support of pro-Soviet leaders and it will open, according to Laurent Casanova, "the perspective toward univeral control, disarmament and the free self-determination of peoples."

Time pressure on Stalinist Party leaders in France is evident. This is why the CONSEIL NATIONAL DU MOUVEMENT DE LA PAIX has been encouraging action "of every kind and on the part of everyone to throw light into the darkest corners". Nevertheless, as Lecoeur has recognized, this gives the Communist Party grave organizational problems. All efforts will be put forward on 15 and 17 July. On 15 July a monster rally is to be held, and the Soviets have ordered an unprecedented effort to have several hundred thousand delegates bearing millions of signatures favoring a Five Power Treaty gather in Paris on the day after the national holiday. The Party will pay special attention to women, capitalizing on their innate opposition to war. A hundred thousand women delegates of "Comites Feminins de la Paix" are expected to be in Paris on 15 July, including 2,000 from Nord, 2,000 from Pas-deCalais and 27,000 from Alpes-Maritimes. Morecver, the "Union des Femmes Francaises" is sending fifty women as delegates to a meeting with German women in Berlin. Fifteen other militant women will be greeted in the USSR by "Anti-Fascist Committees of Soviet Women," while another delegation will be sent to Korea to observe the savagery of American soldiers in massacring children. This plan should not be scoffed at, for it is part of a well concerted action carried on over several years to arouse hatred of Americans among the French masses.

6.

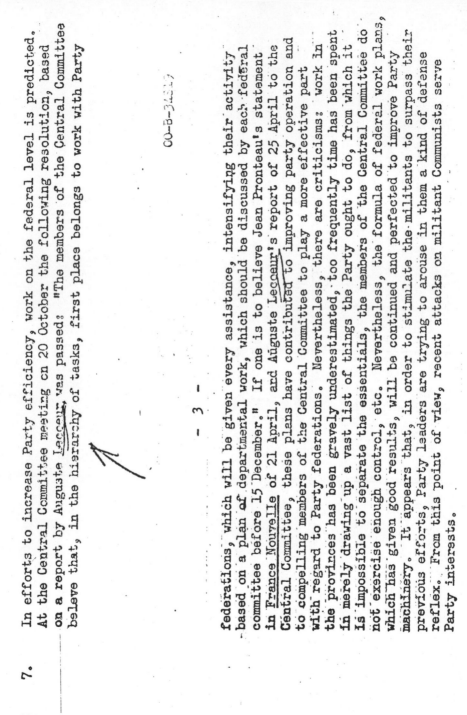

7.

In efforts to increase Party efficiency, work on the federal level is predicted. At the Central Committee meeting on 20 October the following resolution, based on a report by Auguste Lecœur was passed: "The members of the Central Committee beleve that, in the hierarchy of tasks, first place belongs to work with Party

- 3 -

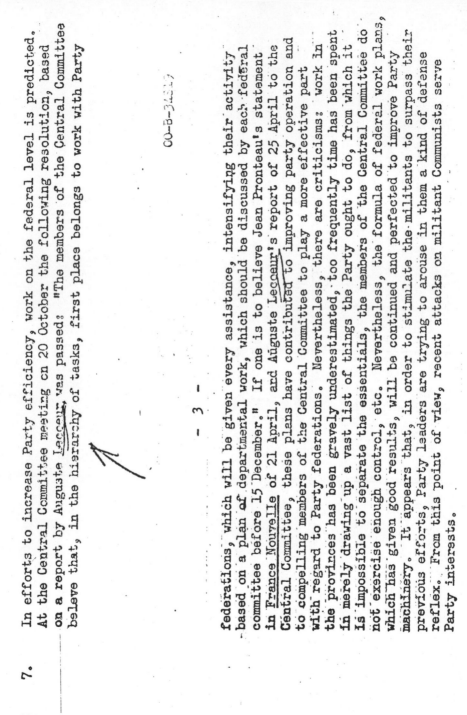

CO-B-34517

federations, which will be given every assistance, intensifying their activity based on a plan of departmental work, which should be discussed by each federal committee before 15 December." If one is to believe Jean Pronteau's statement in France Nouvelle of 21 April, and Auguste Lecœur's report of 25 April to the Central Committee, these plans have contributed to improving party operation and to compelling members of the Central Committee to play a more effective part with regard to Party federations. Nevertheless, there are criticisms: work in the provinces has been gravely underestimated, too frequently time has been spent in merely drawing up a vast list of things the Party ought to do, from which it is impossible to separate the essentials, the members of the Central Committee do not exercise enough control, etc. Nevertheless, the formula of federal work plans, which has given good results, will be continued and perfected to improve Party machinery. It appears that, in order to stimulate the militants to surpass their previous efforts, Party leaders are trying to arouse in them a kind of defense reflex. From this point of view, recent attacks on militant Communists serve Party interests.

204

8.

The Struggle Against Western Rearmament: It seems likely that the Russians will demand greater sacrifices from their agents in France who have the mission of struggling against Western rearmament and against all forms of national defense. Lecoeur has given precise directives on this subject—no isolated actions, but mass actions, in which workers in the war industries and, in fact, the whole population, should be aroused by pamphlets, posters and meetings, to take part. Doubtless direct Communist sabotage methods will be undertaken, and almost every-where careful tests have been made to this end. The confession of the aviation mechanic, Stefane Wigos, who, at the SNCAN factory at Meaulte, sabotaged the fuel lines of Vampire fighters to produce fires while in flight, was embarrassing to the Communist leaders. Fortunately for them, the lawyer of the Secours Populaire saw his client very soon afterward and he retracted his confession.

- end -

205

INFORMATION REPORT

CD NO.

DATE DISTR. 13 Jul 1951

COUNTRY France

SUBJECT Dissolution of the French Longshoremen's Union

NO. OF PAGES 1

PLACE
ACQUIRED Paris

NO. OF ENCLS.
(LISTED BELOW)

DATE
ACQUIRED BY SOURCE 22 Jun 51

SUPPLEMENT TO
REPORT NO.

DATE OF INFORMATION

GRADING OF SOURCE BY OFFICE OF ORIGIN						SOURCE'S OPINION OF CONTENT					
COMPLETELY RELIABLE	USUALLY RELIABLE	FAIRLY RELIABLE	NOT USUALLY RELIABLE	NOT RELIABLE	CANNOT BE JUDGED	TRUE	PROBABLY TRUE	POSSIBLY TRUE	DOUBTFUL	PROBABLY FALSE	CANNOT BE JUDGED
A.	B.	C. X	D.	E.	F.	1.	2. X	3.	4.	5.	6.

THIS IS UNEVALUATED INFORMATION

SOURCE

1. A source in close contact with the French labor movement reports that for several months the French press has been discussing the dissolution of several international Communist organizations by Government decree. Particular attention was paid to the "Departement Professionnel des Marins et Dockers" of the "Federation Syndicale Mondiale" (World Federation of Trade Unions), which has offices on Place de la Joliette, Marseille. The Communists registered solemn protests against such anti-union measures and launched a number of slogans against the authorities.

2. The interdiction decree was duly served against the offices on Place de la Joliette, and the General Information Service of Marseille seized all the archives. Despite a very meticulous search, police say they found nothing of interest. This is not astonishing to those who know the General Information Service, for the seizure was more in the nature of a salvage operation. As a matter of fact, since the seizure the former personnel of the "Marins et Dockers" have gradually quite publicly returned to their offices on Place de la Joliette, reinstituting their services under one pretext or another.

3. Soviet representative Goudanov (Vice-President of the "Union Internationale des Marins et Dockers") has retreated somewhat into the background. But Secretary-General Andre Freyssinet (also Secretary of the "Syndicat Des Marins de Marseille") and Gagnaire (Secretary of the "Syndicat Des Dockers de Marseille", long an agent of the Comintern) are back at their posts on Place de la Joliette. They have recently been assisted by Jean-Paul Comiti, a Counsellor of the "Union Francaise",

living at 21 rue Custine in Paris and at Sospel (Alpes–Maritimes). Comiti, a teacher and former Federal Secretary of Alpes–Maritimes, has recently fallen into disfavor with the Communist Party for having shown lack of energy in the longshore–men's strikes. He is a member of the Commission for the Study of Overseas Pro–blems of the Communist Party.

—end—

CLASSIFICATION

STATE	EV	X	NAVY	X	NSRB	X	DISTRIBUTION		
ARMY		X	AIR	X	FBI				

208

INFORMATION REPORT

COUNTRY France

SUBJECT Communist Party Preparations for Its Possible
Outlawing

PLACE
ACQUIRED Paris

DATE
ACQUIRED BY SOURCE 3 Aug 51

DATE OF INFORMATION

DATE OF DIST. / Oct. 1951

NO. OF PAGES 1

NO. OF ENCLS.
(LISTED BELOW)

SUPPLEMENT TO
REPORT NO.

	GRADING OF SOURCE BY OFFICE OF ORIGIN						SOURCE'S OPINION OF CONTENT					
COMPLETELY RELIABLE	USUALLY RELIABLE	FAIRLY RELIABLE	NOT USUALLY RELIABLE.	NOT RELIABLE	CANNOT BE JUDGED		TRUE	PROBABLY TRUE	POSSIBLY TRUE.	DOUBTFUL	PROBABLY FALSE	CANNOT BE JUDGED
A.	B. X	C.	D.	E.	F.		1.	2. X	3.	4.	5.	6.

THIS IS UNEVALUATED INFORMATION

SOURCE

1. Although the Communist Party is preparing for its eventual suppression (which is desired by the parliamentary majority) it is nevertheless convinced that the French Government will hesitate to outlaw the labor organizations connected with the Communist Party. Preparing for the worst--dissolution of the Party and its return underground--the directors of the French Communist Party have given confidential instructions that the unions--and not only branches of CGT (General Confederation of Labor)--should become the refuge of the Communists if they should have to go underground.

2. There will thus be an increase in Communist penetration of labor unions and a large dispersal of militant Communists into the various unions, if dissolution of the Party takes place. Some statements of the Left Wing minority in CFTC (Confédération Française des Travailleurs Chrétiens) indicate that this group will not be inclined to bar the inclusion of Communists if the Party is persecuted.

3. It is certain that the eventual dissolution of CGT will present the gravest danger of infiltration for the other labor unions. The Communist Party, in preparing for the possibility of dissolution and in order to reinforce its position in the labor unions, has abandoned its aggressiveness on domestic matters. This position conforms with orders of the Cominform, which wants to diminish agitation on domestic matters in order to support the peace offensive of the Kremlin.

- end -

CLASSIF^ATION

CENTRAL INTELLIGENCE AGENCY

INFORMATION REPORT

REPORT NO. 00 -B-40835

CD NO

DATE DISTR. 5 Nov 1951

NO. OF PAGES 1

NO. OF ENCLS.
(LISTED BELOW)

SUPPLEMENT TO
REPORT NO.

COUNTRY France/Italy/Czechoslovakia/USSR

SUBJECT Communist Strike Action Planned for France and Italy/
Czech Government Publication in Paris

PLACE
ACQUIRED Paris

SANITIZED COPY

DATE
ACQUIRED BY SOURCE 19 Sep 51

DATE OF INFORMATION

GRADING OF SOURCE BY OFFICE OF ORIGIN						SOURCE'S OPINION OF CONTENT					
COMPLETELY RELIABLE	USUALLY RELIABLE	FAIRLY RELIABLE	NOT USUALLY RELIABLE	NOT RELIABLE	CANNOT BE JUDGED	TRUE	PROBABLY TRUE	POSSIBLY TRUE	DOUBTFUL	PROBABLY FALSE	CANNOT BE JUDGED
A.	B. X	C.	D.	E.	F.	1.	2. X	3.	4.	5.	6.

THIS IS UNEVALUATED INFORMATION

SOURCE

1. ACTION-ECLAIR—Swift strike actions and disturbances are being organized in France by the Communists to demonstrate social unrest and dissatisfaction in the labor unions. They will be called in the last half of October, in connection with similar actions in Italy. It is important to note that these disturbances are being prepared by the Cominform without the approval of the Communist Party leaders in France and Italy. These leaders are following instructions from Moscow and still insisting on the political anti-US aspect of their present actions. This issue has not been decided yet in the French Politburo.

2. Giuseppe Bappi, an Italian holding a Hungarian passport, arrived in Paris from Budapest. Bappi is charged by the Cagburo of the Cominform with coordinating social agitation in France and Italy in the Autumn of 1951. Since his arrival in France, Bappi has been in daily contact with Frachon and other CGT (General Confederation of Labor) leaders. He is also a personal friend of Gustav Soucek, the new Czechoslovak Ambassador in France, who arrived in Paris on 15 Sep 51, and of the Spanish Republican General, Lister, directing the Communist underground in France.

3. A large amount of money has been put at the disposal of Bappi by Henri Thimonier, Managing Director of Parallele 50, a weekly magazine of the popular democracie, edited by the Czechoslovak Government in France at 18 rue Bonaparte, Paris 6. These funds were sent on 2, 7, and 13 Sep 51 from Prague through the Banque Commerciale pour l'Europe du Nord, 21 rue de l'Arcade, Paris. Parallele 50 is registered as a French weekly magazine and is supervised on behalf of the Cominform by French Communist deputy Cogniot.

— end —

212

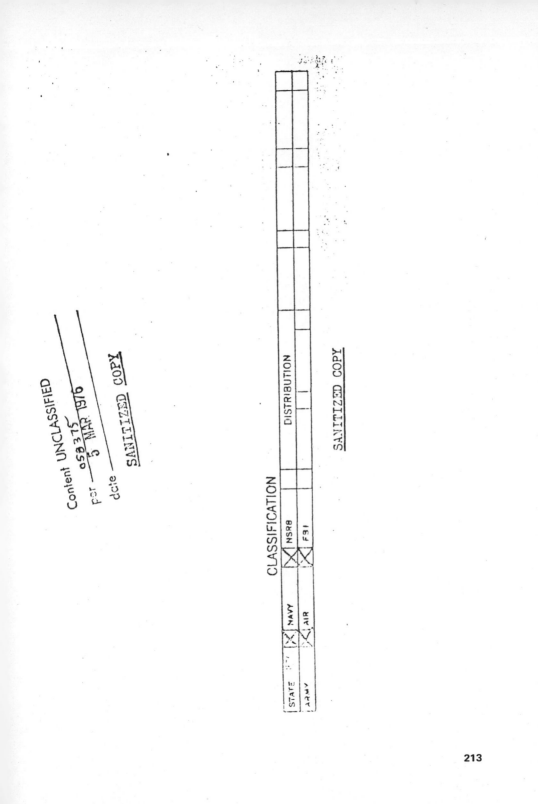

CLASSIFICATION

STATE		NAVY		NSRB	
ARMY		AIR		FBI	

DISTRIBUTION

SANITIZED COPY

Bibliography

PRIMARY SOURCES

American Federation of Labor. *International Free Trade Union News.* 1946–1956.

_____. *Proceedings of the Convention,* 42nd–72nd. Washington, D.C., 1922–1953.

_____. *Slave Labor in Russia, the Case Presented by the American Federation of Labor to the United Nations.* 1949.

American Federation of Labor, Free Trade Union Committee. Archives 1944–1952.

American Federation of Labor, International Labor Relations Committee. "The AFL at Work: Towards Democracy in Germany." October 1947.

_____. "American Labor Looks at the World." September 1951.

_____. *Minutes and Reports.* AFL-CIO archives 1944–1952.

_____. "The Rights of Labor: Democracy vs. Totalitarianism." October 1947.

_____. "What Happened to the Trade Unions Behind the Iron Curtain." 1947.

American Federation of Labor–Congress of Industrial Organizations. *Free Trade Union News.* 1958–1976.

———. *Proceedings of the Convention,* 1st–11th. Washington, D.C., 1955–1975.
American Federationist XXIX–LXXXIII (1922–1976).

Brown, Irving. "Alternatives to Attrition, The Role of Democratic Forces in a Political Solution." In *Labor and International Affairs.* Washington, D.C.: Georgetown University International Labor Program, 1976.

Confédération Générale du Travail. *XXVI Congrès National de Paris.* Paris, 1946.

Confédération Générale du Travail–Force Ouvrière. *Bulletin d' Information de la Manche.* January–February 1950.

———. *Congrès Constitutif.* Paris, 1948.

———. *Force Ouvrière.* 1948–1952.

———. *2e Congrès Confédéral.* Paris, 1950.

Dubinsky, David. "The European Scene–Highlights and Shadows," *American Federationist* LV (November 1948): 10.

———. "Labor Standing by the Atlantic Charter." *American Federationist* LI (June 1944): 6–7.

———. "World Labor's New Weapon." *Foreign Affairs* XXVIII (April 1950): 451–462.

European Economic Community Commission. "The Economic Situation in the Community." Brussels: Directorate General for Economic and Financial Affairs, 1975.

Green, William. "The AFL and World Labor." *American Federationist* LII (September 1945): 6–9.

———. "The AFL and World Labor Unity." *New Leader,* August 4, 1945.

———. "American Labor and World Affairs." *American Federationist* L (July 1943): 9–11.

———. *Labor and Democracy.* Princeton: Princeton University Press, 1939.

House of Lords. *Hansard* 356(52) (February 1975).

International Brotherhood of Teamsters, Chauffeurs, Warehousemen and Helpers of America. *Proceedings of Sixteenth Convention.* Washington, D.C., 1952.

International Labor Organization. Legislative Series. *Germany 6.* Geneva, 1933.

———. Legislative Series. *Germany 1.* Geneva, 1934.

———. Legislative Series. *Spain 1.* Geneva, 1938.

International Ladies' Garment Workers Union. *Justice.* 1945–1950.

———. *Proceedings of the Convention,* 25th–29th. New York, 1944–1950.

International Transport Workers Federation. *Journal.* 1946–1951.

———. "Report on Activities and Financial Report for the Years 1946–1947." *Proceedings of the Congress.* London, 1948.

"John Herling's Labor Letter." 1965–1976.

Labor League for Human Rights. *Memorandum to International and National Unions, State Federations of Labor, Central Labor Unions.* December 31, 1946.

Labor League News I (1945).

_____. "Report on Activities and Financial Reports for the Years 1948–1950." *Proceedings of the Congress*. London, 1950.

Meany, George. "Address to the American Labor and International Affairs Course." AFL-CIO Labor Studies Center, Washington, D.C., April 22, 1974.

_____. "Free Enterprise: What It Means to Labor." *American Federationist* LI (June 1944): 3–5.

_____. "We Back America." *American Federationist* LIII (July 1946): 3–7.

_____. "Why Labor Supports the Marshall Plan." *American Federationist* LV (January 1948).

_____. "The Vienna Conference and the ICFTU." *Vital Speeches* XXI (August 1, 1955).

Miners' International Federation. *Proceedings of Thirty-Fourth Miners' International Federation Congress*. London, 1946.

Mutual Security Agency. *Trans Atlantic*, Labor Newsletter, I and II, 1948, 1949.

United Brotherhood of Joiners and Carpenters of America. *Proceedings of the Convention*, 25th–26th. Washington, D.C., 1946–1950.

United Nations. *Multinational Corporations in World Development*. ST/ECA 10. New York, 1973.

_____. *Yearbook of Human Rights, 1947*. New York, 1949.

U.S. Congress, House, Committee on Foreign Affairs, *Hearings on Détente*, 93rd Cong., 2d sess., 1974.

U.S. Congress, Senate, Committee on Foreign Relations, *Hearings on U.S. Assistance to European Economic Recovery*, 80th Cong., 2d sess., 8 January 1948, pts. 1 and 2.

U.S. Department of State. *Foreign Relations of the U.S.* Diplomatic Papers 1945–1949.

_____. General Records, RG 59, Box 6107, Decimal File 1945–1949.

_____. "White House Daily Summary" 1946–1950. General Records, RG 59.

Woll, Matthew. "A Reply." *Labor and the World Crisis*. New York: Workers Education Bureau Press, 1940.

_____. "The Communists Move in on French Labor." *American Federationist* LIII (July 1946): 10–13.

_____. "World Issues and the AFL." *American Federationist* LV (May 1948): 10–11.

SECONDARY SOURCES

Books

Acheson, Dean. *Present at the Creation*. New York: Signet, 1970.

Adam, Gérard. *La C.F.T.C., 1940–1958*. Paris: Armand Colin, 1964.

Allen, V. L. *Trade Union Leadership*. London: Longmans, 1957.

Alperovitz, Gar. *Atomic Diplomacy: Hiroshima and Potsdam*. New York: Simon and Schuster, 1965.

———. *Cold War Essays*. Garden City: Anchor Books, 1970.

Aron, Raymond. *The Century of Total War*. Boston: Beacon Press, 1954.

Barbash, Jack. *American Unions: Structure, Government, and Politics*. New York: Harper, 1967.

Barjonet, André. *La CGT*. Paris: Seuil, 1968.

Barkin, Solomon, ed. *Worker Militancy and Its Consequences, 1965–1975*. New York: Praeger Special Studies, 1975.

Barron, John. *KGB*. New York: Readers Digest Press, 1974.

Bergeron, André. *La Confédération Force Ouvrière*. Paris: EPI, 1972.

Bergounioux, Alain. *Force Ouvrière*. Paris: Seuil, 1975.

Blackmer, Donald M., and Tarrow, Sydney, eds. *Communism in Italy and France*. Princeton: Princeton University Press, 1975.

Blackmer, Donald M., and Kriegel, Annie. *The International Role of the Communist Parties of Italy and France*. Center for International Studies, Harvard University, 1975.

Bohlen, Charles. *Witness to History 1929–1969*. New York: Norton, 1973.

Borkenau, Franz. *European Communism*. London: Faber & Faber, 1953.

Bothereau, Robert. *L'Organization de la CGT-FO et du Mouvement Syndical*. Paris, undated.

Brezhnev, Leonid. *On the Policy of the Soviet Union and the International Situation*. Garden City, N.Y.: Doubleday, 1973.

Brown, Seyom. *The Faces of Power*. New York: Columbia University Press, 1968.

Byrnes, James. *Speaking Frankly*. New York: Harper & Row, 1948.

Cantril, Hadley. *The Politics of Despair*. New York: Basic Books, 1958.

Coates, David. *The Labor Party and the Struggle for Socialism*. New York: Cambridge Univeristy Press, 1975.

Cohen, Saul B. *Geography and Politics in a World Divided*, 2d ed. New York: Oxford University Press, 1973.

Curtis, J. S., ed. *Essays in Russian and Soviet History*. New York: Columbia University Press, 1963.

Dale, Leon. *Marxism and French Labor*. New York: Vantage, 1956.

Duclos, Jacques. *Mémoires 1945–1952*. Paris: Fayard, 1971.

Einaudi, Mario, et al. *Communism in Western Europe*. Ithaca, N.Y.: Cornell University Press, 1951.

Einaudi, Mario; Bye, Maurice; and Rossi, Ernesto. *Nationalism in France and Italy*. Ithaca, N.Y.: Cornell University Press, 1951.

Epstein, Melech. *Jewish Labor in the U.S.A. 1914–1952*. New York: Trade Union Sponsoring Committee, 1953.

Feis, Herbert. *Between War and Peace*. Princeton: Princeton University Press, 1960.

_____. *Churchill, Roosevelt and Stalin*. Princeton: Princeton University Press, 1967.

Filene, Peter G. *Americans and the Soviet Experiment 1917–1933*. Cambridge: Harvard University Press, 1966.

Ford, Carey. *Donovan of the OSS*. Boston: Little, Brown, 1970.

Fox, William T. R. *The American Study of International Relations*. Columbia, S.C.: Institute of International Studies, University of South Carolina, 1968.

Frachon, Benoît. *Au Rythme Des Jours*. Paris: Editions Sociales, 1967.

Freedman, Robert O. *Soviet Policy toward the Middle East*. New York: Praeger Special Studies, 1975.

Friedland, Edward; Seabury, Paul; and Wildavsky, Aaron. *The Great Detente Disaster*. New York: Basic Books, 1975.

Galenson, Walter. *The CIO Challenge to the AFL*. Cambridge: Harvard University Press, 1960.

Goulden, Joseph. *Meany: The Unchallenged Strong Man of American Labor*. New York: Atheneum, 1972.

Green, William. *Labor and Democracy*. Princeton: Princeton University Press, 1939.

Greenstone, J. David. *Labor and American Politics*. New York: Knopf, 1969.

Halle, Louis. *The Cold War as History*. New York: Harper & Row, 1967.

Hamilton, Richard F. *Affluence and the French Worker in the Fourth Republic*. Princeton: Princeton University Press, 1967.

Harmon, Joseph L. *The Public Services International*. Washington, D.C.: U.S. Department of Labor, 1962.

Harrington, Michael. *Socialism*. New York: Saturday Review Press, 1972.

Harris, André, and de Sedouy, Alain. *Voyage a l'Intérieur de Parti Communiste*. Paris: Seuil, 1974.

Harrison, Martin. *Trade Unions and the Labor Party since 1945*. London: Allen & Unwin, 1960.

Herz, Martin F. *Beginnings of the Cold War*. Bloomington, Ind.: Indiana University Press, 1966.

Hibbs, Douglas. *Industrial Conflict in Advanced Industrial Societies*. Cambridge: Center for International Studies, Massachusetts Institute of Technology, April 1975.

Holborn, Hajo. *The Political Collapse of Europe*. New York: Knopf, 1951.

Horowitz, Daniel. *The Italian Labor Movement*. Cambridge: Harvard University Press, 1963.

International Labor Organization. *The Trade Union Situation in the USSR*. Geneva, 1960.

Jacobs, Eric. *European Trade Unionism*. New York: Holmes & Meier, 1973.

Jenson, Vernon H. *Hiring of Dockworkers and Employment Practices in the Ports of New York, Liverpool, London, Rotterdam, and Marseilles*. Cambridge: Harvard University Press, 1964.

Kassalow, Everett M. *Trade Unions and Industrial Relations*. New York: Random House, 1969.

Kendall, Walter. *The Labor Movement in Europe*. London: Allen Lane, 1975.

Kennan, George. *Memoirs*. New York: Bantam, 1962.

Knorr, Klaus. *Military Power and Potential*. Lexington, Mass.: D.C. Heath, 1970.

Kohler, Foy; Harvey, Mose; Goure, Leon; and Soll, Richard. *Soviet Strategy for the Seventies: From Cold War to Peaceful Coexistence*. Miami, Fla.: Center for Advanced International Studies, 1973.

Kolko, Gabriel. *The Politics of War*. New York: Random House, 1968.

Kriegel, Annie. *The French Communists*. Chicago: University of Chicago Press, 1972.

Krock, Arthur. *Memoirs, Sixty Years on the Firing Line*. New York: Funk & Wagnalls, 1968.

Lang, Lucy R. *Tomorrow Is Beautiful*. New York: Macmillan, 1947.

La Polombara, Joseph. *The Italian Labor Movement: Problems and Prospects*. Ithaca, N.Y.: Cornell University, 1957.

Laurens, André, and Pfister, Thierry. *Les Nouveaux Communistes*. Paris: Stock, 1973.

Laqueur, Walter. "Detente: Western and Soviet Interpretations," Strategic Studies Center, Stanford Research Institute, Stanford, Calif., January 30, 1975.

_____. *Europe since Hitler*. Baltimore: Penguin, 1972.

Laslett, John M. *Labor and the Left*. New York: Basic Books, 1970.

Lasswell, Harold D., and Kaplan, Abraham. *Power and Society*. New Haven: Yale University Press, 1950.

Lecoeur, Auguste. *Le Partisan*. Paris: Flammarion, 1963.

Lefranc, Georges. *Les Expériences Syndicales en France de 1939 à 1950*. Paris: Montaigne, 1950.

Lens, Sidney. *The Forging of the American Empire*. New York: Crowell, 1971.

Levinson, Charles. *International Trade Unionism*. London: Allen and Unwin, 1972.

Lorwin, Lewis. *The International Labor Movement*. New York: Harper & Row, 1953.

Lorwin, Val R. *The French Labor Movement*. Cambridge: Harvard University Press, 1954.

Macridis, Roy. *French Politics in Transition*. Cambridge, Mass.: Winthrop, 1975.

Maddox, Robert James. *The New Left and the Origins of the Cold War*. Princeton: Princeton University Press, 1973.

Madison, Charles A. *American Labor Leaders*. New York: Harper, 1950.

Magill, John H. *Labor Unions and Political Socialization: A Case Study of Bolivian Workers*. New York: Praeger Special Studies, 1974.

Marchetti, Victor, and Marks, John D. *The CIA and the Cult of Intelligence*. New York: Knopf, 1974.

Mayne, Richard. *The Recovery of Europe 1945–1973*, rev. ed. Garden City, N.Y.: Doubleday, 1973.

McInnes, Neil. *The Communist Parties of Western Europe*. London: Oxford University Press, 1975.

McKenzie, Robert. *British Political Parties*, 2d ed. New York: St. Martins Press, 1963.

Meynaud, Jean. *Les Groupes de Pression en France*. Paris: Armand Colin, 1958.

Micaud, Charles. *Communism and the French Left*. New York: Praeger, 1963.

Millis, Walter, ed. *The Forrestal Diaries*. New York: Viking, 1961.

Moch, Jules. *Rencontres avec Léon Blum*. Paris: Plon, 1970.

Modelski, George. *Principles of World Politics*. New York: The Free Press, 1972.

Morgan, Roger. *West European Politics since 1945*. New York: Capricorn, 1973.

Morgenthau, Hans. *Politics among Nations*. New York: Knopf, 1972.

Morris, George. *The CIA and American Labor*. New York: International Publishers, 1967.

Mosely, Philip. *The Kremlin and World Politics*. New York: Vintage, 1960.

Novick, Peter. *The Resistance versus Vichy: The Purge of Collaborators in Liberated France*. New York: Columbia University Press, 1968.

Nye, Joseph, and Keohane, Robert, eds. *Transnational Relations and World Politics*. Cambridge: Harvard University Press, 1971.

Peck, Sidney M. *The Rank and File Leader*. New Haven, College and University Press, 1963.

Perlman, Mark. *The Machinists: A New Study in American Trade Unionism*. Cambridge: Harvard University Press, 1961.

Pipes, Richard, ed. *Soviet Strategy in Europe*. New York: Crane, Russak, 1976.

Puchala, Donald. *International Politics Today*. New York: Dodd, Mead, 1971.

Radosh, Ronald. *American Labor and U.S. Foreign Policy*. New York: Random House, 1969.

Reynaud, Jean Daniel. *Les Syndicats en France*, I. Paris: Seuil, 1975.

Rieber, Alfred J. *Stalin and the French Communist Party 1941–1947*. New York: Columbia University Press, 1962.

Rioux, Lucien. *Clefs pour le Syndicalisme*. Paris: Seghers, 1972.

Robrieux, Maurice Philippe. *Thorez*. Paris: Fayard, 1975.

Romualdi, Serafino. *Presidents and Peons: Recollections of a Labor Ambassador*. New York: Funk & Wagnalls, 1967.

Rostow, Eugene. *Peace in the Balance*. New York: Simon and Schuster, 1972.

Saposs, David. *Left Wing Unionism*. New York: Russell and Russell, 1967.

Seguy, Georges. *Lutter*. Paris: Stock, 1975.

Selznik, Philip. *The Organizational Weapon*. New York: McGraw-Hill, 1952.

Shorter, Edward, and Tilly, Charles. *Strikes in France 1830–1968*. New York: Cambridge University Press, 1974.

Smith, R. Harris. *OSS: The Secret History of America's First Central Intelligence Agency*. Berkeley: University of California Press, 1972.

Sorenson, Jay B. *The Life and Death of the Soviet Trade Unions 1917–1928*. New York: Atherton, 1967.

Stettinius, Edward R., Jr. *Roosevelt and the Russians: The Yalta Conference*. Garden City, N.Y.: Doubleday, 1949.

Sulzberger, C. L. *A Long Row of Candles*. New York: Macmillan, 1969.

Taft, Philip. *The AF of L from the Death of Gompers to the Merger*. New York: Harper, 1959.

———. *The AF of L in the Time of Gompers*. New York: Harper, 1957.

———. *Defending Freedom, American Labor and Foreign Affairs*. Los Angeles: Nash, 1973.

Tiersky, Ronald. *French Communism 1920–1972*. New York: Columbia University Press, 1974.

Tollet, André. *La Classe Ouvrière dans la Résistance*. Paris: Editions Sociales, 1960.

Truman, Harry S. *Memoirs*, I. Garden City, N.Y.: Doubleday, 1955.

Tucker, Robert. *A New Isolationism: Threat or Promise*. New York: Universe Books for Potomac Associates, 1972.

Ulam, Adam. *Expansion and Coexistence*, 2d ed. New York: Praeger, 1974.

———. *The Rivals*. New York: Viking, 1971.

Valtin, Jan. *Out of the Night*. New York: Alliance Books, 1941.

Whitney, Fred. *Labor Policy and Practices in Spain*. New York: Praeger, 1965.

Windmuller, John P. *American Labor and the International Labor Movement 1940–1953*. Ithaca, N.Y.: Cornell University, 1954.

Wolfe, Thomas. *Soviet Power and Europe*. Baltimore: Johns Hopkins Press, 1970.

Wolfers, Arnold. *Discord and Collaboration*. Baltimore: Johns Hopkins Press, 1962.

Articles

Adam, Gérard. "Eléments d'Analyse sur les liens entre le PCF et la CGT." *Revue Française de Science Politique* XVIII (June 1968): 524–539.

Braden, Thomas. "I'm Glad the CIA is 'Immoral.' " *Saturday Evening Post*, May 20, 1967, pp. 9–13.

Chernikov, C. "The Economic Crisis and the Deepening Class Struggle in the Capitalist Countries." *World Trade Union Movement*, January 1975, pp. 5–9.

Crozier, Brian. "New Light on Soviet Subversion I." *Soviet Analyst*, March 28, 1974.

———. "Soviet Interest in Industrial Unrest." *Soviet Analyst*, February 14, 1974.

———. "Soviet Unions, New Takeover Bid." *Forum World Features*, August 1973.

"David Dubinsky, the ILGWU and the American Labor Movement." *Labor History*, Special Issue (Spring 1968).

Ford, Charles. "The Role of the Trade Unions in the Economic Development of Europe." ICFTU, Brussels, 1966.

Frachon, Benoît. "Interventiones." *Cahiers du Communisme* XXX (June–July 1954).

Godson, Roy. "American Labor's Continuing Involvement in World Affairs." *Orbis*, Spring 1975, pp. 93–116.

Guibert, Roger. "France, A Crisis or *the* Crisis." *World Trade Union Movement*, January 1975, pp. 10–12.

Handlin, Oscar. "Failure of the Historians." *Freedom at Issue*, September–October 1975.

Jolis, A. E. "The OSS and the Labor Movement." *New Leader*, August 31, 1946.

Laqueur, Walter. "Rewriting History." *Commentary*, March 1973, pp. 59–63.

"Les Effectifs de la CFDT." *Les Études Sociales et Syndicales*, December 1965.

Lorwin, Val. "French Trade Unions since the Liberation 1944–1951." *Industrial and Labor Relations Review*, July 1952.

Mire, Joseph. "Labor under Hitler." *American Federationist* L (April 1943): 15.

Moore, Barrington, Jr. "Revolution in America." *New York Review of Books*, January 30, 1969, pp. 6–11.

Nossiter, Bernard. "Italy's Fate Turns on the Role of Unions." *Washington Post*, June 23, 1974.

Perline, Martin M. "The Trade Union Press: An Historical Analysis." *Labor History* X (Winter 1969).

Pimenov, Petr. "Towards Unity on a Class Basis." *World Trade Union Movement*, March 1973.

Ranger, Robert. "Les Liens entre le PCF et la CGT, Eléments d'un Débat." *Revue Française de Science Politique* XVIII (November 1968): 182–187.

Reynaud, Jean Daniel. "Trade Unions and Political Parties in France: Some Recent Trends." *Industrial and Labor Relations Review* (January 1975).

Riesel, Victor. "Inside Labor." *New York Post*, April 29, 1947.

Schlesinger, Arthur, Jr. "Origins of the Cold War." *Foreign Affairs*, October 1967.

Simes, Dimitri. "Monthly Report on Foreign Policy, Arms Control, and Strategic Issues in the Soviet Media." No. 10, Georgetown University Center for Strategic and International Studies, Washington, D.C., October 15, 1975.

Velie, Lester. "The Soviet Design for Free World Labor." *Readers Digest*, June 1975.

Weitz, Peter. "Labor and Politics in a Divided Movement." *Industrial and Labor Relations Review* (January 1975).

Windmuller, John P. "Cohesion and Disunity in the ICFTU, the 1965 Amsterdam Conference." *Industrial and Labor Relations Review* XIX (April 1966).

Theses

Carwell, Joseph. "The International Role of American Labor." Ph.D. thesis, Columbia University, 1956.

Chalfin, Seymour. "Causes Leading to Communist Domination of the French Labor Movement, 1944–1947." M.A. thesis, University of Illinois, 1949.

Davies, Margaret. "The Role of American Trade Union Representatives in the Aid-to-Greece Program." Ph.D. thesis, University of Washington, 1960.

Godson, Roy. "The International Confederation of Free Trade Unions and Spanish Politics." M.A. thesis, Columbia University, 1967.

Morrell, Edwin. "Communist Unionism: Organized Labor and the Soviet State." Ph.D. thesis, Harvard University, 1965.

Schwartz, Morton. "Soviet Policies in the WFTU." Ph.D. thesis, Columbia University, 1963.

Index

AFL, *see* American Federation of Labor

Air, Terre, Mer, 121

Alexander, Robert, 39

American Federationist, 42, 52, 76

American Federation of Labor (AFL): aid policy, 116–122; archival documentation, 163–164; background, post-WWII, 32–34; cooperation with CIO, 114–115; decision-making structure, 34–37; and Europe's economic and political status, 151–157; foreign policy choices, 104; and global balance of power, 140–141; and international labor movement, 124–126; moral and psychological support for anticommunists, 107–110; organizational leadership policy, 110–116; perceptions of European labor movement, 75; perceptions of French labor movement, 75–76; perceptions of WFTU, 72–75; postwar European involvement, 7–10; and postwar European unions, 31; and Russian goals and capabilities, 141-146; ultimate goals, 55-57;

American Federation of Labor (AFL): views on domestic politics, 57–59; views on free trade unionism and internal threats to democracy, 59–64; views on Russian policy, 66–69; and world balance of power, 2–3; *see also* Free Trade Union Committee; labor movement; unions

AFL-CIO, 153, 155; current state of affairs, 160–162; openness to involvement in Europe, 157–159

Amis de Force Ouvrière, 90, 119, 134, 135; and CGT split, 129-130

Anticommunists, AFL moral and psychological support for, 107-110

Anti-Nazi League, 41

Antonini, Luigi, 36, 40

Atlantic Alliance, 22

Balance of power; global, 2-3, 140-141; prewar vs. postwar, 15-16; and unions, 29-31

Barge workers, Communist tactics among, 83-84